THE RETURN OF STORYTELLING IN CONTEMPORARY GERMAN LITERATURE AND FILM
PETER HANDKE AND WIM WENDERS

THE RETURN OF STORYTELLING IN CONTEMPORARY GERMAN LITERATURE AND FILM
PETER HANDKE AND WIM WENDERS

David N. Coury

Studies in German Language and Literature
Volume 36

The Edwin Mellen Press
Lewiston•Queenston•Lampeter

Library of Congress Cataloging-in-Publication Data

Coury, David N.
 The return of storytelling in contemporary German literature and film : Peter Handke and Wim Wenders / David N. Coury.
  p. cm. -- (Studies in German language and literature ; v. 36)
 Includes bibliographical references and index.
 ISBN 0-7734-6320-8
  I. Title. II. Series.

This is volume 36 in the continuing series
Studies in German Language and Literature
Volume 36 ISBN 0-7734-6320-8
SGLL Series ISBN 0-88946-578-0

A CIP catalog record for this book is available from the British Library

Front cover: *Homer* by Rembrandt
            Courtesy of the Royal Cabinet of Paintings, Mauritshuis, The Hague, Holland

Copyright © 2004 David N. Coury

All rights reserved. For information contact

The Edwin Mellen Press	The Edwin Mellen Press
Box 450	Box 67
Lewiston, New York	Queenston, Ontario
USA 14092-0450	CANADA L0S 1L0

The Edwin Mellen Press, Ltd.
Lampeter, Ceredigion, Wales
UNITED KINGDOM SA48 8LT

Printed in the United States of America

for Cristina

~ CONTENTS ~

FOREWORD by Sara Friedrichsmeyer ... ix
ACKNOWLEDGMENTS ... xi

INTRODUCTION ... 1

1 The Art of Storytelling: Origins and Definitions ... 15
    Walter Benjamin and the Death of the Storyteller ... 19
    Modernism and the Crisis of Verisimilitude in the Turn of the Century
    German Novel ... 22
    Postwar Literature and the Birth of the New Novel ... 38
    The Return of the Story ... 43

2 Peter Handke and the Transformation of a Storyteller ... 49
    Handke's Early Aesthetics ... 51
    The Early Novels: Experimentation and Anti-Narratives ... 55
    Crossing the Threshold to Narration: The Return of the Storyteller ... 62
    Another Way of Telling ... 73

3 Cinema and the Narrative Tradition ... 85
    Images and Narration ... 89
    The *Autorenfilm* and the End of the Story ... 92
    The Death of the *Autorenfilm* ... 103
    The New German Comedy and the Return of Narrative ... 110

4 Wim Wenders: a Cinematic Storyteller ... 115
    Der ewige Erzähler ... 116
    Wenders's Cinematic Aesthetics: Visual Storytelling ... 119
    Wenders and the *nouvelle vague* ... 126
    Todesboten: Stories and Film ... 131
    Storytelling and the Power of Redemption ... 135
    Vidioten and the Ubiquity of Images ... 142
    The Morality Plays: *Der Himmel über Berlin* and *In weiter Ferne, so nah!* ... 147

CONCLUSION
**Towards a New Narrative: German Literature and Film
at the End of the Twentieth Century** ... 153

NOTES ... 171
BIBLIOGRAPHY ... 195
INDEX ... 203

~ FOREWORD ~

In this study, Professor Coury offers a persuasive analysis of the return of storytelling in contemporary German literature and film, situating his investigation in a scholarly study of the crisis of narration that has plagued writers and filmmakers of the past century. The development that he is charting is represented most fully in this study by the prose works of Peter Handke since the late 1980s and the recent films of Wim Wenders, but his wide-ranging references to other contemporary writers and filmmakers makes indisputable his claim that German literature and cinema of the recent past have struggled to synthesize the populist aspects of storytelling with postmodernist expectations.

This work presents a scholarly contribution in many important ways. First of all, from a methodological perspective, the author offers a quite obviously successful example of interdisciplinary scholarship. Further, he advances a well-argued interpretation and analysis of the works of two of Germany's most prolific and controversial creative artists. Studying Wenders and Handke within the context of the much-discussed demise of narration, Coury demonstrates that they are representative of a new group of German writers and filmmakers who, in their search for communal, shared experiences, are resuscitating the art of storytelling.

In an informed introductory chapter, the author investigates the twentieth-century crisis of narration, a crisis that he follows through its various surfacings in, for example, the writings and theories of early twentieth-century critics such as Walter Benjamin, Alfred Döblin and Thomas Mann. And after considering the fate of storytelling during and immediately after the Third Reich, Coury tracks its further deterioration through the thinking of writers identified with the avant-garde and/or postmodernism, beginning with Alain Robbe-Grillet, and then in the works of late twentieth-century thinkers (among them Michael Roemer, Uwe Wittstock, Peter Brooks, and Paul Ricouer). To this on-going discussion Coury is able to offer strong interpretation of the recent works of Handke and Wenders as representing, even heralding, a counter movement: as his analysis demonstrates, both have incorporated storytelling and discussions about it into their works since at least the 1980s. His insights will lead readers to a renewed appreciation for the experimental work of both Handke and Wenders as attempts to recapture the communal pleasure and focus of early forms of storytelling, but in ways well-suited to a postmodern age.

Coury offers further proof for his thesis with brief analyses of well-received recent novels by Patrick Süskind, Robert Schneider, Sten Nadolny, and Uwe Timm, all of whom, in Coury's view, have focused on narration and storytelling, not least of all with their creations of reliable narrators, narrative voices that do not feel called upon to refuse all claims to experience or truth. He provides similar analysis of several recent films, among them an examination of Tom Tykwer's highly successful film *Lola rennt*. Coury perceptively points to this film as one that not only claims a German legacy (as he points out, the name of the protagonist resonates with those of many figures from the past), but as one that announces a return to storytelling while nevertheless acknowledging a postmodern rejection of an authorial voice. By going beyond the works of Handke and Wenders to investigate the works of creative artists firmly rooted in the 1990s, he lends credence to his claim that contemporary German literature and cinema have come to embrace storytelling and the various structures that support such forms of narration.

In his conclusion, Coury cautions that the development he has traced does not provide a permanent solution to the crisis of narration. Although the new forms of literature and cinematic expression he has defined do synthesize what he calls "the populist aspects of storytelling" with postmodern tropes, they will inevitably be supplanted by others. Challenge will come, Coury cautions, but for the time being—and his arguments are compelling—the possibilities opened up by what he calls the "neo-narrative" are far from exhausted.

Sara Friedrichsmeyer
Department of German Studies
University of Cincinnati

~ ACKNOWLEDGEMENTS ~

Many people deserve thanks for their support of this study from its inception as a doctoral dissertation through the many revisions and expansions that it has since undergone. First, I would like to thank Sara Friedrichsmeyer and Rick McCormick for their enthusiasm, suggestions and readings of my manuscript. Their comments and critiques have been very useful in helping me to refine my thesis. Colleagues and students, both past and present from the University of Cincinnati and the University of Wisconsin–Green Bay have provided stimulating insight and conversation, which has allowed me to re-think some of my suppositions as well as to expand on others. Both institutions have additionally at various times and in various ways provided financial support that helped me complete the work. I'm grateful as well to various friends both in the U.S. and in Germany who have also been very helpful in providing materials and fruitful conversation. The Stiftung deutscher Kinemathek, Berlin and the Mauritshuis, Den Haag, have provided access and use of materials for this study as well. Additionally, thanks to Justin Connaher for the author's photo.

    I would also like to express my gratitude to Tricia Hill for her fine work in designing and laying out the book in such a professional manner. Finally, special thanks goes to my family and to Cristina and Lucas for indulging me for so long while I worked on this book.

~ INTRODUCTION ~

At the end of every year, critics and pundits of all sorts reflect on the trends and issues which, over the course of the preceding twelve months, helped shaped society and culture. In 1999, however, they had the rare opportunity to consider not only the past year, but the preceding century and millennium and then to determine which events and issues shaped our culture in the twentieth century. Inevitably, though, such reflection leads to endless lists and debates over what was included and what was overlooked, which events were more crucial than others and which developments represent lasting change and which were merely passing trends.

In one such ambitious effort, the *New York Times Magazine* decided to construct a time capsule as a means of giving readers a framework for thinking about the past.[1] In doing so they decided to remain with "millennial themes," a term which they recognized was as ambiguous as the project itself. Nevertheless, they asked writers, critics, artists and intellectuals what they felt were the true "millennial themes" worthy of inclusion in this special end of the century issue. Interestingly, although the answers covered a wide spectrum of topics in modern society—from women's rights and human rights violations to the relationship between nature and the individual—they all reflected central themes of contemporary art and literature. One of the respondents, however, selected a structural and formalist theme: storytelling. When considering the nature of artistic endeavors and how they have changed and been transformed in the last millennium, Mary Schmidt Campbell, the Dean of the Tisch School of the Arts at New York University, stated quite simply: "The tools will change but the artistic skills of storytelling will endure" (28). Indeed, the enduring legacy of storytelling in literature and the arts has been the focus of much attention in the waning years of the twentieth century, a preoccupancy that reflects a larger formalist and social development within western culture. In fact, just two months earlier, the *New York Times*

Book Review published an essay by Wendy Steiner in which she argues that the American novel had abandoned "metafictional fireworks" and returned instead to issues of love and the tradition of the "premodern" nineteenth-century novel.[2] Gone were the "clever, verbose metafictionalists . . . concocting fables of absurdity" and in their place are now works "rich in imagery and emotion, consumed by the desire to recover a lost or hidden past." This type of work, Steiner argues, is concerned with individual experience more than with the paradoxes of existential being and as such, it speaks and appeals to a much wider readership than its literary predecessor, the postmodern novel and its primary target group, intellectuals and literary critics. Moreover, what guides many of these more recent works is indeed masterful storytelling. As Campbell argued, although the tools (and themes) have changed at the end of the millennium, the skill of a well crafted story has seemingly endured.

Oftentimes, though, critics are want to dismiss works that demonstrate strong storytelling skill by arguing that they lack an intellectual rigor; what constitutes a true literary work, so the theory goes, is linguistic irony, self-referentiality and literary genius. In his seminal work on reading and narratology, *Reading for the Plot*, Peter Brooks argued against this notion, but at the same time recognized that story and plot (its corollary) have long been rejected as unbefitting of literary study: "Plot has been disdained as the element of narrative that least sets off and defines high art—indeed, plot is that which especially characterizes popular mass-consumption literature: plot is why we read *Jaws*, but not Henry James" (4). Brooks set out to debunk that myth by showing the value and importance of the plot. Still, a long tradition firmly entrenched within literary aesthetics argued that linear narratives, stories and plot are populist and lacking in creativity and originality and thus constitute "trivial literature."[3] Nowhere has this notion been stronger than in Germany, where plot and narrative have been questioned since the Enlightenment and rejected at least since the beginning of the twentieth century with the advent of the modernist novel, and where in the post-WWII era, stories and plot have been viewed as artifices used to avoid engaging in sociopolitical concerns.

In fact, in a recent review of German-language writings in the *Economist*, the author, commenting on the state of German language fiction, noted that most Anglo-American publishers feel that "while foreign writers from . . . America,

Britain or Scandinavia can turn out well written works with interesting story lines and even arresting thoughts, modern German novelists have tended to disdain writing readable, entertaining books altogether" ("Tell us . . . " 14). Although such an assessment is somewhat overstated, many critics have lamented a certain lethargy in contemporary German literature, especially given the relative critical neglect afforded it outside the German-speaking realm. How and why this has come to be the case has been the object of much discussion, prompting on the one hand, careful analyses of the reading public, market forces, and the detrimental influence of the media on reading and, on the other hand, a reproaching of German writers for being, what the former literary editor of the *Frankfurter Allgemeine Zeitung*, Uwe Wittstock, has deemed "schwierig, unsinnlich und weltfern" (Wittstock 10). In 1995, Wittstock, now lector at the S. Fischer Verlag, published an extended exegesis on the state of German language fiction which he titled, *Leselust, oder Wie unterhaltsam ist die neue deutsche Literatur?* The answer to his somewhat rhetorical question was "not very." Despite recent popular successes in the late 1980s and early 1990s like Patrick Süskind's *Das Parfum* and Robert Schneider's *Schlafes Bruder*, and more recently Bernhard Schlink's *Der Vorleser* and Ingo Schulze's *Simple Stories*, the German public continues to shun contemporary German fiction in favor of works by U.S. American, South American and Scandinavian writers.[4] The reason, Wittstock argues, is the continued aversion amongst German writers toward notions of *Unterhaltung* and the underlying perception that *Unterhaltung* is anathema to literature and serious writing. Wittstock in fact makes a plea for a more "entertaining," "unterhaltsame Literatur," yet he never relinquishes the demand for literary quality. In fact, he defines *unterhaltsam* to mean: "mit literarischen Mitteln beim Publikum Interesse für ein Thema, Anteilnahme an einer Figur, Neugier auf ein Geschehen oder auch Lust an einem ungewöhnlichen Sprachspiel zu wecken und wachzuhalten" (22). He notes further: "Für welche der zahllosen Formen von Unterhaltung sich ein Autor entscheidet, unterliegt keinem Gesetz, wichtig ist nur, daß er diesen Aspekt nicht aus den Augen verliert" (22).

What Wittstock is making a case for is renewed attention to the reader on behalf of the author. With the rise of the novel in the nineteenth century and its dominance in the following century, so too came the isolation of the writer and thus a decided break between the storyteller and the audience. As Walter Benjamin has argued: "Die Geburtskammer des Romans ist das Individuum in seiner Einsamkeit, das sich über seine wichtigsten Anliegen nicht mehr exemplarisch auszusprechen vermag, selbst unberaten ist und keinen Rat geben kann" (II.2 443). Concomitant to this was a crisis in modes of narration and in the possibility of verisimilitude. Since the beginning of the twentieth century, literary critics and theorists in the western tradition have recognized and attempted to define this crisis in the modern novel. Paramount to this was the proclaimed death of the narrator and narrated stories and eventually the death of literature itself. The novel, it was felt, could no longer convey the same sense of reality and experience as the stories and storytellers of preceding generations. In Germany, the crisis was especially pronounced as writers themselves, including Alfred Döblin, Thomas Mann, and Robert Musil, problematized this situation in essayistic form and responded in practice by searching for new ways to break from the traditions of the past. Literary critic Horst Steinmetz has maintained that this rejection of narrative forms in literature stems from the belief in the early part of the twentieth century that reality could no longer be reflected through traditional conventions and that the undermining and destruction of these conventions was necessary for the creation of new ways of portraying reality.[5] More important than reflecting reality became the question of how to depict reality. More and more, the narrator became suspect, and the process of ordering reality, which resulted from such narrative techniques, was rejected as insufficient in portraying the world and modern reality in writing. In 1936, Benjamin proclaimed in an essay dealing with the death of the storyteller: "Der Erzähler—so vertraut uns der Name klingt—ist uns in seiner lebendigen Wirksamkeit keineswegs durchaus gegenwärtig" (II.2 438). This thesis soon found its realization in the works of Joyce and Beckett as well as in Döblin and Musil in the German-speaking realm.

But German literature has long maintained a philosophical tradition, from Kant and Hegel to Adorno, which posited that reality is not narratable.[6] Moreover, the increased expansiveness and subjectivity of the modernist novel led in the early part of the twentieth century to counter-narratives and an amplification of narrated time and space. The overcoming of this tradition in twentieth-century poetics that argues against a narratable reality as well as the critical tradition that views innovation as the true mark of literary talent,[7] is not easily achieved. The complex issues of subjectivity and narratable time which so pervaded the modernist novels in the first half of the century further eroded the tradition of storytelling and certainly of linear narratives in the second half. With Adorno's proclamation in 1954 that, given the current state of literature in society, "es läßt sich nicht mehr erzählen," and continuing with Alain Robbe-Grillet's theoretical formulations of the *nouveau roman* in the 1960s—"narration in the actual sense of the word has become impossible"(34)—the story and storytelling as a narrative trope were summarily rejected as artifices incapable of grasping the complexities of a modern and, later, a postmodern society. The discussion on the death of the novel and narration had in the 1950s and 1960s also become so ubiquitous that it had even reached the point of parody as evidenced in Günter Grass's *Die Blechtrommel*. Oskar Matzerath, the protagonist and sometimes narrator of the novel, ponders how he should begin telling his story:

> Man kann eine Geschichte in der Mitte beginnen und vorwärts wie rückwärts kühn ausschreitend Verwirrung anstiften. Man kann sich modern geben, alle Zeiten, Entfernungen wegstreichen und hinterher verkünden oder verkünden lassen, man habe endlich und in letzter Stunde das Raum-Zeit-Problem gelöst. Man kann auch ganz zu Anfang behaupten, es sei heutzutage unmöglich, einen Roman zu schreiben, dann aber, sozusagen hinter dem eigenen Rücken, einen kräftigen Knüller hinlegen, um schließlich als letztmöglicher Romanschreiber dazustehen (11).

Keith Bullivant, in his study of realism in the contemporary German novel, attributes the tendency toward rejection of traditional narratives, in part, to the staying power of the anti-realist novel of the 1920s and 1930s,[8] whereas other literary critics and philosophers, especially French cultural critics like Paul Ricouer and Jean-Francois Lyotard, have developed this idea even further, positing a larger, more complex cultural phenomenon which has culminated in the death of the narrator and narration itself.[9] As a result, many writers and critics in the 1970s and 1980s found the impetus for rejecting the realist and narrative traditions under the guise of postmodern aesthetics, thus continuing the anti-narrative trend away from literary realism.

In his recent study of twentieth-century German narrative, Patrick O'Neill suggests that the move away from stories and linear narratives parallels a shift in literary aesthetics in the twentieth century, whereby the discourse of the novel has come to supersede its story.[10] In a broad overview summarizing the development of narrative in the twentieth century, he argues that "realist texts focus on the story, modernist texts focus on the relationship between story and discourse, postmodernist texts treat the discourse as the story" (7). Throughout this century, he demonstrates, literary narratives have increasingly shifted from story-driven texts to discourse-driven texts, to the point where discourse has become primary and story secondary, for at the end of this century "that is exactly what makes literary texts literary. To read literary texts as literary texts is therefore always necessary to engage in critical analysis of the semiotics of discourse" (9). O'Neill ends his study of the contemporary German novel convincingly with an analysis of Thomas Bernhard's 1970 novel *Das Kalkwerk*, a text much like Grass's *Die Blechtrommel*, Uwe Johnson's *Zwei Ansichten* and Peter Handke's *Die Angst des Tormanns beim Elfmeter*, the other three postmodernist texts he treats, in which "the story presented is entirely inextricable from the discourse that presents it" (157). Common to these and other "postmodernist" texts is the characteristic that the "discourse pervasively *hinders* us in determining what exactly the story it tells really is" (157), a device drawn from the experimental and avant-garde texts of the *nouveau roman* and one which came to predominate literary narratives in the 1970s and early 1980s.

Postmodernist and poststructuralist theorists have seized upon this trend and have attempted to search for the root of this disintegration of form and tradition, leading to a myriad of theories and postulations. Poststructuralists, like Michel Foucault and Roland Barthes, see an even greater tendency that encompasses a more far-reaching phenomenon, namely the death of the author and possibilities of authorship. In extreme cases, some critics, like Jean Baudrillard, have gone so far as to postulate that the world has surpassed a definitive end point in which all new forms and possibilities of innovation have been exhausted and only simulation remains. Others, however, especially those in the German tradition of Jürgen Habermas and the Frankfurt School, maintain that the project of the Enlightenment is not over and that meaning is still to be had from literature, narratives, and the arts.

This aversion to narration and storytelling in German literature appears to be changing, however, as an undeniable trend in German literature since the 1980s has become discernable, namely the return of the storyteller. The recent international commercial success of writers like Schlink and Schulze demonstrate a willingness on behalf of a newer generation of writers to appeal to the reader and to write *unterhaltsame* works. Indeed since the 1980s there have been signs of a change in the narrative constructs of German fiction, one which has evidenced a restitution of the storyteller; and with the return of the storyteller, the story itself has begun to reassert its dominance over the literary discourse embodied in the text.[11] This return to storytelling instances and traditions can be explained in perhaps two ways: Steinmetz argues that the recipients of nonnarrative literature, the readers, have often rejected storyless literature, thereby expressing a profound need for stories and the harmonious meaning they impart. But beyond that, stories also represent basic patterns for the cultivation and conveyance of experience, Steinmetz argues, echoing in many ways Benjamin's views of the story (75). Moreover, artists and writers have continually found themselves faced with the dilemma of having to find ways of relating human experience, something which the "experiment" of anti-narratives was unable to accomplish. Many postwar writers, however, have maintained all along that traditional forms of narration were not only alive but necessary. Uwe Timm, for instance, a long-time practitioner of literary storytelling, maintains that, while the art of storytelling is not dead, it is, in Germany at least, endangered. However, there is still hope, he feels, for storytelling has not died out but is experiencing a re-birth of sorts.[12]

Even postmodernist writers like Peter Handke have in the late 1980s and 1990s embraced the story and the act of storytelling as a literary trope central to the construction of narratives and linked to explorations of the self and the formation of personal identity. Handke's three essays, or *Versuche,* from 1989 to 1991 explore the possibilities and complexities of the literary narrative. Not surprisingly, the title of the English translation, *The Jukebox and Other Essays on Storytelling,* reflects this newfound identity of the storyteller. For a writer who once proclaimed the uselessness of the story, his current stance represents a profound shift in his conception of writing, yet it is also representative of a larger paradigmatic shift in contemporary literary aesthetics. Brooks maintains that "there have been some historical moments at which plot has assumed greater importance than at others, moments in which cultures have seemed to develop an unquenchable thirst for plots and to seek the expression of central individual and collective meanings through narrative design" (*Plot* 5). Similarly, Steinmetz has argued that the return to storytelling has, in part, been necessitated by social concerns and demands. Thus it stands to reason that such a phenomenon would not be limited to the realm of literature. Indeed, other cultural and artistic forms of expression have similarly experienced a comparable return to narrative, especially the cinema. After a long period of growth (and some would argue stagnation) in the early part of the twentieth century, in which the cinema embraced narrative traditions and even established the linear narrative cinema as the dominant form, a group of young French filmmakers in the 1950s and 1960s took their cue from their literary counterparts and ushered in a new wave of composition, a *nouvelle vague*, which emphasized anti-narrative constructs. Its most prominent practitioner, Jean-Luc Godard, made a number of films that purposely broke with and deconstructed traditional narrative filmmaking. In Germany, another group of young filmmakers embraced this practice in the 1960s and proceeded to proclaim the death of the old cinema and the birth of the new, a position which informed the approach of a second wave of filmmakers and the so-called New German Cinema (NGC) of the 1970s and 1980s.

As with literature, however, the German cinema has recently seen a similar return to narrative form and tradition. Above all, Wim Wenders, the most active and highly regarded of the new wave of filmmakers of the 1970s and 1980s still working today and one who early on challenged traditional conceptions of filmmaking, has come in recent years to call for a return to cinematic storytelling as a way of again relating human experience and establishing order and meaning in the world. His two-part cycle on Berlin and angels, *Der Himmel über Berlin* (*Wings of Desire*) and *In weiter Ferne, so nah!* (*Far Away, So Close!*), deals directly with this issue via characters representing storytellers of the literary and cinematic tradition. Furthermore, through his essays, he has made an impassioned plea for the restitution and rehabilitation of storytelling as a way of overcoming societal ills and the destructive forces of modernity.

This study, then, will focus alternately on the return to narratives and stories in contemporary German literature and film. In order to examine a more specific manifestation of this trend, I focus on the more recent works of Handke and Wenders as exemplary of this shift. Both Handke and Wenders are highly respected in their individual fields in both Europe and North America, have won numerous international awards and have found distribution for their works in most major markets. Moreover, they are artists who have a body of work that has undergone a transformation from disdaining narratives to embracing the story. Both began their careers in the spirit of the avant-garde, creating works which rejected stories as structuring principles. However, in the 1980s, both began to reassess the function and utility of narrative and slowly, yet individually, became advocates for stories. In many ways, their careers serve as excellent examples of a larger phenomenon in cultural aesthetics.

Although the two have collaborated on a number of projects throughout their careers, their evolution and artistic development has nevertheless been separate. This is perhaps best evident by the fact that each lists practitioners of his own respective genre as dominant influences on his career and ideology; that is, Wenders views himself strongly in the cinematic tradition while Handke is well versed in the German literary tradition. Nevertheless, they continue to work together on occasion based on their shared sense of visual and literary aesthetics and both are acutely aware of the developments in the other medium. In interviews, Wenders shows a strong literary acumen; Handke, on the other hand, has made three feature films on his own. Thus a study of their works and poetics is revealing, for not only are they accomplished artists in their own right, but they are both well versed in other areas of artistic and cultural production. Furthermore, both have been alternately praised and criticized for the shifts in their theoretical and ideological views. Some critics maintain that these changes are opportunistic, others that they are merely at the vanguard of cultural production and thus an important litmus of current ideas and trends.[13] In either case, their works serve as a reflection of concomitant ideological debates and concerns, and thus stand as representative of these trends.

Handke's and Wenders's more recent demands for stories and narratives call into question many of the basic tenets of postmodernism, the leading philosophical and theoretical basis for art and cultural studies of the past twenty years. In Chapter 1, I will present an overview of and discuss the philosophical discourses leading to the so-called death of the narrative. As many critics, from Benjamin to Ricouer and Brooks, have noted, prose fiction, and especially the novel, has inherited the oral narrative tradition. Therefore the crisis of the novel in the twentieth century is at once a crisis of the narrative tradition. Chapter 1 thus presents a historical overview of the narrative crisis in the novel with the intent of establishing the basis for the return to stories and narrative at the end of the twentieth century. In order to contextualize this debate, I will first define and analyze the importance of the story, for both historical and narrative purposes, using Benjamin's essay as a theoretical basis of an understanding of the cultural significance of storytelling. Although hundreds of books and articles have been written on the crises of narration, subjectivity, and the novel itself in the last hundred years, I wish to focus not on reiterating what has already been done, but to highlight the correlation these discussions have with regard to the death and subsequent rebirth of narrative stories. In doing so, I will concentrate on the novel as the literary form which has carried on or, as Benjamin would argue, supplanted the oral narrative and storytelling tradition. By demonstrating that the novel inherited this tradition from the epic, it becomes clear that the decline of storytelling and the sense of shared communal experience it imparted was inevitable. However, the distinct trend in recent years toward a restitution of the narrator and of literary storytelling coupled with the reappearance of the novella and the birth of traditional narratives parallels a shift in society which calls for a greater sense of community and exchange of experience, both elements inherent in the story.

Chapter 2 will then focus specifically on Peter Handke's most recent works as exemplary of this trend. With Handke, too, there exists a great deal of secondary literature dealing with both his early fiction and his dramas as well as his more recent works with their existential thematics.[14] For the purposes of this study, I do not intend to concentrate on analyzing his entire narrative *oeuvre*; rather, by focusing on key works of the 1980s and 1990s and contrasting their narrative constructs to those of his earlier works, I intend to show how Handke has returned to more traditional narratives and especially how these works reevaluate the narrator as storyteller. Handke's reversal, from a writer who early on openly disdained linear narrative to one who now exalts storytelling, is especially telling, as Handke has always been an artist who continuously redefines himself in reaction to the most current philosophical and ideological trends. As such, focusing on Handke serves a twofold purpose: on the one hand, he represents a writer who arose from the postwar avant-garde movement and adopted aesthetic notions associated with non-traditional narrative forms, yet has come to reject these origins in favor of a postmodern sensibility that reconciles narration and text. On the other hand, Handke is, as has been stated, representative of a larger trend in German literature, both traditional and postmodern, which has brought forth an affirmation of stories and narrative storytelling.

Chapter 3 parallels Chapter 1 by looking at the development of postwar German cinema and its rejection in the 1960s and 1970s of the dominant narrative cinema. The repercussions in Germany of the French *nouvelle vague* and Godard's anti-narrative cinema had a similar effect on cinematic style as the *nouveau roman* had on the novel: linearity and storytelling were rejected in favor of episodic, essay films that often served a more didactic purpose than a communicative one. This chapter will focus more on a thematic and contextual discussion of this trend as opposed to structuralist and semiotic approaches to narrative analysis.[15] Chapter 3 will analyze German film history with an emphasis on the varying approaches taken toward cinematic storytelling. Although most silent films necessarily used narrative as a structuring principle, this was not always the case with sound film. In the post-World War II era, European cinema as a whole developed an alternative style of filmmaking which rejected the constructs of the dominant narrative cinema and has since been termed the "Art Film." In Germany, this influence resulted in a blossoming of the cinema in the 1970s and 1980s known as the NGC. As there have once again been many studies on this period,[16] my concern is with its legacy on German narrative film. With the first wave of post-NGC directors now releasing films, there is a decided trend toward narrative filmmaking with an emphasis once again on story. The second half of this chapter will look at recent ideological shifts in the German film industry that mirror the same calls for stories and narratives as in contemporary German literature.

Although most of the filmmakers involved in the NGC now only irregularly make films, Wim Wenders continues to create films that receive both popular and critical acclaim. Chapter 4 will concentrate on Wenders's approach to narrative cinema, from his early films which were influenced by the French anti-narrative, cinema to his more recent forays into Hollywood-style filmmaking. Currently, Wenders is one of the few German filmmakers who is striving to combine aspects of the European Art Film with the more accessible constructs of narrative filmmaking. Wenders's essays on the importance of stories and narratives, not only as artistic principles but as elements central to the dynamic between the artist and the audience, will also be discussed.

The paradigmatic shift back to stories and narratives in contemporary German literature and film is, I feel, quite significant. In the past several years there has not only been a marked increase in the number of cinemagoers (suggesting that the communal nature of shared vision has not succumbed to the isolation of video watching), but also of literary storytelling. The Austrian city of Graz has, for instance, been host the past few years to one of the world's largest storytelling festivals that includes storytellers and tales from across Europe. In the promotional material for the festival, director Folke Tegetthoff writes:

> The art of storytelling is much more than a "stage art," and much more than "entertainment." Therefore, this festival—unique in Europe and dedicated to this rediscovered art form—is much more than just a cultural attraction. The art of storytelling is simply the "living"—hearing, seeing, and feeling—of what life is about; namely our past, present, and future.[17]

Interestingly, Tegetthoff emphasizes not only the performivity of storytelling but also the entertainment value as well as the notion that stories and storytelling are crucial to conceptions of identity, an aspect that many writers and filmmakers underscore as well. He also posits the idea that stories can indeed convey meaning and comment on a society's past, present and future, a concept that was rejected both by modernist writers in the first half of the twentieth century and then again by postmodernists in the latter half.

In the united Germany, this appreciation for the innate value of story can been seen in the renaissance of the literary salon as well. Like their nineteenth-century counterparts, these salons emphasize friendship, intellectual exchange and the nurturing of new talent. The current president of the Berlin-Brandenburg Academy of Arts, Györgi Konrad, together with the Society for Friends of the Academy of Arts, plans to open a permanent salon in the heart of Berlin and to invite established cultural and political leaders from Germany and abroad to participate.[18] This type of salon is interesting in its goal of uniting the literary and political spheres through the act of open, public readings. In a recent article on this phenomenon, appropriately entitled "Die neue Lust am Erzählen," the opening of the Berlin Wall is linked to the renewed interest in telling stories: "Mit der Einheit war die so lange eingemauerte Geschichte wieder in Bewegung geraten und setzte Geschichten frei, die nur aufgesammelt werden mussten, um erzählt zu werden."[19] Moreover, the article maintains, with the renewed interest in stories has come a vitality to the German literary scene, which had up through the 1990s a reputation of being antipathetic to narrative.[20]

To this end, then, I bring together in the Conclusion this phenomenon of a renewed interest in the story and manners of storytelling in the larger context of the future of German literature and film, by examining select works of fiction and film that represent a new narrative literature and cinema. Although such a neonarrative aesthetic does not in and of itself signal the death of the avant-garde, it nonetheless does represent a challenge to some of the avant-garde tropes that have been accepted by the cultural establishment. Moreover, that two once iconoclastic artists, both steeped in the protest and experimental movements of the 1960s, now reject antinarrative principles in favor of the story, which many cultural historians have directly condemned as "bourgeois," is further telling. Whether this return to the story represents a conservative trend toward the restitution of bourgeois elements in the artistic world or a new exploration of the possibilities of narrative remains to be seen. Through an exploration of these ideas, I hope to demonstrate the importance of these new narrative constructs for contemporary German literature and film, and in doing so, to show how storytelling is central to questions of modernity, technology, history, and redemption.

~ 1 ~

The Art of Storytelling: Origins and Definitions

The art of storytelling and the need and desire to tell stories is older than recorded time. Recent studies have suggested that storytelling can be traced back as far as Neanderthal and Cro-Magnon beings, who, by simply recounting an everyday event or situation and by ordering them into some sort of chronology, began the tradition of storytelling and narration (Harrell 10–11). These two acts, recounting events and creating order, would become central components of the story in both society and in literature. Before the advent of writing, these early stories began to serve a purpose greater than that of merely informing, namely, they became, as Horace later mandated for art in general, a source of both entertainment and education, and as such they were handed down from generation to generation, creating a tradition of oral narrative. The development of this tradition into an art form was inexplicably linked to the development of language, in that as greater linguistic possibilities evolved, the abilities of the teller expanded correspondingly and the act of narration became enriched with suspense and excitement.

The art of oral narration created by prehistoric humans and continued by the Sumerians, Greeks, and Romans is, however, viewed today by many ethnologists as a dying art. The development of writing—and later of the printing press and mass media—has threatened this art and jeopardized not only its niche in society but its very existence. The true "näive" storyteller was a product of an illiterate, analphabetic society, in which oral narrative served not only as a source of entertainment, but also as the only means of preserving traditions, of educating, and of elucidating certain rituals and religious beliefs (Rooth 11–12, Harrell 61f.). Thus today in order to trace the origins of stories and storytelling and to determine their function and importance within a society, ethnographers are studying the cultures of analphabetic, indigenous peoples that have not been tainted by modern developments that threaten the oral narrative tradition.¹ In such cultures, oral narratives still play an important part in their lives and customs.

Opinions on the importance and relevance of storytelling in modern society, however, vary. One ethnologist has maintained that, with the reduction in illiteracy, storytelling has "diminished in importance" and in Western society is "considered obsolete" (Rooth 11–12). On the other hand, writer and literary critic, Reynolds Price, is still convinced of the importance of narrative, arguing that the need to "tell and hear stories is essential to the species *Homo sapiens*—second in necessity apparently after nourishment and before love and shelter."² Whatever decline in oral narration Western society may have experienced over the centuries, it seems clear that narration and storytelling are still popular, as evidenced by the number of storytelling contests in America, the popularity of traditional tales, myths, fables, and *Märchen* throughout the world, as well as the scholarly debates over the years on the importance and function of narrative. It is telling as well that the final Nobel Prize for Literature in the twentieth century was awarded to Günter Grass, for, according to the Nobel committee, his "frolicsome black fables portray the forgotten face of history."³ As an iconoclastic writer who himself has problematized the use and abuse of narrative, it was fitting that the final Literature Prize of the century should go to a master storyteller and especially to someone from a literary culture that for so long has spurned the uses of story and narrative. In his acceptance speech, Grass emphasizes the oral origins of storytelling and speaks of the need for the story in art and culture as an "Überlebens- und Kunstform."⁴ Furthermore the recent resurgence of studies on fairy tales and myth as well as the acceptance of children's narrative literature into the realm of academic study attest to the power and influence stories and tales have within modern culture and on the human psyche. Although no one can be sure of its exact origins—either historically, psychologically, or sociologically—storytelling certainly did not die with the development of writing, rather it became transformed into written narratives and as such reached new levels within the genre of epic prose.

Although much has of late been written on the origins of storytelling, defining exactly what constitutes a "story" or "narrative" is somewhat problematic. The *Oxford Dictionary of English Etymology* traces the origins of the word *story*—itself meaning a "historical anecdote" or "narrative designed for entertainment" (872)—to the Old French *estoire* or *histoire* (872). *History*, in turn, is derived from the Greek *historía*, meaning "learning or knowing by inquiry, narrative, history" (442). Thus the interconnection between historicity and narrative is contained within the word itself. Similarly, the German word *Geschichte* today has the dual meaning of both "story" and "history," yet according to the Grimm *Wörterbuch* is etymologically derived from the Old and Middle High German *gesciht*, which has the denotation of both "schickung" and "geschehen" (5:3857), implying a correlation between fate and experience. The connection then to narrative comes from its extended meaning: "mündliche oder schriftliche erzählung von etwas wirklich geschehenem, dann auch von etwas ersonnenem, das aber im grunde als wirklich geschehen gedacht ist" (5:3862). Thus with the very beginnings of the word, claims of verisimilitude were questioned, and, consequently, the word *Erzählung* counts as its Latin equivalents both *narratio* and *fabula* (Grimm 3:1078). The connection between the story and reality would be one debated throughout the course of history and the breakdown of this connection would inevitably contribute toward the decline of narrative in the twentieth century. Moreover, in both English and German, the linguistic and conceptual development of *story* and *narration* implies concepts of both historical preservation as well as entertainment, thus delineating these two words from the process of mere informing or from a factual recounting.

But the word *story*, as Reynolds Price notes, is also related to "wisdom" and "vision," thus making it "an account of something seen, made visible in telling" (15). He argues further that the origins of the word and implicit in the definitions given in dictionaries is a natural association with the teller; that is, that the word is defined from the viewpoint of the teller, and the audience is only the "object to be 'interested or amused'" (15). Over time, this distinction changed and the concept of storytelling came to encompass an implicit understanding between teller and listener. Michael Roemer elucidates the linguistic relationship between *narration* and *connection*, concluding that to know something is to have the ability to make connections.[5] Correspondingly the definition of a story necessarily changed over time as well, whereby it was imparted a certain degree of openness and ambiguity so as to allow the listeners the opportunity to interpret or understand what was being told based on past experience and using their imagination (Harrell 65). This connection and interdependency between teller and listener is crucial to the art of oral narration, for a story cannot be told without a listener.

With the onset of written narrative, however, this assumption began to change radically. No longer was it necessary to have an audience at hand, as the writer/teller could now narrate in the confines of his/her own study, committing a story to paper for posterity. Consequently, Price argues that with the development of the novel in the eighteenth century and the newfound consciousness of the possibilities of literary narrative, the assumption that "verbal narrative actively seeks an audience" became increasingly invalid.[6] (16) Indeed by the twentieth century, written narrative had in many cases ceased to seek an audience actively, returning instead to a situation not unlike that implied by its linguistic origins, namely, one in which stories were being told for the teller's sake rather than as a mutual act of communication between narrator and receiver.[7] The increased de-emphasis on the reception of a work served as the basis for a new trend of hermetic narrative, which in many ways came to represent the literary counterpart to the artistic concept of *l'art pour l'art*: the literary teller no longer needed nor, in many cases, cared about an audience or its ability to comprehend the story.

Why then tell stories if the linguistic and aesthetic nature of a text is itself the true art form? Here again theories vary, yet the basic tenet that a storyteller or artist needs or desires to relate something, be it to an audience or merely for his/her own sake, has remained constant.[8] Price answers this question by arguing that narrative provides numerous types of nurture essential to human survival. The value of stories, he writes, is:

> the simple companionship of the narrative transaction, the union of the teller and the told; the narrator's opportunity for exercise of personal skill in telling and its ensuing rewards; the audience's exercise of attention, imagination, powers of deduction; the spiritual support which both parties receive from stories affirming our importance and protection in a perilous world; the transmission to younger listeners of vital knowledge, worldly and unworldly; the narcotic effect of narrative on pain and boredom; and perhaps most importantly, the chance that in the very attempt at narrative transaction something new will surface or be revealed (26).

This argument could, of course, be made for both oral as well as literary narration, answering both the question "why tell stories?" as well as "why read?" Written narrative does, however, decrease the establishment of such a "companionship" with regard to the narrative transaction between teller and the told. Nevertheless with the transition from oral storytelling to written narratives came a shift from a shared communal experience to a more isolated reception of the text; storytelling lost its embeddedness in a shared experience.

Walter Benjamin and the Death of the Storyteller

This shift from the oral tradition of communicating experience to fictional narration is, according to Benjamin, "[d]as früheste Anzeichen eines Prozesses, an dessen Abschluß der Niedergang der Erzählug steht" (II.2 442). In his seminal essay, "Der Erzähler," Benjamin argues that the material which can be handed down orally is fundamentally different than that which constitutes the elements of the novel. Whereas the storyteller draws upon personal experience and transforms it so as to make it appear part of the experience of those listening to the tale, the novelist remains isolated, creating a work in solitude: "Die Geburtskammer des Romans ist das Individuum in seiner Einsamkeit, das sich über seine wichtigsten Anliegen nicht mehr exemplarisch auszusprechen vermag, selbst unberaten ist und keinen Rat geben kann" (II.2 443).

The ability of the storyteller to "counsel" others, Benjamin writes, stems from the fact that the story or tale has a particular usefulness in society:

> Dieser Nutzen mag einmal in einer Moral bestehen, ein andermal in einer praktischen Anweisung, ein drittes in einem Sprichwort oder in einer Lebensregel—in jedem Fall ist der Erzähler ein Mann, der dem Hörer Rat weiß. (II.2 442)

However, since the story is "eine Begleiterscheinung säkularer geschichtlicher Produktivkräfte," wisdom and truth, he argues, were at the beginning of the twentieth century dying out and, as a result, narrative was becoming removed from the realm of living speech (II.2 442). If the didactic quality of the story together with its ability to establish connections between teller and audience does indeed constitute the two primary elements central to its usefulness and importance in literary narrative, then the question as to how writers and artists view the relative importance of these two qualities then determines the value placed on narrative and stories at any given time. Beginning at the turn of the century, the importance of the story within the literary work was greatly debated and for the first time called into question based on this very relationship. Benjamin argues that the decline in wisdom and truth in modern society in fact precipitated the demise of storytelling and that information has supplanted the story in importance. With the increase in the dissemination of information and the emphasis on specialization, larger notions of truth and wisdom become increasingly invalid, a concept which would, of course, become central to postmodern aesthetics in the latter half of the century.

With the decline in the value of experience, the basis for narrative, the desire and hunger for information in modern society increases. Information, in contrast to narrative, is immediately verifiable, and as such removes the necessity of establishing a psychological connection between the events on the part of the audience by providing an immediate causal explanation. For Benjamin, half the art of storytelling is keeping the story free from explanation, for information demands explanation without personal connection (II.2 445). Roemer makes a similar point, but shows the inherent ironic contradiction. Using the example of tragedy, Roemer relates that, on the one hand, stories present themselves as a means of making sense out of the world; by presenting the cause and effect of someone's action, we see the consequences. But in actuality they do not create order out of chaos, for while they do present a series of events in a plausible causal sequence, they fail to give any clear meaning or explanation for why these events occurred in the first place (44). In fact, stories are more closely related to myth, he argues, for they give the illusion that we understand the world, when in reality they show that the world is inexplicable. Thus Benjamin's contention that storytelling by its very nature remains free of explanation posits the question as to what the story's mimetic function is. If indeed, as Roemer maintains, the traditional story is paradoxical in that it "renders events that cannot be averted and problems that cannot be solved" (48), then perhaps it portrays a somewhat accurate view of the world. However, the desire to represent the world through art has resulted in a continuous search for increasingly new ways of approximating reality, a search which also contributed to the rejection and death of narrative in the twentieth century.[9]

With the advent of telecommunication and mass media, modern society has become inundated with information and facts, but lacking in stories. This has, in turn, altered the nature of society. Brooks, one of the first literary critics to argue for the value of narrative in a postmodern culture, has noted that the "familial and communitarian circles which fostered the telling of the *Tales of Mother Goose* and the *Kinder- und Hausmärchen* collected by the Grimm Brothers" are no longer present in a society in which literature is "in the process of becoming commercial, even industrial, and . . . urban" (*Tale* 285). Even in the earliest days of an industrial, urban society, Benjamin saw the inevitability of the decline in the dissemination of wisdom, which he terms the "epische Seite der Wahrheit" (II.2 442). This loss is brought about by a new state of narrative in an age of mechanical reproduction, in which the mass production of books has created a situation in which narratives are both produced and consumed in solitude. No longer do people gather around the storyteller to hear the wisdom bound in the form of story. Instead, the writer has become isolated from an audience and is no longer the traveler who practices a craft of preserving traditions and histories. The reader too is equally isolated, and in solitude jealously seizes upon the material presented, destroying meaning in the process (II.2 456). In a lengthy exegesis on this phenomenon, Benjamin shows that the novel, and thus the process of reading a novel, is inexorably tied to the quest for the "meaning of life," and that the preeminence and foreboding of death sanctions the storyteller and imparts authority to his story (II.2 450). Thus "[d]as was den Leser zum Roman zieht, ist die Hoffnung, sein fröstelndes Leben an einem Tod, von dem er liest, zu wärmen" (II.2 457).

Brooks has read Benjamin's essay less as a plea to return to an era of oral narration—which is irretrievably in the past—than as a protest against the state and place of the text in the modern world. He sees the essay as an objection to the "decontextualization of discourse, [and is thus] an effort to rediscover certain coordinates of narrative in narrative voice, in the transmission of a certain 'wisdom' from narrator to narratee, in the transaction or transference that takes place every time that one recounts something to someone" (*Tale* 290). Nineteenth-century novelists, in fact, sought to reproduce this situation in written narrative by expanding the numbers of the narrative voice in the novella by means of framing devices. Such stories and novellas attempt to reconstruct storytelling situations by introducing a second level of narrative. Brooks feels that the attraction writers felt at that time toward oral communication lies above all in their "deep wish to believe in the cognitive value of narrative, its capacity to make a difference through the transmission of experience" (291). However, this construction was not suited for the lengthier narratives of the novel, and, instead, novelists began experimenting with the possibilities of structuring narratives even further. Modern (and later postmodern) narratives forgo this attempt altogether, emphasizing instead the *act* of narration, or in many cases the narrative itself, creating new forms of meta-narratives, which are completely removed from all semblance of the oral tradition.[10]

Indeed, Ricoeur, in his three-volume study *Time and Narrative* (1985), shares the same concerns that Benjamin expressed some fifty years earlier, namely that in modern society human beings have lost the desire to share experience and thus modern narratives can no longer achieve the same sense of closure that oral narratives could. Even the centrality of death, which Benjamin maintained was the ultimate means of closure for novelistic forms, is no longer possible due to the discordance of discourses in modern society. Consequently, Ricoeur writes:

> Perhaps, indeed, we are the witnesses—and artisans—of a certain death, that of the art of telling stories, from which proceeds the art of narrating in all its forms. Perhaps the novel too is in the process of dying as a form of narration. Nothing, in fact, prevents our excluding the possibility the cumulative experience that, at least in the cultural space of the West, provided a historically identifiable style might be dying today (28).

Thus the postmodern novel has perhaps once again reached an impasse, not unlike the crisis experienced in Europe and in Germany at the beginning of the century, in which, rather than having reached a limit, novelists were exploring the possibility of destroying narrative boundaries. In both cases, however, many critics and writer alike heralded the novel's ultimate demise.

Modernism and the Crisis of Verisimilitude in the Turn of the Century German Novel

Most literary critics and historians agree that the Golden Age of the novel in Europe was the nineteenth century. In France, England, and Russia, as well as in Scandinavia, novels of great scope and power were published, mirroring in many ways the dimensions of the modernizing society which had produced them. By the beginning of the twentieth century, however, the novel began experiencing significant changes and, in many ways, narrative prose no longer resembled the novels of the preceding century. Experimentation and new means of artistic production coupled with a rapidly changing society resulted in new theories and ideas of what the novel could and should be; and, in some cases, the validity of the genre as a whole was even called into question. Consequently, a wide-ranging debate ensued in which writers, critics, and intellectuals all discussed what came to be known as the crisis of the novel. Just as there were a multitude of opinions as to the cause of the crisis, so too were there countless pronouncements as to what it all meant. Invariably, discussions both then and now turned to narration and what the purpose and function of narration should be within the novel. This, in turn, led to a growing excitement on the one hand for the newfound possibilities of the novel, but also to numerous lamentations on the death of the novel and of narration.

This debate was no less pronounced in Germany, where novelists such as Thomas Mann, Alfred Döblin, and Robert Musil all expressed their views on the topic, with varying degrees of optimism.[11] However, the German novel had, unlike its European cousin, reached an earlier high point in the late eighteenth century, with the development of a form unique to German literature, the *Bildungsroman*. According to Thomas Mann, German novelists produced very little in the nineteenth century that could be considered great art or seen as a contribution to the development of the European novel (XI 470). In an essay from 1939 tracing the development of the novel in Germany, "Die Kunst des Romans," Mann speaks of a "Fremdheit des Romans in Deutschland," arguing that Germany's contribution to art in the nineteenth century was not in the realm of the literary, but in the field of music (XI 470). With the exception of Goethe, Fontane, and some of the Romantics, Germany, in his view, contributed very little to further the art of the novel in the nineteenth century. The corollary to this was the failure of German Realism to take hold, in part due to the fact that the prose of German Realists suffered from what various critics have seen as their provinciality and, as one has termed it, the "political backwardness of the social group to which they belonged."[12] Mann, however, connects this not to a lack of artistic talent or to the social background of certain writers, but to the *Geist* of the German nation as a whole and the sociopolitical atmosphere of the time:

> Man sagt nicht zuviel, wenn man den Roman europäischer Prägung für eigentlich landfremd in Deutschland erklärt—womit Bedeutsames ausgesagt ist über das Verhältnis des deutschen Geistes nicht nur zu dem eingeborenen Demokratismus des Romans als Kunstform, sondern zur Demokratie überhaupt im weitesten und geistigsten Sinne des Wortes. (XI 470)

Mann infers here that the novel is not only a mirror of the *Zeitgeist* of a nation, but also that there is an interrelationship between the mind set of a nation and the accepted forms of literary expression. This postulate lies at the heart of the debate surrounding the state of the novel and the possibilities of narrative, as twentieth-century novelists increasingly viewed the novel as the truest reflection of society and thus the spirit of the nation.[13]

Mann's summation of the Germans' relationship to democracy comes as perhaps no surprise given the year of its writing, but more unusual perhaps is his view of the novel as the most democratic of art forms. By virtue of its ability to reflect the spirit of a nation, its natural ability to give expression to modern life and its social and psychological passion, the novel "[wurde] zur repräsentativen Kunstform der Epoche und den Romandichter selbst mittleren Formats zum modernen literarischen Künstlertyp par excellence" (Mann XI 468–469). This had not always been the case in Germany, however, as the novel had always struggled for recognition as an art form in part due to the historical importance and esteem bestowed upon the epic. For many, Mann argues, the novel remained a long time the poorer cousin to the more majestic verse epic: "Es ist wahr, historisch gesehen bedeutet der Roman regelmäßig ein späteres, unnaiveres, sozusagen, 'moderneres' Stadium im epischen Leben der Völker, und das Epos stellt im Vergleich mit ihm immer etwas vor wie die gute alte, die klassiche Zeit" (XI 458). Thus the novel came to be seen as a *Verfallsform* of the higher prose form, the epic. With this came the beginning of the gradual displacement of the narrative tradition; since the epic was, as Benjamin maintains, the keeper of the storytelling tradition, and the novel its successor, with the degeneration of the novel came then the disintegration of narrative. Moreover, up until the twentieth century, prose fiction was, as Mann points out, itself considered inferior to the drama, "welches alle übrigen Dichtungsarten in sich vereinigt und in der Tat der Gipfel der Poesie, die Königin in ihrem Reiche ist" (XI 457). This subjugation of the novel to the drama led not only to the former's inferior position, Mann argues, but, at times, even to its disregard within literary history.

But Mann views the novel not as merely the *Verfallsform* of the epic; rather he sees the epic as a "primitive Vorform des Romans" and the "Verfall" of the novel not as a process of degeneration and death, but as a development, a "Verfeinerung, Vertiefung, Veredelung" of the novelistic form (XI 464). It is a form which has struggled throughout time for recognition, but due to its inherent qualities, is superior to other forms by virtue of its inclusiveness and all-encompassing epic nature. This view has important implications for the stature of stories and narration, given their relationship to the epic. Whereas Benjamin had argued that the epic was the literary bearer of the oral tradition and that the novel contributed to its demise, Mann's view of the novel as the successor to the epic underscores the novel's claim to being the keeper of the oral narrative tradition. In contrast to Benjamin, Mann makes a strong case for the novel as having a positive influence on the oral tradition, in that the novel reflects a refinement of narrative possibilities.

Such high praise for the novel is not surprising, coming from a writer of epic, historical novels. Benjamin, though, agrees with Mann's distinctions between the epic and the novelistic, but differs on his assessment of the two genres. In another essay on the novel, Benjamin writes:

> Was den Roman vom eigentlichen Epos trennt, fühlt jeder, der an die homerischen Werke oder an das dantesche denkt. Das mündliche Tradierbare, das Gut der Epik, ist von anderer Beschaffenheit als das, was den Bestand des Romans ausmacht. Es hebt den Roman gegen alle übrigen Formen der Prosa-Märchen, Sage, Sprichwort, Schwank-ab, daß er aus der mündlichen Tradition weder kommt noch in sie eingeht. (III.1 230–31)

Benjamin argues here, as he does in "Der Erzähler," that the isolation of the novelist and the lack of oral source material for the novel threatens not only to diminish shared, communal experience, but may lead to a "Verstummen des inneren Menschen" whereby the writer is no longer able to convey inner thoughts and feelings (III.1 231).

Ironically, Benjamin chose to express this view in a review praising Döblin's *Berlin Alexanderplatz*, a novel which, Benjamin maintains, marks an attempt toward novelistic storytelling. What distinguishes the novel, he claims, is its foundation on the stylistic principle of montage, a style that enables the proclamation of the "Alleinherrschaft des Authentischen" (III.1 233). Döblin is, according to Benjamin, a born *Erzähler* who protests the death of a "natural" use of language by incorporating Bible verses, statistics, headlines, and reports in his novel and thereby imparts a sense of authority and authenticity to the work not unlike that found in the epic. As such, Benjamin views *Berlin Alexanderplatz* as one of the first works with the potential to reconcile narration with the novel, albeit one that breaks from the "natural" use of language and telling, reflecting a new understanding of the function of language in narrative conveyance. Ultimately Döblin's attempt at constructing a new novel fails, Benjamin feels, for at the point in which Bieberkopf's "Dasein" can no longer benefit the reader (by symbolically imparting a higher meaning), he ceases to be exemplary and "ist lebendig in den Himmel der Romanfiguren entrückt worden" (III.1 236). As a result the novel becomes the "äußerste, schwindelnde, letzte, vorgeschobenste Stufe des alten bürgerlichen Bildungsroman" (III.1 236). While Benjamin's review of *Alexanderplatz* is somewhat harsh, it nonetheless follows closely the ideas he formulated in "Der Erzähler" by utilizing similar commentary and argumentation. In his review, however, he delineates the elements of Döblin's novel which have story-like and thus epic characteristics, based primarily on the possibilities afforded by Döblin's montage technique, which imparts a truer sense of documentation. The documentary aspect functions not unlike the oral narrative in that both use language similarly as a means of reproducing reality or, in the case of *Alexanderplatz*, the reality that is Berlin. In this sense, Benjamin is in agreement with Mann in that the novel can be a refinement of the narrative possibilities of the epic. But their different conception of the use of language reflects the split in theories of the novel: for Mann the novel in all its expanse allows for the telling of epic narratives in the greatest of detail; for Benjamin the novel allows for linguistic and narratologic experimentation not possible in the epic that are more "authentic" and reflective of social and cultural reality.

Although Benjamin maintained his reservations about the future of the novel, Mann undeniably classifies the novel as an art form and a "Kunstgattung" of the highest rank. It is the *Geist* and genius of the writer which has elevated the novel to great heights, for it, unlike any other literary form, has the patience and the time to develop and portray "nicht den Ausschnitt, die Episode," but "das Ganze, die Welt mit unzähligen Episoden und Einzelheiten" (XI 461). Thus as the ultimate literary democratizer, the novel is able to deal with an infinite array of topics and themes too broad for the epic or the drama. Mann cites, for example, a passage from Goethe's *Dichtung und Wahrheit* which served as a motto for his own undertaking of the material in his *Joseph* cycle: "Höchst liebenswürdig ist diese natürliche Geschichte: nur erschient sie zu kurz, und man fühlt sich berufen, sie in allen Einzelheiten auszuführen" (XI 447). What the story in its Biblical telling lacked was the space and time to provide extensive detailed descriptions of Joseph and his story, an aspect which the novel as a literary form affords and which Mann utilizes in his novelistic cycle. Basing his argument for the validity of the artistic novel on Schopenhauer's view that the novel reached a higher, nobler position through a principle of *Verinnerlichung*,[14] Mann argues that the true art of the novel and thus the task of the writer is nevertheless not to tell of great events, but to make the little, the quotidian, interesting. The connection between this inner turn of narrative and the ability to make the mundane interesting is the secret and key to the development of the novel, and, ultimately the source of a story's popularity. Historically seen, the novel has thus changed very little, Mann claims, for even the German *Bildungs-* and *Erziehungsroman* is not representative of a progression or development of the novel, but is little more than the "Verinnerlichung und Sublimierung des Abenteurer-Romans" (XI 466). This novelistic form, however, represented for Benjamin as well neither progress for the novel nor a deviation from its norm: "Indem [der Bildungsroman] den gesellschaftlichen Lebensprozeß in der Entwicklung einer Person integriert, läßt er den ihn bestimmenden Ordnungen die denkbar brüchigste Rechtfertigung angedeihen. Ihre Legitimierung steht windschief zu ihrer Wirklichkeit. Das Unzulängliche wird gerade im Bildungsroman Ereignis" (II.2 443).

But it is the very expansive nature of the novel, with its detailed descriptions, discussions, and discourses that Mann praises, which Benjamin deems detrimental to the art of storytelling: "nichts tötet den Geist des Erzählens so gründlich ab wie die unverschämte Ausdehnung, die in unser aller Existenz das Romanlesen annimmt" (III.1 231). The breadth and scope of the novel, which in Mann's view allows it above all other prose forms to explore the world best, kills the essence of storytelling. In Benjamin's view, though the novel never had the ability to simulate the oral narrative tradition, novels of epic scale provide even less an opportunity for a restitution with storytelling or with the epic narrative, which manages to maintain its innate affinity to narrative due to the oral nature of the genre. This fundamental characteristic of the novel, its expansiveness, would continue to increase the gap between storytelling and the novel throughout the twentieth century, as novelists exploited this difference resulting in the demise of the few remaining elements of the oral tradition.

But the apparent limitlessness of the novel would lead to further problems with regard to story. In his examination of twentieth-century narrative prose, Wilhelm Emrich argues that the novel had found itself in a state of crisis as a result of the inability to achieve a sense of closure.[15] He cites the novels of Musil, Thomas Mann, Rilke, Broch and Kafka as exemplary works that demonstrate the limitations of the novel and maintains further that narration no longer existed as a possibility within the novel, as novelists had become more interested in detail and discussion than with narration and storytelling. Above all Thomas Mann, Emrich maintains, "erzählt nicht mehr, sondern erörtet, diskutiert, beschreibt, zergliedert" (59). Moreover, the very precision of Mann's analysis and the exactitude of his reflections and perceptions stood in direct opposition to the essence of *Erzählkunst* (59). Emrich's assessment reflects in many ways Benjamin's view that, whereas storytelling had become threatened by the novel, the novel too was in danger of dying out due to the proliferation of information and the newfound compulsion to convey it. While Benjamin pointed to the inundation of facts and statistics from newspapers and brochures, Emrich extends this notion to narration, stating that this type of description had overtaken storytelling in the twentieth-century novel resulting in epic scale novels which revel in description at the expense of narrative economy.

Both Emrich and Benjamin share a common view of what is lost and sacrificed when description and detail supplant storytelling: namely the transference of shared experience. Emrich, for example, defines the goals and the aims of *Erzählkunst* based on its effect: "Sie erweckt im Leser oder Hörer die Illusion ein Wirkliches mitzuerleben oder zu erfahren" (60). Narration and storytelling have the ability to transmit through fiction a sense of understanding and shared experience which discursive narratives lack. To illustrate his point, Emrich cites Mann's speech on his *Joseph* novel-cycle in which Mann claims that the rhetorical devices used in the novel are all "Täuschung, Spiel, ein Kunstschein," leading Emrich to question the ability of the novel overall to achieve verisimilitude. Mann, however, saw these characteristics not only as positive but as the strength of narrative fiction, for although such devices are deceptive, they are nevertheless a means "zur Erzwingung von Wirklichkeit" (XII 448). Emrich, on the other hand, viewed them, and what he similarly sees in Musil as "der Wille zur Genauigkeit," as a hindrance to storytelling and narration.

The proliferation and spread of information and the resulting trend toward description had a decisive effect on storytelling. Benjamin claims that information, as a form of communication, "zeigt sich, daß sie der Erzählung nicht weniger fremd aber viel bedrohlicher als der Roman gegenübertritt, den sie übrigens ihrerseits einer Krise zuführt" (II.2 444). This crisis stems from the fact that information by nature demands comprehension and shuns ambiguity; as a result, its value does not survive the moment it is new and, unlike the story which has a certain timelessness about it, lives only for the moment (II.2 445). As such, Benjamin defines the value of storytelling based on its permanence and, in doing so, he establishes a dialectic between the limitedness of information and the transcendency of the story. This shift in literature from timelessness to immediacy parallels the growing demands in society for facts and information as opposed to broader parables and narratives. Nowhere does this dialectic become more integral in the novel than in Döblin's *Berlin Alexanderplatz*, a novel which deals with, among other things, the increased tempo of modern society.

In an essay on the structure of the epic work, Döblin proposes that "der Bericht," as opposed to narrative, forms the basis of the epic novel. He then offers three postulates as to the function of the epic: "Das epische Werk berichtet von einer Überrealität"; "Das epische Werk lehnt die Wirklichkeit ab"; and "Die Epik erzählt nicht Vergangenes, sondern stellt dar."[16] By suggesting that the epic represents the present as opposed to the past and further creates an "Überrealität," Döblin establishes a form which perhaps most closely approximates Benjamin's conception of a literary oral narrative. In his review of *Alexanderplatz*, Benjamin praises Döblin's radical break with tradition and states that Döblin's essay on the structure of the epic is "ein meisterhafter und dokumentarischer Beitrag zu jener Krise des Romans" (III.1 231). He further contrasts Döblin's narrative theory with André Gide's conception of a *roman pur*, arguing that the two represent opposite poles of the dialectic, whereby the *roman pur* "reines Innen [ist], kennt kein Außen, und somit äußerster Gegenpol zur reinen epischen Haltung, die das Erzählen ist" (III.1 232). At first, this would appear to be contradictory, for Döblin's theory rejects realism and, in his novel, facts and reports serve as a primary structure, something which Benjamin maintains stand in direct opposition to storytelling.

However, it is more than just realism and narrative style which is important, for the story should also present something useful, Benjamin argues. In this regard, Döblin is just such a writer, for *Alexanderplatz* offers the reader a moral, an element crucial to its function as a story, and in the process, it incorporates facts and reports in such a way so as to maintain its "story-like" qualities. And so it is on these grounds that Benjamin judges the novel: "Es ist lohnend, der Kur an Franz Bieberkopf nachzugehen" (III.1 233); but it is also on these grounds that the novel falters.

However, as Mann has stated and as Döblin himself has admitted, these stylistic devices are nevertheless lies and as such reject reality, once again calling into question even the so-called "epic" novel's claims to verisimilitude. To this end, Emrich has summarized the inherent conflict and consequently the major question confronting modern narrative: "Ist es möglich, an Stelle der falschen Kategorien, mit deren Hilfe unsere schlechten Romanschreiber, Wissenschaftler und Staatsmänner eine zweite utopische Wirklichkeit schaffen, die Lüge ist, mag sie nun dichterische Fiktion oder Ideologie sein, eine befriedigende Totalität zu gestalten, in der der potentielle Mensch, der Mensch als Inbegriff seiner Möglichkeiten, sich zu entfalten und eine sinnvolle Existenz zu leben vermag?" (66). What Emrich is in fact questioning is if the principles of the *Bildungsroman* are still meaningful and if enlightened thought, or, what Habermas would later term the project of the Enlightenment, has come to an end. This has important ramifications for the utility and need for literary stories, for, if stories are didactic, as they have traditionally been throughout the course of history, then what happens if the belief in edification (*Bildung*) through narrative is lost? Moreover, if the novel ceases to lay claim to reality and its constructs are self-acknowledged lies and games, then what becomes of the literary story?

Central to this problematic was a concurrent debate on the position of art and the artist within society, a relationship which had also begun to change at the beginning of the twentieth century. At that time, both the concept of "high" art and the elevated position of the writer were beginning to dissolve, in favor of art and literature which reflected the cold, objective reality of modern society. Moreover, the historical, bourgeois novel quickly became antiquated. With it, the long-standing tradition in German literature and philosophy of the artist as an Olympian outsider who through his/her isolated yet elevated status is able to look out upon the world and create a work of art reflective of the world's greater truths was becoming equally suspect. The modern novel, as a product of the modern artist, was also no longer capable of fulfilling this vision. Modern society and the individual in the twentieth century had become too complex for the artist to grasp. As a result, many of the fundamental categories once assigned to the novel had lost their validity: "keine menschliche Handlung ist überschaubar, kein Mensch als Charackter definierbar," Emrich states with regard to modern society (64). The conception of the artist as an outsider offering his/her view of the world and of mankind is no longer possible within a complex society, not even through the medium of the novel, a form which is, in principle, unlimited in scope. Although novels of epic proportion attempted at this time to approximate the reality of their characters and their respective worlds—the preeminent example being Joyce's *Ulysses* with the amplification of one day in the life of the protagonist into an epic novel—they all failed to reach a sense of closure or finality that is normally associated with storytelling and narration. It becomes impossible to convey a sense of shared experience and reality via a narrative form which essentially has no limits. Consequently, writers began experimenting with narrative forms and intentionally broke down traditional narrative constructs in an attempt to redefine the novel; and the story was no longer a valid tool for reflecting reality or for imparting meaning and insight.

As a result, the novel came to be defined in the twentieth century so as to include a vast array of styles and types of narrative works, including the idea of an "anti-novel," a form which inherently expressed the discontent with the limitations and confines of the novel.[17] In an essay from 1913, Döblin, for example, wrote: "Der Erzählerschlendrian hat im Roman keinen Platz; man erzählt nicht, sondern baut. Der Erzähler hat eine bäurische Vertraulichkeit. Knappheit, Sparsamkeit der Worte ist nötig" (17). As such, Döblin rejects Mann's assertion that the novel is within the realm of art, maintaining instead that the primary object of the novel is "die entseelte Realität" and that, as such, it has no claims to the realm of art (17). Furthermore, the novel should emphasize occurrences rather than characters, action as opposed to thought; and in doing so it functions more as a report (*Bericht*) than as an extended narrative.[18]

As an expression of this theory, *Berlin Alexanderplatz* can be read as one of the first novels to cast off narrative in favor of conveying the reality and experiences of modern city life through a montage of styles and literary techniques.

Döblin's approach, which Theodore Ziolkowski has termed "fictional disintegration," stands in direct contrast to Mann's, who attempts to convey a sense of totality in the world by "isolating certain elements of reality and intensifying them to a point where they become symbolically representative of the world as a whole."[19] Döblin, on the other hand, allows for greater freedom within his novelistic structure, thereby permitting individual elements to be loosely linked to the greater whole. Whereas stories create connections and an understanding of the world by presenting cause and effect, Döblin's novel does not provide this totality or sense of connectedness. What results is the beginning of the breakdown of conventional linear narrative, a process which will continue throughout the century, leading inevitably to the final end-stage of narrative, the anti-narrative.

Despite the "disintegration" of fictional techniques employed in the novel, *Alexanderplatz* nonetheless maintains one central aspect of traditional storytelling—the experiential narrative. Werner Welzig, for example, has called the novel "ein Stück selbsterlebte Realität, der Erfahrungsbereich des Berliner Arztes Döblin" (114). While Döblin's goal was not, to be sure, to create a work in the mode of the traditional narrative, it does convey a sense of shared experience. As such, *Alexanderplatz* has served as a model for a number of later novelists who would attempt with ever greater frequency to incorporate personal experience within fictional narrative.[20] However, Döblin was still concerned with the collective (as evidenced by the novel's title, a collective space where people gather and congregate) and how the individual becomes shaped by external as opposed to internal forces. Yet modernist novels increasingly tended toward subjectivity and the inward reality of its protagonists, a tendency which Mann also notes in his essay on the novel and one which would have a profound impact on the course of the novel as well in relation to narrative voice.

Over the course of the nineteenth century, the narrative voice had shifted from the commonplace third-person narrator of Victorian novels to a more introspective "Ich-erzähler" within the context of literary modernism. This narrative shift brought about not only a more personalized narrative voice, but also allowed for greater flexibility in literary style and form. In turn, new techniques of literary expression arose, including stream of consciousness and inner monologue, which gave greater insight into the psyche of the narrator but, in time, also led to a crisis of reliability and the further demise of novelistic storytelling. Adorno attributes the increased suspicion toward the interrelationship between the mimetic potential of the novel and its claims to objectivity as stemming from the rise of subjectivity, "der kein unverwandelt Stoffliches mehr duldet und eben damit das episches Gebot der Gegenständlichkeit unterhöhlt" (61). Consequently, the rise of subjectivity forced a further break between the traditions of the epic and the novel by virtue of its opposition to objectivity and verisimilitude, two aspects that are central to the art of storytelling.

In his study of the rise of the modern German novel, Russell Berman attempts to determine why a "cultural rupture" occurred in Germany, which led to the aesthetic practices of "modernist" writers, after 1900 (vi). Berman argues that the answer lies within the rhetorical devices of the literary works of this period which reflect a certain "communicative strategy designed to produce a relationship with the recipient," one that is necessarily social and reflective of social changes within society (vi). Such a communicative strategy suggests the intents of storytelling through the establishment of a more solid relationship between teller and audience. This resulted, he argues, from a fundamental artistic crisis in the latter half of the nineteenth century, namely the breakdown of social realism. Berman sees the erosion of poetic realism as stemming from both external and internal factors: "external because industrialization aggressively transforms the structure of the literary public; internal because the immanent categories of the realist texts diverge increasingly from the character of monopoly capitalistic society" (57). Thus with the loss of realism's "cultural viability," new forms of literary experimentation arose and flourished, all with the fundamental goal of establishing a connection between aesthetics and social change. Berman further sees a process of "social delegitimation of the individual" within the context of modernist society, which had the consequence of undermining the viability of the third-person omniscient narrator and which gave rise to the epic collectivity of leftist modernism (58). This crisis of the individual and the disintegration of the self led to a profound shift in narrative constructs in the early part of this century that would, in the end, culminate in a greater crisis of narration and narrative possibilities. In many ways, Berman echoes the primary thesis of Lukàcs' *Theorie des Romans*, which sought to analyze the novelistic form at the beginning of the century from a philosophic-historical point of view. In his *Vorwort*, Lukàcs summarizes the fundamental conception of his study: "die Problematik der Romanform ist hier das Spiegelbild einer Welt, die aus allen Fugen geraten ist. Darum ist hier die 'Prose' des Lebens nur ein Symptom unter vielen anderen dafür, daß die Wirklichkeit nunmehr einen ungünstigen Boden für die Kunst abgibt" (12). Lukàcs recognizes and establishes a relationship between form and reality which later formed the crux of the debate on novelistic form. The rejection of verisimilitude as a basis for art likewise facilitated, at least theoretically, the introduction of psychological elements into the novel, Lukàcs argues, and this practice, as Döblin and later Adorno would show, would lead further to the downfall of narration.[21]

Both the introduction of the psychological as well as of modernist literary devices to the novel had as their source a shift in the overall conception of the novelistic narrator. In his study on the development of the novel, Wolfgang Kayser argues that it is indeed the evolution of the *Erzähler* which characterizes the modern novel. Kayser attributes Sterne's *Tristram Shandy* to being the first novel to show, "worin das Neue der modernen Romanform gegenüber dem Barockroman lag: in dem fiktiven, aber so merklichen persönlichen Erzähler mit seinem persönlichen Blick auf das Dargestellte und seinem persönlichen Verhältnis zu dem (fiktiven) Einzelleser" (19).[22] The development of a personal narrator and a correspondingly personal view of the represented lays the foundation for what Kahler refers to as the inward "turn" of narrative.[23] This predilection for the personal and the emphasis on the self would become the hallmark of the modern novel. Milan Kundera has in fact argued that it is one of the fundamental questions on which the novel is based: "All novels, of every age, are concerned with the enigma of the self. As soon as you create an imaginary being, a character, you are automatically confronted by the question: What is the self?" (23). Kayser agrees, arguing that this very problematic, though, led to an internal crisis of the German novel at the turn of the century, the death of the third-person narrator and the rise of subjectivity. This rise of subjectivity and the emphasis on the self were then ruinous to the communal and communicative nature of storytelling. But the predominance of first-person narrators was in and of itself not incongruous to storytelling for many oral tales themselves utilize this form. However, the increasing stylistic innovations and experimentation that first-person narratives afforded increasingly distanced the texts from their orally told cousins.

Already by the end of the nineteenth century, writers had begun experimenting with the narrator and forms of narration, searching for new means of expression. Although such change and formal experimentation were certainly not new, the underlying conception was: for the first time a sense of mistrust with regard to the conventional novel was beginning to arise, arousing the suspicion that the novel's conception of reality was no longer "real" and no longer a "getreuer Ausdruck des heutigen Verhältnisses zum Dasein und Sein" (Kayser 28). The sense of trust and security that the novel once provided was now lacking and, as a result, writers began to attack everything associated with the novel's form. As Kayser put it: "Im einzelnen richten sich die Angriffe gegen alles, was wir als wesentlich für die Form des modernen Romans erkannten: gegen das Erzählen vom persönlichen Standpunkt aus" (28). This attempt at eliminating the third-person, "objective" narrator in favor of first-person, stream-of-consciousness narratives and techniques of inner monologue led to a dissolution of the relationship between the reader and the narrator and eventually to the complete disappearance of the *Erzähler* (32).

As a result of an increasingly modernized and mechanized society and with the impending decline and fall of social and familial structures in early industrial society, new attempts were made to adjust the structure of the novel to the changes in society. The ultimate goal for many modernist novelists was to find better ways of objectively reflecting reality in a world in which security and relationships of trust no longer existed. As such, a debate arose throughout Europe as to the function and the direction of the novel. Central to this debate was the sense that simple narration could no longer describe and depict the complexities of modern society. However, this resulted in a peculiar paradox with regard to the novel; as Adorno formulated it in a 1954 essay on modernism, "es läßt sich nicht mehr erzählen, während die Form des Romans Erzählung verlangt" (61). As a result, new methods and techniques of narration were sought. Within the fine arts as well as within the relatively new medium of cinema, the concept of montage entered into literature, as writers abandoned attempts at linear narrative in favor of fragmented scenes which better approximated the hectic rhythms of city life. The proliferation of information and facts brought about a fractionalization of the continuity that many artists and intellectuals perceived as reality[24]. As larger, "grand narratives" began to lose their importance and meaning, so too did a sense of connectedness and unity within both society and art. Lukàcs termed this sense of unity that was once found in reality "Seinstotalität" (12). Further, he maintained that as reality ceased to serve as a source of artistic creation, so too did literary forms change as the sense of closure and totality became increasingly invalid. As a result, writers felt compelled to reject realist tendencies and to experiment with narrative technique in an attempt to expand the boundaries of prose so as to capture reality more faithfully. Adorno calls for a similar path: "Will der Roman seinem realistischen Erbe true bleiben und sagen, wie es wirklich ist, so muß er auf einen Realismus verzichten, der, indem er die Fassade reproduziert, nur dieser bei ihrem Täuschungsgeschäfte hilft" (64). The Expressionists' experimentation with episodic structures as well as the newly incorporated technique of montage served literature well, as did the use of inner monologue and stream-of-consciousness narration. This break from tradition was not merely a question of writers exploring new ideas but it constituted what Alan Bance has termed "a revolution in the writer's expectations of the reader, a refusal to provide the usual narrative guidewords or 'markers' being only one symptom of the change" (53). Many writers were heavily influenced by similar movements in the fine arts. Both the Dadaists and the Surrealists began challenging the recipients' expectations and began calling into question the boundaries and limits of art. Döblin himself acknowledged the influence of the avant-garde on his writing and Benjamin similarly noted the influence of André Gide's *roman pur* on Döblin.[25]

Such increasing experimentation in style and form led to widespread debates in modernist circles on the function of art and its relationship to form.[26] In Britain, for example, where Joyce's influence was becoming increasingly felt, there were two schools of thought concerning the novel: there were writers who wished to expand the boundaries of the genre and to elevate the novel to a higher art form, and there was a public who simply wanted a "good read" and was not interested in, or for that matter, could not understand, any sort of narrative experimentation.[27] The dichotomy arising in the first half of the twentieth century between artistic vision and audience expectation would remain a primary point of contention throughout the century, but it would also, some argue, influence the direction of the novel and play an important role in the return to novelistic storytelling toward the end of the century. However, with innovations in printing and publishing as well as a change in the consumer consumption at the turn of the century, the novel nonetheless enjoyed new freedoms in formalistic and stylistic technique. What ensued was "an intense concern for the potentialities of the instrument itself, for the latent and neglected capacities of narrative fiction" (Kermode 9). For the first time, narrative technique was analyzed and scrutinized to the same degree that music, painting, and philosophy were, all in an attempt to break from the traditional constraints of narrative. Kermode notes, however, that this experimentation was not singular to Britain, but that across Europe it had become "commonplace to decry mere story" (10).

Literary experimentation as well as the literary modernist and avant-garde movements came to an abrupt end in Germany with the rise of National Socialism and its strict rejection of such principles.[28] If anything, the novel experienced a regression stylistically in Germany during the 1930s and 1940s and those writers sanctioned by the government returned to traditional forms and structures of narration. A distinction should be made, however, between novels written during this time by exiled writers and those written under the aegis of National Socialism. Although these novels are clearly quite different thematically, it is quite interesting that structurally, there is little evidence of a crisis of form while thematic concerns took precedence over experimentation or issues of aesthetics. In the case of the former, writers often turned to the historical novel, revitalizing the long, descriptive, linear narrative characteristic of such works. The so-called *Deutschlandromane* and *Exilromane* both attempted to describe the situation in Germany as well as in exile, incorporating personal first-person narratives, but showed little interest in breaking down narrative constructs. In many ways, these novels represented a temporary restitution of literary storytelling, for they conveyed and shared personal experiences abroad using conventional methods of narration. However, as the emergence of exile literature was inexorably connected to the historical, social, and political situation which produced it, such literature cannot be considered a major influence on the further structural and intellectual development of the novel on the European continent. Those writers who returned to Germany after the war (Thomas Mann, Anna Seghers, Bertolt Brecht, for example) were, to be sure, influenced by this trend, and often continued with a similar style. However, their works came to represent for many young postwar German writers the establishment, and would subsequently be rejected in the 1960s in favor of a more experimental type of literature.[29]

Similarly the novels written during the period of National Socialism in Germany exhibited, with few exceptions, no development or resolution of the theoretical debates which led up to the period. Often these novels oriented themselves toward the *Entwicklungsroman*, but with the necessary depiction of the protagonist's development into a model citizen (quite often the author him/herself). As nontraditional narratives were rejected and suppressed, the National Socialist novel would have little influence on future writers, with the notable exception that it served as an antipode for postwar literature. While many writers in the postwar era would once again come to reject both stories and narrative, the connection of both to National Socialist literature constitutes only part of what would be a greater skepticism with regard to reliability and believability in narrative constructs.

Postwar Literature and the Birth of the New Novel

The literary productivity in the immediate postwar era in Germany has been characterized—rightly or wrongly—as a period of "Neubeginn," "radikaler Neubau," "Kahlschlag" and as a historical "Stunde Null."[30] As a result of attempts by a new, younger generation of writers to minimize and simplify prose and literary language, the novel did not play a decisive role in the immediate postwar period due primarily to its expansive nature; the short story, however, took on new importance, in part, because it corresponded well to the aesthetic goals of *Kahlschlagliteratur*. However, the short story did not share many of the characteristics of the traditional oral narrative, as it often lacked the traditional narrative structure of a beginning, middle, and end. Moreover, its goal was usually not to convey a sense of shared experience, but to present a "slice" of reality. Wolfgang Weyrauch's introduction of the term *Kahlschlag* in 1949 stood as a programmatic statement about the desire of postwar writers to cut through the "Dickicht" in German literature. Individuals and literary groups alike participated in projects aimed not only at rejecting their immediate literary heritage, but looking forward to new means of expression and reconciliation with the past.[31] Moreover, a number of German authors in exile (including Thomas Mann and Hermann Hesse in Switzerland) were involved in a negation of Nazism through the restitution of pre-Nazi literary traditions and cultural values.

Consequently, by the early 1950s, a debate about the future of the novel, whose development had for all practical purposes ceased during the period of National Socialism, resurfaced and once again, centered around the problematic of representation and mimesis, but this time from a decidedly different perspective. Whereas writers and theorists in the past questioned the ability of prosaic forms and language to capture the complexities of a modern reality, postwar writers were concerned with the contamination of language and words and resorted to a complete *Kahlschlag* of tradition and historicity. This rejection of language and tradition culminated in a skepticism of form and expression, a skepticism which would again lead to the rejection of literary storytelling. Writers like Wolfgang Koeppen and Grass found direction from their Weimar models, Broch and Döblin, while others rejected all Germanic influences and sources and turned instead to American and French writers for inspiration.

The debate over narration and the validity of stories was again at issue in the 1950s. Adorno's assertion in his 1954 essay "Standort des Erzählers im zeitgenössischen Roman," that "es läßt sich nicht mehr erzählen" (61), referred primarily to works of the past (namely those of Proust, Mann, and Joyce), but was nevertheless a reflection of an atmosphere pervasive in German literary circles of the time; namely the general skepticism and rejection of the traditions of the "bürgerlicher Roman," which included the defining device of the third-person omniscient narrator.[32] While Adorno advocated "einen neuen Roman" in the sense of the anti-realist, *antibürgerliche* novels of the 1920s and 1930s, a number of young German writers came under the influence of a reformed, new novel of a different tradition, the French *nouveau roman*.

In the 1950s and 1960s, Alain Robbe-Grillet heralded what would become known as the *nouveau roman* through a series of essays discussing the state of the European novel and the need for new ideas and experimentation. Central to his argumentation was his view that the novel had reached a state of stagnation and that the nineteenth-century bourgeois novel as well as the psychological and naturalistic novels of the earlier part of the century had become antiquated (17). The novel, he maintained, has always been in a state of flux and has thus continually reinvented itself. In the 1950s, there was once again a need for imminent change, as the "destitution of the old myths of 'depth'" had necessitated a radical break from the traditional means of understanding prose fiction (24). Whereas literature had in the past consisted of writers burrowing below the surface of the outer world in order to excavate some deeper truths, such notions of greater truths below the surface of reality were becoming obsolete. His contention that literature had lost claims to greater truths would be echoed more and more in the second half of the twentieth century by postmodernist theorists and critics. But Robbe-Grillet's theories also played a significant role in the demise of literary stories, for, by their very nature he claimed, stories represent greater truths and contain meaning. With the loss in the belief of such truths, the story must necessarily be rejected as an invalid literary trope.

Furthermore, concern for an understanding of the human condition had superseded explications of Nature, and consequently, the composition of literary language changed as well. As Robbe-Grillet noted: "From day to day, we witness the growing repugnance felt by people of greater awareness for words of a visceral, analogical, or incantatory character. On the other hand, the visual or descriptive adjective, the word that contents itself with measuring, locating, limiting, defining, indicates a difficult but most likely direction for a new art of the novel" (24). In theory, the *nouveau roman* should in effect reject traditional usages of language and embrace a new method of descriptiveness which explores the human condition as opposed to that of the exterior world. Moreover, such language is anathema to storytelling, for stories are not concerned with defining and locating, but with describing and relating a given occurrence. A new language which concentrates on analyzing and deciphering the world would exclude the possibility of using the traditional story as a narrative trope; with a new language, a new means of fictional structuring is also required.

Robbe-Grillet's ideas and conceptions of literature and literary language appealed to a number of younger German writers seeking new means of expression and a break from stagnant traditions.[33] Exemplary among these writers was Peter Handke, whose first two novels were self-styled works in the tradition of Robbe-Grillet and Nathalie Sarraute.[34] Moreover, Handke gained notoriety through his attacks on the German literary establishment at the 1966 meeting of the *Gruppe 47*, in which he criticized the *Beschreibungsimpotenz* of a literary group founded under the pretext of creating a new literature. Handke's criticism of his literary peers reflects an understanding of description and aesthetics similar to that expressed by Robbe-Grillet, in that both reject the goals the art of description once served. Whereas description once "claimed to reproduce a preexisting reality," according to Robbe-Grillet, "it now asserts its creative function," thus serving the aesthetic nature of language as much as of reality (147). Handke makes a similar argument in an essay justifying his remarks at the meeting of the *Gruppe 47*:

> Ich habe nichts gegen die Beschreibung, ich sehe vielmehr die Beschreibung als notwendiges Mittel an, um zur Reflexion zu gelangen. Ich bin für die Beschreibung, aber nicht für die Beschreibung, wie sie heutzutage in Deutschland als "Neuer Realismus" proklamiert wird. Es wird nämlich verkannt, daß die Literatur mit der Sprache gemacht wird, und nicht mit den Dingen, die mit der Sprache beschrieben werden. (29)[35]

This emphasis on language reflects a major concern for Handke as well as a central theme in his early works: namely, the ability of language to accurately convey and express reality.[36] This connection between language and reality—or lack thereof—forms a substantive aspect of the *nouveau roman* in that the term is, according to Robbe-Grillet, "merely a convenient label applicable to all those seeking new forms for the novel, forms capable of expressing (or creating) new relations between man and the world, to all those who have determined to invent the novel, in other words, to invent man" (9). The ability to "invent man" and thus construct the world, as it were, is possible only through a reevaluation of the meaning of words. A corollary to this is a need for the reexamination of the constructs of narration, for, as at the turn of the century, the validity of narration had to be questioned in order to attempt to convey the complexity of this newly constructed world.

For the proponents of the new novel, narration had lost much of its impact and importance. Telling stories was no longer an end in itself nor a means to a creative end. As Robbe-Grillet most bluntly put it:

> ... it is enough to read the great novels of the beginning of the century to realize that, while the disintegration of the plot has become insistently clearer in the course of the last few years, the plot itself had long since ceased to constitute the armature of the narrative. The demands of the anecdote are doubtless less constraining for Proust than for Flaubert, for Faulkner than for Proust, for Beckett than for Faulkner .... Henceforth, the issue lies elsewhere. To tell a story has become strictly impossible (33).

Part of the reason for demise of the story lies with the overall rejection of the nineteenth-century novel and its tropes and constructs. Many among this new wave of writers[37] rejected the idea of the novel as a literary form which told stories and developed characters according to the principles of the nineteenth century. As Susan Sontag has noted, cinema inherited much of the novelistic tradition and became its leading exponent as it could better serve the mimetic and narrative demands of nineteenth-century realism.[38] The novel, then, she claims, must "record without comment the direct and purely sensory contact with things and persons which the 'I' of the novelist experiences" (108). This transformation meant the inevitable death of one crucial aspect of the novel, the third-person narrator, and with it the novel's storyteller.

This newfound supremacy of language and form over content served as an underlying foundation for poststructuralist aesthetics as well as for much of modern literary criticism as a whole, whereby many of the long-standing assumptions about literary aesthetics began to be questioned. The implications for storytelling and narration were, consequently, quite far-reaching. Barthes, one of the first to herald not only the end of narration but also the death of the author, views the creator of the modern text no longer as a storyteller-narrator but as nothing more than a "scriptor" who is born simultaneously with the text, having neither a past nor a "message" to convey.[39] The modern text has eliminated the necessity of an author-narrator in the traditional sense and has supplanted it with a scriptor engaged in a performative, linguistic act. Similarly, Barthes writes, the scriptor "no longer bears within him passions, humours, feelings, impressions, but rather this immense dictionary from which he draws a writing that can know no halt: life never does more than imitate the book, and the book itself is only a tissue of signs, an imitation that is lost, infinitely deferred" (147). With the disintegration of fiction to a series of encoded signs, the experiences and accumulated knowledge once associated with the storyteller are no longer extant, thus diminishing one of the primary functions of narration. Moreover, this transformation from author to scriptor reflects a broader tendency toward a more hermetic type of postmodern literature in which the traditional connection between teller and receiver, one of the last remnants of the oral narrative tradition, dissolves. It is at this point that the teller (now scriptor) no longer actively seeks an audience and the literary act thus ceases to serve a primarily communicative function.

Furthermore, as Barthes maintains, when the text becomes transformed into a "multidimensional space in which a variety of writings, none of them original, blend and clash," then "meaning" in the more traditional sense becomes lost as well (146). Poststructuralist and postmodernist theories similarly reject traditional notions of "meaning" and "message" in the text in general, for the text no longer lays claim to verisimilitude or mimesis.[40] Such texts, and indeed such a view toward literary production as a whole, signal an end for the need for storytelling and its basic function of communicating shared values and communal experience. This loss has prompted Paul Ricoeur to speculate that we are perhaps "at the end of an era in which narrating no longer has a place . . . because human beings no longer have any experience to share" (28).

Such an outlook is at once quite pessimistic, yet nonetheless concurrent with the very nature of the postmodern, for it reflects the notion put forth by Jean Baudrillard and other French critics that the world has surpassed an end point in which all new forms and possibilities of innovation have been exhausted and only simulation remains. In such a state, experience, history, and communication become in themselves meaningless as they no longer serve the functions with which they were once associated. This condition is reflected in a great number of "postmodern" literary works of the later half of the twentieth century, all of which reject notions of historicity and conveyed experience in favor of inwardly directed journeys of self-discovery, a period heralded in Germany as the "Neue Innerlichkeit" or "Neue Subjectivität."[41]

The Return of the Story

Nevertheless, at the very end of the twentieth century, a trend toward the restitution of history, communication, and narrative has taken place. Huyssen has argued that postmodernism has always been in search of tradition while just pretending to innovation (170). Moreover, he writes, postmodernism has not been completely ahistorical but rather has sought a historical tradition, a tradition that is intricately bound with the search for cultural identity. To his mind, such quests point dramatically to the "exhaustion of the tradition of the avant-garde, including post-modernism" (172). To be sure, there have all along been voices and theories of opposition to anti-narratives as well as postmodernism. Habermas' claim that the project of modernity has not fully been completed has been attacked by most theoreticians as a neoconservative struggle to hold onto the last remnants of modernism. Central to Habermas' argumentation, however, is the idea that art has not lost aesthetic value and function, or, at least, that these qualities must be reaffirmed.[42] If indeed art continues to possess a sense of value, then its communicative function in society is perhaps also still valid, albeit endangered. Habermas' views, standing in the philosophical tradition of Adorno and Benjamin, in many ways indirectly affirm the value and importance of narrative and stories in literature based on the central idea of storytelling as a means of conveying truth. While Benjamin maintained that "[d]ie Kunst des Erzählens neigt ihrem Ende zu, weil die epische Seite der Wahrheit, die Weisheit, ausstirbt" (II.2 442), Habermas seems to be arguing that this art (and art in general) is not dead and can still impart truth and wisdom, suggesting as well that through literature and storytelling, wisdom is still to be found.

Even some of the most ardent supporters of postmodernism acknowledge the validity of stories. Jean-François Lyotard has, for instance, affirmed the value of narration and storytelling: "Narration is the quintessential form of customary knowledge, in more ways than one . . . [S]tories themselves recount what could be called positive or negative apprenticeships (*Bildungen*): in other words, the successes or failures greeting the hero's undertakings" (19–20). Lyotard argues further that a "work can become modern only if it is first postmodern. Postmodernism thus understood is not modernism at its end but in its nascent state, and this state is constant" (79). Given Lyotard's understanding of postmodernism, it becomes much easier then to reconcile the reemergence of narrative and storytelling, as he himself does, by allowing for the necessity of transmitting traditional forms of knowledge, namely stories. Huyssen makes a similar case for the coexistence of story and innovation and experimentation, arguing that the preservation of certain elements of the avant-garde tradition is "not at all incompatible with the recuperation and reconstitution of history and of story" (174). In fact, he cites Handke's early works as being exemplary of merging of the two traditions.

Indeed, there are many indications to suggest that literature and art have not fully relinquished their claims to truth and knowledge. As Horst Steinmetz has noted, in his analysis of the old and new function of the storyteller in the modern media world: "Seit etwa der Jahrhundertmitte hingegen sind nun, soweit ich sehe, im Roman Entwicklungstendenzen erkennbar, die auf Restitution der Geschichte und auf eine Rehabilitierung des Erzählens hinauslaufen. Der Erzähler kehrt zurück beziehungsweise ist bereits zurückgekehrt" (72). Steinmetz agrees that with the break from traditional means and methods of narration in the first half of the century, art and literature lost its function and ability to create meaning and order, which further became victims in postmodernist literature. Thus twentieth-century literature shifted from attempting to portray and convey reality to providing ways of dealing with reality. However, this lack of structure and of constructs for interpreting reality led to complexities and difficulties on the part of its recipients. As Steinmetz writes:

> Die Abwesenheit der Geschichte erschwert vor allem die Konstitution desjenigen, was man die Botschaft, die Aussage, das Anliegen des Werkes zu nennen pflegt, seine Bedeutung. Aus der Perspektive des Werkes formuliert: Die Erfahrung des Wirklichen als eines nicht in einer Geschichte sich Verwirklichenden kann ohne Geschichte nur schwer vermittelt werden. Das hat seinen Grund darin, daß Wirklichkeit, Erfahrung von und über Wirklichkeit offenbar vornehmlich, wenn gar nicht ausschließlich, über und mittels Geschichten wahrnehmbar und gleichzeitig auch mitteilbar werden (74).

Although justification for the restitution of stories and narratives based on an analysis of the reception of literary works may seem arbitrary, Steinmetz also bases his arguments on anthropological and philosophical arguments not unlike those of Reynolds Price, who maintains that there is a certain need and demand for stories. Moreover, at the end of the twentieth century, the desire for order, meaning, and a sense of connection in the world became even greater.

Throughout the twentieth century, literary critics and philosophers have argued that there is a tendency as well as a necessity to understand life and thus reality through stories,[43] and, as Benjamin has maintained, ancillary to that is the need to exchange experience so as to understand better both the world and ourselves. Furthermore, Steinmetz shows that the return to storytelling and literary narrators has been enabled, if not necessitated, by other forms of media. Contrary to Benjamin's assertion that the ubiquity of information, especially as transmitted by mass media, would lead to the inevitable death of the novel and thus literature, Steinmetz maintains that visual media has in time satisfied our need for stories and thus necessitated the return and restitution of storytelling within literature by forcing it to reestablish its competitive position with the visual arts.

Although purists would perhaps scoff at the notion that literature would adapt itself in order to "compete" with other art forms (especially with electronic media), there are undeniable indications that literature (and books in general) is experiencing a renaissance, and this may be in part due to changes within literature itself that have made it again appealing to the public. In a *Time* magazine article about the rise of book sales and of so-called superstores in the U.S., the author notes that in a time and culture "where book reading is supposed to be an endangered habit, it is an oddly heartening sight [that] book reading has suddenly gone aggressively public."[44] What is happening more and more is that book stores are becoming cafes and social gathering spots where customers can come to browse, talk, and read. The article notes that many stores sponsor social events as well as lectures, readings, and discussion groups. What is odd is that in a country not known for cafes and European-style salons and in the age of on-line books and information, book sales and literary readings are on the rise and are developing an associated social element as well. In a peculiar sort of way, this rise and rebirth of literature and of open and public readings and discussions reverses the trend of the isolation of the reader which Lukàcs and Benjamin saw as destructive to the oral narrative tradition.

Sociobiologists and evolutionary psychologists explain this and other similar trends as the result of atavistic and visceral yearnings for community and familiarity.[45] Politically, this need has manifested itself in the rise and growth of communitarianism, an international movement which defines itself as "people committed to creating a new moral, social and public order based on restored communities, without allowing puritanism or oppression."[46] Narratives and storytelling in many cases play an integral role in the creation of such moral and social orders, for, as Benjamin argues, the storyteller is akin to the sage: "So betrachtet geht der Erzähler unter die Lehrer und Weisen ein. Er weiß Rat-nicht wie das Sprichwort: für manche Fälle, sondern wie der Weise: für viele. Denn es ist ihm gegeben, auf ein ganzes Leben zurückzugreifen" (II.2 464). In a postmodern culture, such figures are rare; however, the need to be presented at least with the illusion that such people still exist is nonetheless strong.

In fact, to claim that storytelling is experiencing a "rebirth" is perhaps in some ways a misnomer as it in many ways never really died out, at least in the Americas. A *New York Times* article from 1991, for instance, tells the curious story of a man, Ray Hicks, who lives in the hills of North Carolina and makes his living from the art of storytelling.[47] The 74 year-old Hicks attained fame through his mastery of 18 tales known as "Jack Tales," which, according to Folklorists "have been transplanted from Europe and handed down to Mr. Hicks in an unbroken oral tradition thought to be eight generations old" and are derived from the same tales collected by the Brothers Grimm in 1812. The article notes that storytelling has been experiencing a newfound popularity, in part due to storytelling festivals around the country and has spawned a new generation of professional storytellers like Garrison Keillor and Spalding Gray. While Mr. Hicks cannot understand how someone could capitalize on such a talent and turn it into a profession, as he feels that money is a corrupting form of motivation (although he did receive a $5,000 award from the National Endowment of the Arts in 1983), he can offer an interesting analysis as to why storytelling is so popular: "It's to help people in living." As the article states, he feels "stories should be told the way scripture is read, for joy and wisdom" (A14), once again reiterating, probably quite unbeknownst to him, not only Horace's definition of art, but Benjamin's similar understanding of the importance of storytelling.

That this resurgence should come from the Americas is not surprising, given the importance writers from both North and South America have always placed on narrative and stories.[48] Uwe Timm, a long-time proponent of literary storytelling, maintains that the disrepute that has fallen on storytelling in Germany stems from a longer German philosophical tradition:

> Es gibt in Deutschland wenig Erzähler, und in Deutschland ist das Erzählen immer so anrüchig. Das hat eine alte Tradition von Hegel über Adorno, daß man durch Erzählen Wirklichkeit nicht mehr darstellen kann, was ich für einen ruinösen Quatsch halte. Das ist eine pessimistische Theorie, während in Lateinamerika, in Amerika, in Schweden, in Italien, in Irland, wo man auch immer hinkommt, immer erzählt wird, wunderbar erzählt, literarisch erzählt.[49]

Timm also acknowledges that in Germany there is a second problem, namely the pervasiveness of the modernist theory that reality is so complicated, "daß man gar nicht mehr erzählen kann" (109). However, there are many good storytellers in the U.S. as well as in Latin America, he feels. Writers in Germany need only have the "courage" to once again tell stories, above all since stories represent, for Timm especially, a type of resistance and opposition (*Widerstand*) to many of the problems in society.[50]

Sociologically a major impetus for authors in Germany once again to write, to narrate and to infuse literature with social import (thus overcoming the postmodern negation of meaning) came from the debates in the late 1970s and 1980s over the possibilities of nuclear war and a coming armageddon.[51] The apocalyptic forebodings found in much of the literature of the time, such as Christa Wolf's *Störfall* (1987) or Günter Grass's *Die Rättin* (1986), were characteristic of a new urgency to write that seemed to overshadow the self-imposed "Schreibverbot" as well as theories on the end of fiction to which many writers and critics ascribed. That German writers were indeed finding the courage once again to narrate is evidenced by the spate of novellas that appeared in the 1990s, a genre which is usually most strongly associated with the nineteenth century.[52] If the novella is the literary genre which best approximates the storytelling tradition, as Peter Brooks has argued, then literary storytelling, and hence the storyteller as well, would appear to be resurgent. Steinmetz, among others, singles out Handke as being exemplary of this trend: "Handkes starke Aversion gegen das Erzählen von Geschichten und gegen den Erzähler, die er im Frühwerk nicht genug betonen konnte, ist inzwsichen völlig überwunden" (72). Indeed, a closer examination of Handke's more recent works, reveals this to be the case.

~ 2 ~

Peter Handke and the Transformation of a Storyteller

In 1994, Peter Handke published three narrative prose works in English translation under the title "The Jukebox: And Other Essays on Storytelling."[1] The curious subtitle given to this collection[2] adds a certain explication to the works which was not present in their original form, but which nevertheless provides insight into Handke's own aesthetics and current view of literature. Handke's views on narratives and storytelling have changed over the course of his career. His more recent praise of storytelling is a prime example of the trend in contemporary German literature toward the use of narratives and literary stories. Handke's change becomes especially evident when comparing his early works and essays which demonstrated a strong aversion to narrative and stories to his recent works of short fiction from the 1980s and 90s and his open embracing of the story. Although his return to stories and storytelling is, to be sure, still of a highly intellectual nature and not (necessarily) of the engaging, "entertaining" sort, he does now nevertheless proclaim the importance of the story as a means of imparting narrative structure as well as a means of establishing personal identity and reclaiming history, issues which have been major themes in contemporary German literature.

Early in his career, Handke established himself not as a storyteller, but as an iconoclastic writer who purposely broke with literary traditions, often with the primary goal of provocation. Steeped in the Austrian avant-garde and borrowing heavily from the French *nouveau roman*, Handke's earliest prose fiction, his 1966 novel *Die Hornissen* (*The Hornets*), the 1967 novel *Der Hausierer* and his 1967 collection of short prose, *Begrüßung des Aufsichtsrats* (*Greetings from the Board of Directors*) dealt predominantly with linguistic questions and was, at times, quite abstruse. In the 1970s, however, he established himself as one of the leading German language writers and helped usher in a wave of self-reflective literature, which came to be known as "die neue Subjektivität."[3] These works of short fiction[4] were experientially based and in some ways resembled extended interior monologues, in that the narrator recounted his feelings and emotions in a pondering, philosophical style, at times in a self-directed Socratic method of questioning and answering.[5]

Not one to remain stagnant, however, Handke soon redesigned his narrative structures and wrote in the early 1980s a tetralogy[6] which reflects what Manfred Durzak has termed a "neues Gesetz": namely the (re)discovery of nature (146). Although nature and city spaces receive great attention in these works, the style is still quite self-reflective and inwardly subjective. Klinkowitz and Knowlton see this phase of Handke's writings as one central to his development into a postmodern writer, as these works discard "sociological and historical categories in favor of epistemological and phenomenological ones, emphasizing production rather than the finished product" (13). The concern for methods of artistic creation and production would remain central themes in most of his works to come. Moreover, this phase of his writing represents a reconfigured consciousness and understanding of the self, in which the "I" reconstructs the outer world as a manifestation of an inner world: "The result is objective knowledge permeated with subjectivity. . . . [T]he rediscovered 'I' discerns, classifies, and describes the perceived world and thus secures it as personal knowledge with an intersubjective component."[7] This approach to writing and perceiving reality, though very much in line with Handke's early aesthetics and writings, stands in stark contrast to the goals and functions of traditional storytelling, which stresses communication and a dynamic relationship between teller and audience based on commonalities and shared perception. Yet at the same time, Handke himself has stated that the writing process for him does not completely exclude his audience. In a 1975 interview, when asked whether he writes for a particular audience, Handke stated: "Ich bin immer mehr dazu gekommen, wie kann ich andere dazu bringen, . . . daß sie in der tiefsten Seele getroffen oder mitbewegt sind bei dem, was ich mache."[8]

This style of writing, with its emphasis on phenomenology, was typical of the literature of the late 1970s and early 80s and concerned itself less with communicating shared experience than with the subjective experiencing and perception of interior and exterior realities, a theme not unlike that promulgated by the *nouveau roman*. As Handke stated, he is less concerned that the reader shares or is moved by his perceptions per se than by what he is doing ("was ich mache"), namely writing. The transference of experience comes from a connection to the linguistic power and beauty of his writing and less with the subject and the signified. What becomes discernible in Handke's writing by the late 1980s, however, is a gradual shift from his early, linguistic-based anti-narratives toward an expression of self-discovery and phenomenology via more traditional forms of narration and finally, storytelling. To be sure, Handke has always been interested in the act of storytelling (*das Erzählen*) itself. Early on, however, he consciously strove toward breaking down traditional elements of the story and narrative techniques so as to reveal the artificial nature of the narrative act.[9] Gradually, though, his works in the late 80s sought a restitution of storytelling as a means of self-discovery and understanding. Thus his collection of essays in the 1990s professing the importance of storytelling can be read as an avowal of his newfound understanding of stories as a poetic methodology which facilitates a greater understanding of self-truths. This transition is in many ways consistent with Handke's continuous search for expression and modes of communication. Handke stands in a long tradition of writers—especially Austrian, from Hofmannsthal and Wittgenstein to Ingeborg Bachmann—who have been plagued by a crisis of language and linguistic expression. Handke's early *Sprachlosigkeit* would be instrumental, as well, in his initial rejection of narrative; having deemed stories part of the problem, he would search for new constructs that would facilitate expression. However, after experimenting with both meta-narratives and anti-narratives, his search for expression inevitably led him back to the framework of linear narratives and stories. This transformation, however, is best elucidated by comparison to his early aversion to narrative.

Handke's Early Aesthetics

A common subtext to all of Handke's works, but especially his early texts, is the fundamental questioning of the narrative act, and the extent to which words can meaningfully convey experiences and feelings. In his 1967 programmatic essay "Ich bin ein Bewohner des Elfenbeinturms," Handke outlines his early aesthetics and poetics, wherein he calls for more realistic methods of narration and description. As a "Bewohner des Elfenbeinturms," he claims to be searching "nach Modellen für eine Literatur . . . , dies schon morgen (oder übermorgen) als realistisch bezeichnet werden wird" (26).[10] His claims for a new, more realistic literature propelled him to prominence, primarily as a result of his attacks on the

Gruppe 47 at their meeting at Princeton in 1967. At that meeting, Handke brashly lambasted the German literary establishment with the reproach that they suffered from a *Beschreibungsimpotenz* and had misappropriated the term "Neuer Realismus," which had, as a result, paralyzed German literature.[11] In an explication of his criticism (actually a sort of apologia), he later stated that he did not oppose description per se, but was against the prevalent type of narratives in Germany at that time which many writers had falsely termed "Neuer Realismus."[12] Moreover, his primary concern in his attack was the lack of understanding about the nature of language and the discrepancy between the objects described and language itself as a linguistic signifier, a theoretical basis highly informed by structuralist theories and linguistics. Although Handke's critique resulted in a polemic which has since often served as the source of judgment for or against his literary output,[13] the substance of his remarks are in fact nothing more than a continuation of the debate over verisimilitude and language in fiction that had begun some fifty years earlier and which formed the basis for the crisis of the novel at the beginning of the century. Handke's remarks and prose helped usher in a similar crisis in the 1960s, which once again led to a rethinking of the concept and poetics of the novel.

Gretel Koskella, in her study of this novelistic crisis of the 1960s, points out that Handke's first two novels[14] are too often overlooked when evaluating his influence on the development of the German novel. Although his contributions to the development of the *Neue Subjektivität* are seen as his primary legacy, these early novels, she argues, were in fact very characteristic of a general movement toward experimentation and abstraction in the 1960s.[15] These novels were also highly influenced by avant-garde tendencies and were characterized by their lack of narrative structure. Furthermore, this period in general marked a turning point in the development of the postwar German novel, as evidenced by the existence of what Koskella terms a "literarische 'Fortschrittsfraktion' von jüngeren Autoren, die sich in Opposition zu herkömmlichen Normen setzten, um neue Richtungen zu erproben" (76). As a former member of the Austrian avant-garde movements *Forum Stadtpark* and the *Grazer Gruppe*, Handke's aesthetics were greatly informed by the search for the new modes of expression that these groups advocated. Handke's protests against the establishment could in fact be seen as a call for new sources of literary inspiration rather than solely as a rejection of previous modes of literary production. Thus Handke's early rejection of narrative had to do, in part, with his attempts at finding new methods of literary and linguistic expression. Indeed, Koskella notes that rather than categorically dismissing Handke and his critique, the *Gruppe 47* embraced his ideas and praised his sense of rebellion (78). Consequently, the group met only once more before disbanding, an indication that his criticism perhaps had some impact, for its members recognized that their circle, which had begun as an opposition group, had, by virtue of becoming the establishment, lost its validity.

Handke's early novels were less models of how literature should incorporate description, than works which expressed structurally the sovereignty of language and the primacy of form over content. As a result, the mimetic nature of the text became secondary to issues of objectivity, an aesthetic clearly informed by principles of the *nouveau roman*, as discussed in the previous chapter. As Koskella argues:

> Über die Ähnlichkeit zwischen den beiden ersten Romanen Handkes und der Romantheorie des französischen *nouveau roman* kann kein Zweifel bestehen. Die Methoden, die Handke anwendet, stammen direkt von den Methoden des Nouveau Romans, vor allem aber von der Romantheorie Robbe-Grillets, dessen Ziel es war, den Roman von Abbildungsfunktionen zu befreien, um Texte zu gestalten, die ihre eigenen Prozesse und ihre eigene 'Literarisierung' reflektieren. (84)

This type of self-reflective literature, which deals thematically with the process of text construction, would become a hallmark of Handke's work to come. Drawing on Robbe-Grillet's theory of the novel, Handke rejected and, in fact, deconstructed many traditional elements of the novel, foremost among them being linear narratives and a storyteller. His texts dealt instead with events and experiences which are molded and formed by language and represent an exploration of the various linguistic possibilities for relating these events. Inherent within these linguistic exercises is then an understanding of the potentials of narrative fiction, and for Handke its greatest potential was to provide a clearer understanding of the self.

Handke's stated conception of literature has always been connected to self-understanding: "Literatur ist für mich lange Zeit das Mittel gewesen, über mich selber, wenn nicht klar, so doch klarer zu werden" (*BE* 19). As such, literature possesses in his view an edifying value, a position which paradoxically has its roots not in the structuralist and poststructuralist theories demonstrated in his texts, but rather in the discourse of the Enlightenment. However, this approach differs primarily from that of the Enlightenment in that literature in his view does not serve a didactic or political function, but an exploratory one, one which should convey personal realities as opposed to greater truths. In fact, in one essay, "Die Literatur ist romantisch," he clearly takes issue with Sartre's conception of a *littérature engagée* by claiming that literature cannot be political, only the writer can, thus rejecting the idea of a politically didactic literature.[16] In his early essays, he outlines further the significance of literature for the development of his own self-conception: "Erst die Literatur erzeugte mein Bewußtsein von diesem Selbstbewußtsein, sie klärte mich auf, indem sie zeigte, daß ich kein Einzelfall war, das es anderen ähnlich ging" (*BE* 19). Literature thus enables both the writer and the reader to view reality critically and to become aware of literary realities. By calling into question existing realities and replacing them with fictive worlds, Handke rejects claims of truth or historical precedent, favoring instead the world and truths of literature: "Ich erwarte von der Literatur ein Zerbrechen aller endgültig scheinenden Weltbilder" (*BE* 20). This renouncing of existing realities and worldviews in favor of a reality based on the self has propelled Handke to the forefront of postmodern writers,[17] and has also served as a central tenet of the "Neue Subjektivität."

Structurally, Handke rejected early on many conventional tropes of modernist literature as well. First and foremost, he emphasized his disdain for stories and his concern for method and methodology. Stories are only bearable, he claimed, when spoken or orally narrated, and as such do not belong in works of fiction. This view represents a clear attempt at distancing storytelling from literature and reestablishing the primacy of form over content. Stories are merely a vehicle for conveying information about the world, he argued, an invention which has become unnecessary: "Immer mehr Vehikel fallen weg, die Geschichte wird unnötig, das Erfinden wird unnötig, es geht mehr um die Mitteilung von Erfahrungen, sprachlichen und nicht sprachlichen, und dazu ist es nicht mehr nötig eine Geschichte zu erfinden" (*BE* 24). Fiction, and its utilization of stories as its primary modus operandi, was too concerned with attempting to describe concretely a preexisting reality which was meaningless for Handke. The exploration and mastery (*Bewältigen*) of reality was the object of study for scientists, he claimed, whereas the exploration and mastery of his personal reality was the subject of his literature (*BE* 25). Such experiences and realities cannot be objectified through words or language, as the relationship between linguistic signifier and the signified object are predetermined by forces outside of his sphere of reality. Nor can they be conveyed through the use of stories, as stories represent something too ordered and "agreeable" for fiction. For this type of literature, a story is only legitimized through its own negation: "als reflektierte Verneinung ihrer selbst: eine Geschichte zur Verhöhnung der Geschichte" (*BE* 26).

By rejecting all conventional forms and methods of narration, the writer is then free to search for new models and modes of expression, ones which are more realistic than those prescribed by tradition. Important as well, he maintains, is the ability to recognize and reject these methods when they too have become mannered. Thus the goal of the writer is to seek continuously new modes of expression and of conveying reality, without losing sight of literature's purpose: to elicit self-understanding and achieve clarity of the self. Such a methodological program is at once reactionary and visionary, in that it demands of the writer continuous evolution and development. At the same time, it gives insight into Handke's gradual shift back to storytelling and narration: for Handke, the forms and tropes of his earlier periods had themselves become hackneyed and manneristic and he therefore felt that new modes of expression once again had to be explored.

Handke rejects the notion, though, that his career is marked by a series of turning points; rather he feels that his literary methodology is in a constant state of transition.[18] In interviews, he has defended his earlier writings, yet acknowledged that his views and convictions have changed so as to reflect more current literary trends and personal conceptions of reality.[19] Thus his change in attitude toward storytelling and narratives can be read not only as the result of a personal evolution but also as a reflection of a greater trend in contemporary literature.

The Early Novels: Experimentation and Anti-Narratives

Given Handke's rather categorical rejection of fiction and novelistic discourses in the 1960s, his earliest prose works can be seen as a reflection of this ideology, for, with them, he sought to define a new genre, namely the *Sprechstück*, a form that is part theater, part prose, and part poem.[20] The underlying principle in these works was a negation of all previous methods and methodologies of literary construction and convention. In their place, Handke proposed a system which establishes a doctrine of anti-narratology (*BE* 27). Similarly, Handke was to approach the novel from this same perspective, although the novel was not a literary form which, he readily admits, was inherently suitable to his ideas. In doing so, he appropriated the scheme of a novel and transformed its conventional elements so as to elicit once again an inner-reality. In describing the process of writing his second novel, he has written:

> Ich habe keine Geschichte *er*funden, ich habe eine Geschichte *ge*funden. Ich fand einen äußeren Handlungsablauf, der schon fertig war, das Handlungsschema des Kriminalromans, mit seinen Darstellungklischees des Mordens, des Sterbens, des Schreckens, der Angst, der Verfolgung, der Folterung. In diesen Schemata erkannte ich, als ich über sie nachdachte, Verhaltensweisen, Existenzformen, Erlebnisgewohnheiten von mir selber wieder. Ich erkannte, daß diese Automatismen der Darstellung einmal aus der Wirklichkeit entstanden waren, daß sie einmal eine realistische Methode gewesen waren. (*BE* 28)

This reappropriation and conscious utilization of the conventional tropes of an accepted genre is the essence of a postmodern aesthetic, one which recognizes the increasing invalidity of traditional genres and yet, through an acknowledged use of their elements, establishes new meaning via the primacy of and concern for form. Moreover, his emphasis on finding (*finden*) as opposed to creating (*erfinden*) narratives mirrors structuralist theories relating to the exhaustion of fictional possibilities: stories could no longer be created, rather only found in preexisting objects or other works of art. Thus, as Klinkowitz and Knowlton argue, the idea behind these novels is not about reality per se; rather, "it is about the medium in which the real manifests itself and in which the reality of the innerworld . . . confronts the outerworld: the medium of language" (22). The concern for the medium and the process of creating this medium, that is, fictionalized meta-narratives, would be a central theme in many of Handke's works to come.

Nevertheless, the early novels reject ideas of plot, character-development and a reliable narrator, a rejection drawn from the theories of the *nouveau roman*. Both works deconstruct the genre in which they are consciously in dialogue: *Die Hornissen*, the novel, and *Der Hausierer*, the mystery story. In *Die Hornissen*,

Handke utilizes multiple narrators and overlapping structures so as to purposely question the progression of the narrative. Firda has shown that this first work was heavily influenced by Handke's reading of Barthes (which Handke himself has acknowledged) and, as such, views the work as an example of an attempt at writing a novel based on structuralist principles (51–57). Firda notes as well that upon its publication Rowohlt issued an introductory statement designed to help the reader better understand the novel (52). In this statement, the work is termed a "new novel" primarily because the course of events are described in such a way that makes it impossible to determine whether they occur to the protagonist or whether they are part of the novel within the novel. This question forms the primary focus of the novel, namely, how to construct and reconstruct memory and thus narrative. What results, Firda claims, is "a new category of the traditional novel," one that supports Barthes' view of the novel as a source of fabricating meaning (56).[21] What it also reflects is the breakdown and deconstruction of the story. The novel consciously questions the nature of plot and story, and forces the reader to consider the usefulness and thus uselessness of traditional plots. Whereas conventional novels emphasize and rely on stories and plotting devices to convey ideas and meaning, *Die Hornissen* provokes an unconventional reading, whereby established meanings are called into question in favor of subjective notions of reality and understanding.

Similarly, in *Der Hausierer* Handke continues his experimentation with form and methodology, once again relinquishing traditional methods of narration and representation. The novel reconstructs a murder by dissecting the elements of the crime and commenting on the various occurrences through both a theoretical and a narrative aspect. Firda categorizes the work as a postmodern novel that "demands a willing reader, especially a reader who brings to the text an innate sense of the content and structure of a genre murder mystery" (57). Handke's challenge to the reader is to create a story of his or her own, by relying on one's previous knowledge and understanding of the given genre. The reader constructs for him- or herself a text and thus a story, which remains unresolved and unexplained.[22] Such a work undermines the reciprocal relationship implicit in the normal course of exchange between the teller and the audience by eliminating the "teller." Instead, the source of the information attempts as objectively as possible to present or represent the events without prejudice. This documentary approach dispenses with the need for establishing order, which ironically is a primary theme of the work.[23]

Handke acknowledges that these works lack a story, but he maintains that the absence of narrative is itself a new type of order: "Diese Erzählungen und Romane haben eigentlich gar keine Geschichte. Das sind nur in eine neue Ordnung gebrachte Alltäglichkeiten. Was daran 'Geschichte' oder 'Fiktion' ist, ist immer nur der Schnittpunkt zwischen den einzelnen Alltäglichkeiten. Das erzeugt den Eindruck von Fiktion" (Schlueter 164).[24] By dissolving the boundaries between fiction and reality and thus creating the impression of fiction, Handke further extends the limits of representation and reference points. The reliability of the narrator, a major concern of much postwar German literature, is no longer an issue, as the novel no longer lays claim to issues of verisimilitude or representation.

In practice, however, Handke's methodology was often greeted less than enthusiastically, and, rather than praised for their realism, his works were often criticized for their obscureness. Klaus Stiller, for example, wrote with regard to Handke's debut novel *Der Hausierer*, that the reader "soll die vom Autor umschriebene Story als Fortsetzung verstehen, Fortsetzung eines verheimlichten, imaginären Geschehens, dessen alleinige Kenntnis den Autor in die Position des Mehrwissers emporlüpfen soll" (48). Herein lies of course the central issue, namely how willing the reader is to forego notions of plot and story (while reading a novel) in favor of creating a narrative of one's own. Such critical responses were not unlike the criticisms of Robbe-Grillet's conception of the *nouveau roman* which was similarly attacked as being unreadable and hermetic.[25]

When asked in 1979, however, whether the novel as a form had run its course and was thus no longer a valid genre, Handke defended the novel, arguing that every generation has a need to read stories and narratives which are more than just journalistic reportage (Schlueter 165). Moreover, he felt the novel can still be beneficial for society, although he does question the terminology and conception of a novel:

> [I]ch denke, daß vielleicht der Roman—nun weiß ich nicht, was Roman wieder ist, aber daß eine bestimmte erzählende Haltung—der Gesellschaft sehr gerecht werden kann. Ich sage nicht "Roman," sondern die Haltung des Erzählens, die Mitvergangenheit: es war einmal, oder ich ging, oder er ging, sie, die Frau ging. Ich stelle mir vor, daß das eine ewige und auch die

freieste Sprache ist. Das heißt nicht "Roman," das heißt die erzählende Sprache (Schlueter 165).

This professed belief in the permanence of narrative language represents a marked contrast from his fellow avant-garde theorists as well as from his earlier statements and programmatic essays.[26] What it shows is the limits of experimentation as well as the necessity of narrative. Despite attempts at eliminating all semblance of narration, Handke begins to maintain that anti-narratives are actually impossible, for not only is narrating language intrinsic to the nature of writing, but it ironically also affords the writer the greatest degree of linguistic freedom.

Handke perhaps realized the limitations of anti-narratives already with the publication of his third novel, *Die Angst des Tormanns beim Elfmeter*, a novel which shows signs of a return to narrative language and structures. This novel, a critical success and one later filmed by his friend Wim Wenders, in many ways demonstrated Handke's view of the necessity of narrating language while at the same time concerning itself thematically with the very limitations of words and narration. The title figure, a soccer goalie named Bloch, is released from his job one day and begins an existential journey through the Austrian countryside in search of meaning in the world around him. Gradually Bloch realizes that his perception is distancing itself from reality and he becomes unable to control the separation between meaning and the outer world with which he must interact. For instance, one morning he awakens and finds that language and perception have lost meaning: "Mit geschlossenen Augen überkam ihn eine seltsame Unfähigkeit, sich etwas vorzustellen. Obwohl er sich die Gegenstände in dem Raum mit allen möglichen Bezeichnungen einzubilden versuchte, konnte er sich nichts vorstellen" (20). The breakdown between word and object and between signifier and signified represents a loss of meaning and the inability for Bloch to relate to the world around him. As a prime element of poststructuralist theory, it is also a reflection of the inability of words to accurately convey reality, a failure which in Bloch's case results in disorientation. He attempts though to overcome this breakdown by ordering and structuring the objects he perceives, i.e. to create a narrative: "Er behalf sich, indem er statt Wörtern für diese Sachen Sätze bildete, in der Meinung, eine Geschichte aus solche Sätzen könnte ihm erleichtern, sich die Sachen vorzustellen" (20). Bloch's attempt to rectify this problem and the failure of narrative to remedy the loss of meaning for the individual word reflects Handke's greater struggle on the whole. For Handke the writer, words too had innately lost the ability to convey either an inner or outer reality; his seeking to link individual words into a narrative would also inevitably be a failure for the sentences and stories they form were similarly lacking in meaning.

Bloch in true existential fashion (and one reminiscent of Camus's *The Stranger*) then commits a senseless murder of a cinema cashier. Unlike Camus's protagonist, however, this act is not one of liberation or self assertion of his fate, rather Bloch finds himself increasingly caught up and entangled in a world which has lost linguistic meaning. By the end of the novel, Bloch no longs finds words for the objects in his immediate reality, rather can visualize them only as objects, a state from which he finally finds no release. This theme, the relationship between word and object, would continue to play a central role in Handke's work, yet a solution to the dilemma would not be presented until the *Langsamer Heimkehr* tetrology.[27]

An important transitional work for Handke, however, is the 1972 novel *Der kurze Brief zum langen Abscheid* (*Short Letter, Long Farewell*) the first of his novels in which the storyteller is no longer disdained but glorified. Perhaps it was Handke's life long interest in the cinema as well as his more recent forays into filmmaking (his collaborative work with Wenders on the film version of the *Tormann* as well as collaborations on several short films) that resulted in the embodiment of the naïve storyteller in this novel in the figure of cult filmmaker John Ford. The novel, too, is very cinematic in structure in that it takes the form of road movie, a genre favored by New German Cinema (NGC) filmmakers as well as the beat poets of the 1950s, a group for which Handke and his generation have shown a decided fascination. Moreover, Handke uses quotes from Karl Philipp Moritz' *Anton Reiser* to set up the referential framework for the novel: namely a *Bildungsroman* of self-discovery. The Austrian protagonist, whose wife has left him and fled to New York, embarks on a transcontinental journey through the States in search of his wife and, in many ways, for a clearer understanding of himself and his own identity. Throughout his journey, the narrator wishes to visit Ford, the aging director who has retired in Southern California. Finally after meeting up with his wife and reconciling certain differences, they travel together to meet Ford. The narrator describes Ford as the quintessential storyteller who holds court on his terrace telling stories to friends and passersby: "[M]eist saß er davor auf der Terasse und redete mit alten Freunden . . . . Für die Besucher gibt es Korbsessel . . . . Wenn man darin sitzt und redet, fängt man bald an, dem anderen eine Geschichte zu erzählen" (186).

Indeed, the narrator, and with him Judith, end up telling their story to Ford at the conclusion of the novel: Judith had come to America, her estranged husband had followed; then she had had him followed, robbed and threatened. Now, however, they had reached a peace accord, reconciled and were able to go their separate ways. By telling their story to Ford, Judith creates a sense of closure to the their personal story as well as to the larger story as a whole. Moreover, their pilgrimage to visit Ford, who himself was one of the great cinematic storytellers, serves as a kind of benediction; through listening to this "wise" storyteller, they find a means of narrating their own story, through which they find resolution and redemption. In their discussions, Ford's one concern, however, is for the veracity of the story. He insists that all of his stories were true and nothing made up. When Judith concludes her story, his one question for them is whether it too is all true, invoking the need for truth in the stories told. The final words of the novel belong to her: "'Ja,' sagte Judith, 'das ist alles passiert.'" (195). At this point truth and fiction collide whereby Judith's assertion is that the events that she has just recounted—which are indeed the very same events that the reader has just encountered—are indeed true, intentionally blurring the line between fiction and reality and between narrative and meta-narrative. Through this postmodern guise of conflating fiction and reality, Handke is here first able to deal with the loss of "truths" and narratives, by creating a narrative in which he plays with the nature of fictitious and realistic stories. By posing the question of narrative veracity at the very conclusion of the work, Handke not only underscores the issue but renders it irrelevant. The characters he has created have been able to define themselves and inevitably find redemption through the creation of their own stories within the larger narrative of his fiction. In doing so, the ability of stories to represent and convey truths—something called into question by modernist and avant-garde writers and ultimately rejected by postmodernists—is once again reconstructed within the framework of a fictive work.

Once liberated from the necessity of veracity and expectations of truth, Handke was free to use the story as a means to his own artistic ends. The next phase of his writing then concerned itself with issues of narratology and how it is related to the dialectic between the individual and the outer world, a tenet which forms the basis for the ideas of the *Neue Subjektivität*. Klinkowitz and Knowlton characterize the "quest" undertaken by these writers whereby through a negation of existing structures, they create "visible antagonisms between individuals and the existing social order by reappropriating the world and displaying this newly created universe of fiction as personally secured knowledge imbued with subjectivity" (78).[28] The subjective approach to constructing a fictitious world would reach its pinnacle for Handke in the late 1970s with the publication of his *Langsamer Heimkehr* tetrology,[29] a series of novels which signals not only a culmination of Handke's search for spatial orientation but also a return, a *Heimkehr*, to Europe, to Austria, and to a search for redemption, for healing, for self actualization and for a new form of literary expression: the narrative act.

Crossing the Threshold to Narration: The Return of the Storyteller

In addition to introducing the new themes of space, orientation, and redemption,[30] *Langsamer Heimkehr* also represents a desire to recreate and reestablish order. Valentin Sorger, the geologist protagonist of the first novel, returns home to his native Austria after a lengthy stay in Alaska where he had been conducting research on the natural forms of the northern landscape. His slow journey home becomes a metaphor for his spiritual quest for a sense of orientation and salvation (as characterized in the book's opening passage: "Sorger hatte schon einige ihm nah gekommene Menschen überlebt und empfand keine Sehnsucht mehr, doch oft eine selbstlose Daseinslust und zuzeiten ein animalisch gewordenes, auf die Augenlider drückendes Bedürfnis nach Heil" [9]) as well as a search for order and form. As Hugo Caviola points out, Sorger inevitably finds the direction he has been seeking, and, as will become typical for Handke, it is manifested in narrative: "Having established a form of spatial orientation in the Alaskan wilderness and a form of social orientation in the city on the west coast, the narrator now realizes that the creation of a *narrative* can provide the form for an experience of continuity" (388). This epiphany, as Caviola terms it, is representative of a larger quest within the realm of Handke's literary journeys, one which involves the desire for unity between the fragmentary perceptions of the outer world and the subjective impressions of the protagonists' inner-world. He notes, for example, that this novel appeared two years after Handke's fragmentary collection of observations and aphorisms, *Das Gewicht der Welt*. The fragmentation as well as the absence of plot typified by his previous fictive works is an extension of avant-garde tendencies which had informed his work up to this point and can be read as a "negation of the 'false' linearity of narrative realism," a view which reflects the charges he made some years earlier against the *Gruppe 47* (388). Both Caviola and Christoph Bartmann assert that with these works, Handke begins to negate the negations inherent in the ideology of the avant-garde in favor of a reconstruction of narrative coherence, a methodology which is applicable to both narrative structures as well as linguistic representation. His subsequent work reveals a rethinking of traditional narrative structures as well as a new understanding of the relationship between language and reality.

In the 1980s Handke embarked on a series of works which both continued the program of *Langsamer Heimkehr* and explored the rediscovered territory of narrative constructs. Whereas his first two novels deconstructed the novel and the murder mystery as literary genres, these works also utilized and worked within the boundaries of preexisting forms, but this time with the intent of exploring the validity and possibilities inherent in these genres. Although the literary aims remained the same, Handke's methodology had clearly changed: rather than negating the story and dismissing the narrative act as a means of expression, he begins experimenting instead with the *Bildungsroman* (*Die Wiederholung*, 1986), the short story (*Nachmittag eines Schriftstellers*, 1987), and the Märchen (*Die Abwesenheit*, 1987) as a means of reestablishing form and as a mode of self-expression. Inextricably connected with these literary forms, of course, is the structured mode of narration found in the story. However, Handke first had to reconcile the incongruous relationship between language and narrative. His 1983 novel *Der Chinese des Schmerzes* took up this very theme.

The protagonist of this work, Andreas Loser, is a teacher of classical languages in Salzburg and an amateur archeologist who defines himself as a *Schwellenkundler* or *Schwellensucher* (24). Loser is also an acute observer who enjoys solitary walks through the city and the countryside, activities which afford him the opportunity to reflect on himself as well as his surroundings.[31] One day, while walking in the mountains, Loser finds a swastika painted on a tree. In a spontaneous act, he hunts down the perpetrator and kills him. Afterwards, he decides to reconstruct and reexamine his life, which leads him to become a listener. He asks various acquaintances to tell him "Schwellengeschichten" and, in the final portion of the story, he himself becomes a teller and his son a listener. He seeks out others to listen to his story as a means of spiritual redemption, finding that the story functions as a method of conveying his own history and his own existence.

This shift from viewer to listener to teller is significant for both the narrator as well as for Handke. Handke divides the novel into three portions plus an epilogue, "Der Betrachter wird abgelenkt," "Der Betrachter greift ein," and "Der Betrachter sucht einen Zeugen," each of which reflects various stages of the protagonist's development (and arguably, Handke's own development as a writer). Loser is thus defined as a viewer, or observer, something which has been typical of Handke's previous protagonists, as well as of himself. It also reflects the type of storyteller Handke the author is and becomes—a teller of observations. Indeed Handke, like his protagonists, is not a teller of tales in the traditional sense, but a recounter or describer of events and experiences. Nevertheless, it becomes clear that, textually, the act of telling serves a function not unlike that of traditional tales and tellers, namely to establish human contact and a sense of community. While at a get-together with friends, Loser asks each person to recount a story about a threshold. In the enthusiasm of their storytelling, they ask the son of the house, who finds the entire bit a nuisance, to participate. His rebuff causes them to fall silent, but, Loser notes, not to cease: "Das Erzählen schien vielmehr in dem Schweigen weiterzugehen und auf diese Weise sogar noch beredter zu werden. Ein jeder rückte immer tiefer in sich selber hinein und traf sich dort mit dem andern, mit dem er jetzt alles zwanglos gemeinsam hatte" (133–34). The act of telling, even in its nonverbal form (a form of communication which Handke holds in high esteem), had produced a bond, a link, among each of the members of the group, the bond of storytelling:

> "Es war einmal wir." (Wieso kann ich sagen: wir?—Wir waren ja nicht viele. Und diesem "wir" vertraute ich. Es war einmal eine Tatsache.) Einer lachte auf, scheinbar unvermittelt, und ein anderer nickte; oder man begann an einem Weinring auf dem Tisch eine Linie zu ziehen, die der nächste dann fortsetzte. (134)

The communicative act had established a sense of community and harmony between the friends at the table, a harmony not unlike that for which Sorger had been searching for in Alaska. This sense of implicit understanding through telling is the threshold that both Loser and Handke are seeking. To cross that threshold is to narrate and to understand, the two central aims for Handke and his protagonists.

Handke's novel, as has been well defined, is in many ways a study of thresholds. What exactly that threshold has come to mean has been a source of greater discussion. The narrator himself, defines *Schwelle* not as *Grenze* but as *Zone* (127), although throughout the novel, the word takes on various meanings. Caviola notes that the concept of *Schwelle* can be "applied to physical thresholds, to narratives, and to a narrator himself" (392), and Bernofsky similarly writes that the threshold is "the source of knowledge and self-discovery, of the story, of existence itself" (64). Bernofsky argues further that all of the thresholds that Loser encounters are "stepping-stones that advance him in his quest, his search for himself" (64), a search which has preoccupied Handke since his earliest writings. However, it is the threshold or the zone of the story which Handke has now come to accept as a form capable of bridging the gap between signifier and signified, between words and experience, whereas mere words had in the past failed him.

But stories and storytelling have also traditionally served as a method of historical preservation.[32] The concept of a teller and a set of narratives which maintained a cultural patrimony was central to the development of the oral narrative tradition. In fact, it was due in part to the connection between narrative and historicity that the German and Austrian avant-garde, as well as many other young writers not associated with a particular ideology, rejected narratives and stories in the 1960s. Thus as a former member and advocate of the Austrian avant-garde, Handke's return to and espousal of narratives is an even greater reversal, as it raises the question to what extent he is calling for a (re)historicizing of literature. Russell Berman contends that Handke is indeed reevaluating the tenuous connections between narration and history. In particular, Berman singles out *Der Chinese* as a novel which not only represents the culmination of Handke's ideological shift, but one which is also representative of a larger trend in German literature. Loser's confrontation with and murdering of the man he finds spray-painting swastikas is symbolic of a larger confrontation with a historical presence which the younger Handke, along with his colleagues in the *Grazer Gruppe*, had rejected. In the novel, however, it leads Handke to a "retrieval of language as narration and to a reconstituted historicism" (*Refusal* 162). Moreover, Berman raises the question as to whether this confrontation should be viewed as a "self-critical reconsideration of Handke's own past" and his early rejection of historical narratives. As self-criticism then, Berman argues, "the novel itself investigates the origins of recent Austrian literature and its foundational fiction of antifascism" (162).

The final scene of the epilogue, which finds Loser standing on a bridge over the Salzach contemplating the sky over Europe, holds the key to understanding Handke's assumptions about narrative. As a "guarantor of peace for the 'sky over Europe,'" the bridge, Berman asserts, "elicits history: both as historiography and as narrative" and thus implicitly "explores the possibility for stories about history" (160). While the tradition of narrative as a locuter of history was rejected in Germany after World War II, it maintained its vitality in other literary cultures. Handke was no doubt familiar with Ivo Andric's Nobel Prize-winning novel *Na Drini cuprija* (*The Bridge over the Drina*), which similarly used a bridge in Bosnia as the embodiment of history and narrative. It is this same tendency toward the reification of history through narrative that characterizes his essays on storytelling in the late 1980s; the desire "ein wenig in der Landschaft lesen zu können" as well as to heed the significance of geography as "Dienerin der Geschichte" (*Jukebox* 126). Story serves history in that it not only allows for a reconsideration of sociopolitical history (in this case, the rise of Austrian fascism, as Berman contends), but also the reassessment of personal history. To tell the story of another person, or of one's self, is to affirm the existence of that person. In many ways, a person with no story ceases to exist. In this manner, story and personal history are intricately linked to identity. Handke's next works would utilize the journey of self-discovery as a means of finding narrative and narrative as a means of affirming identity. Through narrative and story, the writer/narrator is afforded a means to express self and reality and thus create the identity of both self and other.

In *Die Wiederholung*, Handke continues both structurally and thematically ideas that he explored in *Der Chinese*, but this time using the structure of the *Bildungsroman*. Like most of his fiction, this work is of a semi-autobiographical nature, in that it is set in a small village in southern Carinthia, not unlike Handke's birthplace, and details, albeit in a disguised manner, memories and events of the narrator's childhood. Whereas his earlier works explored social and political problems, *Die Wiederholung* introduces the theme of linguistic and ethnic identity. The novel traces the journey of Filip Kobal, the protagonist, across the border of Austria into Slovenia in search of his long-lost brother who had disappeared during World War II, carrying with him two books, a treatise Kobal's brother wrote on fruit-growing and a Slovenian-German dictionary, in which his brother had annotated select words. These books come to symbolize the greater themes of Filip's quest for spatial and linguistic identity.[33] It is significant that Handke should return to the *Bildungsroman*, a genre he had previously explored in *Falsche Bewegung*, at this juncture in his writings. Whereas *Falsche Bewegung* deconstructed the *Bildungsroman* by creating an anti-*Bildungsroman*, *Die Wiederholung* functions as a reaffirmation of the tenets of the genre, namely the education of the protagonist.

In the first part of the story, "Das blinde Fenster," Filip's familial background and childhood are revealed in a long reminiscence which establishes him, as Firda has stated, as Handke's "ideal figure to begin this special journey into the linguistic and cultural elements of his ethnic past" (127). This affinity is based primarily on the similarity between Filip's childhood and adolescent history and Handke's own. In this way, he serves, as do many of Handke's protagonists, as his alter-ego. However, this relationship is not based solely on biographical and geographical similarities, but also on an identification with storytelling. Filip recognizes that storytelling played a central role in the dynamics of his family when he was growing up. His father, a Slovene who harbored anger and rage as a result of his family's displacement from their native land, is the only member of the family conversant in Slovene. However, his mother, a native speaker of German but sympathetic to her husband's ancestral and linguistic origins, creates for Filip, through storytelling, an image of Slovenia which, he recalls later, really had nothing to do with reality. However, it is her ability to conjure up the past and another reality which spurs Filip on to seek out his brother. Thus in his later recollections, he envisions his parents as storytellers: "Wenn ich dazu das Bild der beiden bedenke, sehe ich einen weinenden und einen lachenden Erzähler vor mir: der eine beiseitestehend, der andere in der Mitte das Recht behauptend" (78).

Early on in his life, Filip recognizes the importance of stories for him and for his ability to function as an outsider in society. He often made up stories for himself and played the role of storyteller for the other children of the village as well: "Diese nahmen mich bereitwillig auf, als Schiedsrichter für ihre Spiele, als Helfer, als einen, der ihnen etwas vorerzählte" (48). This ability as well as the necessity of telling stories and relating occurrences was inexplicably connected to the linguistic borders and barriers within his family and within the society they lived. Filip recalls that it was a beating from another child which "löste mir die Zunge" and enabled him to recount as well as to objectify the child who became, through this event, his enemy: "ich konnte der Mutter (ja, ihr) von dem Feind erzählen. Jene Erzählung begann mit einem Befehl: 'Hör zu!,' und schloß mit einem anderen Befehl: 'Tu etwas!'" (30). Thus at the early age of twelve, the narrator had grasped the power and function of storytelling: it was a vehicle for conveying experience as well as for prompting action. Moreover, it is the central method for the process of reification, an act which constitutes the central event of the novel: namely the objectification of his brother Gregor through story. Just as his mother was able to conjure up an idyllic image of Slovenia through storytelling, so too is the narrator able to conjure up an image of his brother, by reliving the events that happened twenty-five years earlier and recounting them in the present. This convergence of past and present is established in the first line of the novel: "Ein Vierteljahrhundert oder ein Tag ist vergangen, seit ich, auf der Spur meines verschollenen Bruders, in Jesenice ankam" (9). It is the repetition or, the *Wieder-Holung* of these events through story which enables Filip to visualize, comprehend, and, as Handke would have it, master (*bewältigen*) the past.[34] Bernd Stiegler has defined a similar function of repetition in this novel: "Der Gestus der Wiederholung ist eine Reaktion auf diesen Wirklichkeitsverlust" (246). Furthermore, Stiegler maintains that memory and remembrance are called forth via a process whereby objects take on meaning through repeated attempts at perceiving them. It is this process which Filip undertakes in his journey through Slovenia: by traveling and repeating the path his brother took, he not only imparts meaning and identity to him but evokes the memory of him in the process. Therein lies the function of the storyteller; for, following Stiegler: "Die Wiederholung ist Erneuerung der Welt durch die Kraft der Erzählung" (247).

Even before he sets out for Slovenia, Filip realizes that his role and calling in life is that of storyteller. When his mother falls sick, each family member takes on a new, almost ceremonial role, from provider to nurse:

> Und ich? Ich trat in der Zeremonie-wehe, wenn jemand aus seiner Rolle fiel!—auf als der Erzähler, konnte, endlich unausgefragt, mich an das Bett setzen, an dessen Mitte, da ja, nach dem

Aberglauben, an Kopf—und Fußende die Todesengel standen, und diese zum Haus hinauserzählen. (87).

By telling his mother his wishes, he is able to transcend reality and enter into the ethereal world of the story: "... und wurden Wort und Wunsch einmal eins, durchfuhr meinen ganzen Körper die Wärme, und in den Augen der ungläubigen Zuhörerin erschien unversehens doch etwas wie Glauben, eine stillere, reinere Farbe—ein Aufschimmern von Nachdenklichkeit" (88). This description of the power of narrative and of the narrative act harkens back to earlier beliefs in the healing power of stories, one still embraced by native peoples around the world.[35] Filip recognizes this and tells stories to his mother to drive away the angels of death. This recognition of the story as healer stands in marked contrast to the idea prevalent in the 1960s and 1970s, which Handke himself had embraced, that narrationand storytelling were no longer possible and served no function. However, this newfound understanding and appreciation of storytelling would continue to form a central part of his works thereafter.

In *Die Wiederholung*, Handke establishes storytelling as a fundamental aspect of his new poetics through the creation of a narrator, who recognizes at the conclusion of the novel that his purpose had not been to find his brother but to tell a story about him. The only way to find him, he realizes, is to find or create his story, a metaphor for Handke's own act of narrative creation. Indeed, the novel closes with a litany to the muse of storytelling in which the narrator/writer exalts the hallowed nature of the story:

> Ich dagegen sehe mich, mag ich auch heute noch sterben, am Ende dieser Erzählung nun in der Mitte meines Lebens, betrachte die Frühlingssonne auf dem leeren Papier, denke zurück an den Herbst und den Winter und schreibe: Erzählung, nicht Weltlicheres als du, nicht Gerechteres, mein Allheiligstes. Erzählung, Patronin des Fernkämpfers, meine Herrin. Erzählung, geräumigstes aller Fahrzeuge, Himmelswagen. Auge der Erzählung, spiegele mich, denn allein du erkennst mich und würdigst mich. Blau des Himmels, komm in die Niederung herab durch die Erzählung. Erzählung, Musik der Teilnahme, begnadige, begnade und weihe uns. Erzählung, würfle die Lettern frisch, durchwehe die Wortfolgen, füg dich zur Schrift und gib, in deinem besonderen, unser gemeinsames Muster. Erzählung, wiederhole, das heißt, erneuere; immer neu hinausschiebend eine Entscheidung, welche

nicht sein darf. Blinde Fenster und leere Viehsteige, seid der Erzählung Ansporn und Wasserzeichen. Es lebe die Erzählung. Die Erzählung muß weitergehen. Die Sonne der Erzählung, sie stehe für immer über dem erst mit dem letzten Lebenshauch zerstörbaren neunten Land. Verbannte aus dem Land der Erzählung, zurück mit euch vom tristen Pontus. Nachfahr, wenn ich nicht mehr hierbin, du erreichst mich im Land der Erzählung, im neunten Land. Erzähler in deiner verwachsenen Feldhütte, du mit dem Ortssinn, magst ruhig verstummen, schweigen vielleicht durch die Jahrhunderte, horchend nach außen, dich versenkend nach innen, doch dann, König, Kind, sammele dich, richte dich auf, stütze dich auf die Ellenbogen, lächle im Kreis, hole tief Atem und heb wieder an mit deinem allen Widerstreit schlichtenden: "Und . . ." (332–34)

This long closing passage reads like a hymn to the muse of the story and presents the multiplicity of uses of the story. Not only is the story the writer's muse, providing inspiration with a mere roll of the dice, it also provides a common pattern for all of mankind, serving to connect individuals through the meanings it imparts and commonalities shared among the listeners. Moreover, the story can provide renewal for the searcher in that it reflects the inner being of the teller, often the key to what the archetypal searcher is seeking. The teller, be it a king or a child, need only begin the act of narration, "Und . . . ," to again receive the rewards, benefits, and power of the story.

Clearly by the mid 1980s, Handke's poetics and understanding of literature were drastically different than that espoused early on in his career when his writings were still very much informed by the avant-garde movements of the 1960s. Now, he not only embraced the story as a valid literary mode of expression, but viewed the story as being inextricably linked to his own conception of self. In a series of interviews with Herbert Gamper in 1986, Handke maintained that the story had always been central to his work and that as a writer, he always felt most comfortable when he could structure a work so that a character could begin to narrate a story (126). In addition, he further characterizes his works as having three key components: a story, dramatic elements and "den Gedicht-Einschlag oder die Gedicht-Möglichkeit, den lyrischen Aufschwung" (128). The combination of these three elements, he feels, constitutes the essence of his literary works; yet, "das Herz meines Schreibens ist das Erzählen, also das lange, ausführliche, schwingende, mäandernde und dann wieder lakonische Erzählen. Das bin ich. Das bin *ich*, das bin ganz ich" (128). Handke's description of his writing and his style is telling. Although the center of his later writings does indeed shift in favor of the story, the stories and narratives one finds in these works are not tight, well developed stories that will immediately engage the reader, rather they are, as he has categorized them, meandering and laconic narratives that have more to do with reflecting the subject than with connecting to the reader. Handke's works have a reputation for being difficult and obtuse, in part due to the fact that they do not typically relate common, shared experiences to which the reader can relate as does the traditional story. Nevertheless, Handke identifies himself with the storyteller and the narrative tradition, suggesting a profound belief on his part in the importance of the story and its ability to posit meaning.

This complete identification with the storyteller and act of telling also betrays a fundamental connection to modernist paradigms. Handke categorizes himself as "vor allem ein episch-lyrischer Schriftsteller."[36] By defining his writings as "lyric epics" and "epic poems," Handke places himself in the tradition of antiquity, and more specifically that of Homer, a figure for whom he has always professed great admiration and whose wandering protagonists have served as a model for many of his own.[37] This connection is significant, for Homer is often considered to be the archetypal storyteller. Thus Handke's identification with the Homeric tradition is at once an identification with the epic and the oral narrative tradition. But the Homeric tradition has close links, not only to the oral popular tradition, but also, as Horkheimer and Adorno have argued, to the bourgeois novel of the nineteenth century: "the hero of the [Homeric] adventures shows himself to be a prototype of the bourgeois individual, a notion originating in the consistent self-affirmation which has its ancient pattern in the figure of the protagonist compelled to wander. The epic is the historico-philosophic counterpart to the novel, and eventually displays features approximating those characteristic of the novel."[38] One of these features, they maintain, is its connection to enlightened thought, rationality and order, all of which destroy myth and mythic thinking in favor of discernible truth. This notion, though, stands in stark contrast to Handke's conception of the story that is very much linked to the mythic, or "das neunte Land," a utopian space which is very much a construction of the poetic mind.[39] Indeed the mythic element of Handke's prose would take on greater significance, as he himself would again move away from a concern with the quotidian in favor of the utopian, a narrative space which allows complete self-expression and self-actualization.[40]

Many of Handke's works have taken on the shape of a journey or a quest and the parallels to and the importance of Homer as the archetypal storyteller are equally clear in these works. In fact, it was around this time, 1987, that Handke worked on the screenplay to Wenders's *Himmel über Berlin*, a script which incorporates the figure Homer as an old man who, in quoting Benjamin, laments the passing of a time when the storyteller was still a respected and revered figure in society. Wenders has stated as well that the idea to include this figure as the archetypal storyteller came from Handke, who had a reproduction of Rembrandt's Homer over his desk and was fascinated with the idea of an eternal storyteller.[41] Through a reconfiguration of the storyteller in his novels, Handke's self-proclaimed "lyric epics" reflect a broader view of literature as an instrument which still posits claims to truth and meaning, a concept Benjamin also assigns to the story. At the same time, it clarifies Handke's position as a postmodern writer, for whom there exists a multiplicity of truths.

To this end, Handke seems to believe that literature is entering a new era. After the release of his epic novel *Mein Jahr in der Niemandsbucht*, he stated: "Wir sind in einer chancenreichen Situation. Wir können wirklich loslegen, von neuem—nicht postmodern, aber im Sinne einer neuen Moderne."[42] His return to modernist tropes and paradigms, and even premodernist forms (both *Niemandsbucht* and his 1987 work *Die Abwesenheit* carried the subtitle "Märchen"), suggests a belief in the power of narratives to impart truth.[43] However, as he stated, this form of neomodernism must be of a type which utilizes a methodology unique to this part of the century. His evocation of the Homeric tradition and its specific connection to the bourgeois novel, however, differs from the intents of the former in that his protagonists do not undertake journeys of conquest but of self-understanding and spiritual awakenings—epics of peace as he would refer to them in the screenplay to *Himmel über Berlin*—not unlike the *Bildungsroman* of the nineteenth century. His figures though, do not seek truth and an understanding of society from the external world but from experience. Like Andreas Loser, Handke's protagonists are viewers and observers who are, in turn, experiential writers, a role which reflects Handke's own position as a writer.

Another Way of Telling

From this perspective, it becomes clear why some twenty-five years after his first collection of essays, Handke has praise for the critic, artist, and storyteller John Berger, whom he writes shows "die Gestik eines Meisters."[44] That Handke is so familiar with and praises Berger's works is itself quite interesting, as Berger's aesthetics represent a decided break from Handke's earlier influences in the French avant-garde. Berger has long been interested in alternative or "other" ways of seeing, looking, and telling. In 1983, Berger along with the photographer Jean Mohr published a work of photographs and essays entitled *Another Way of Telling* in which the very question of how images relate and tell stories is explored, a question which Handke addresses in *Langsam im Schatten*. For Berger, stories are "discontinuous" and based on an implicit agreement between the teller and the listener about what is not said: "The discontinuities of the story and the tacit agreement underlying them fuse teller, listener and protagonists into an amalgam. An amalgam which I would call the story's *reflecting subject*. The story narrates on behalf of this subject, appeals to it and speaks in its voice" (285). This "reflecting subject" is not unlike the self-reflective narrator/subjects of Handke's three *Versuche*-essays from the early 1990s. Indeed, the "Ich" narrative form of each of these three essays mirrors the narrative technique which Handke praises in Berger: "daß er zwischendurch auch Erzähler seines Ich wird, und zwar manchmal sogar des Ich ohne Rollenspiel, kein Sprecher und Anwalt der anderen mehr, nicht mehr ihr selbsternannter Geschichtenschreiber, weder von Begriffen noch von Wissen starrenden Ich-selbst" (164). Berger, according to Handke, simply does nothing more "als gehen und sehen . . . um darüber zu schreiben" (164), the epitome of the experiential writer.

However, the struggle to "find" stories (*finden* versus er*finden*), or to find the words to express personal experiences and realities through stories, is a problem and a major theme in Handke's later works. In many ways, Handke has come full circle, in that he was once again faced with a crisis of creative ability. Whereas in the past, this crisis manifested itself in the inability of words and narrative to express reality, now the struggle of the writer-storyteller is with the ability to find inspiration to tell stories using the very same structures that were once rejected. The inward journey of self-reflective literature, which characterized the novels of Handke's middle period, was now interconnected with the story, for the story is now the narrative trope which can best evoke the inner subjectivity of the narrator. Or, as expressed by the narrator in *Die Wiederholung*: "Auge der Erzählung, spiegele mich, denn allein du erkennst mich und würdigst mich" (333). The challenge for Handke now would be how best to incorporate experience into art and observation into story. These questions were also at the heart of *Nachmittag eines Schriftstellers*, which drew on a similar story, "Afternoon of a Writer," by an American modernist writer, F. Scott Fitzgerald.

The concept of an experiential writer as well as the relationship between art and life have long been central to Handke's oeuvre. Most of his protagonists, from Bloch, the Goalie, to Filip Kobal, have been wanderers or figures who set off on a journey of discovery and, in the process, rely on their faculty of observation to create order or understanding of the world (or lack thereof, in the case of the early novels). In *Nachmittag eines Schriftstellers*, Handke directly addresses the question: how does a writer achieve a balance between art and life? The narrator of the story is a writer living in a city not unlike Salzburg (Handke's own residence at the time). Like Fitzgerald's writer, Handke's has reached an impasse and sets off into the city, i.e., the "real" world, to seek inspiration. In turn Handke's story becomes a metaphor for the artistic process and examines the relationship between art and experience, whereby the artist must utilize his sense of observation and intuition to create or, in the case of the writer, to write.

The dynamic Berger describes between the narrator and the event is similar to that depicted by the narrator-writer of Handke's story. The narrator begins his reflections by discussing the writing process:

> Seit er einmal, fast ein Jahr lang, mit der Vorstellung gelebt hatte, die Sprache verloren zu haben, war für den Schriftsteller ein jeder Satz, den er aufschrieb und bei dem er noch dazu den Ruck der möglichen Fortsetzung spürte, ein Ereignis geworden. Jedes Wort, das, nicht gesprochen, sondern als Schrift, das andere gab, ließ ihn durchatmen und schloß ihn neu an die Welt. (5)

However, the success of communication and of writing was transitory and could disappear with every coming day. Thus it is the fear of being unable to write, unable to tell, which causes him the greatest consternation. But how can he find the impetus to write? The ideal storyteller was, in his mind, "[der] schweigsame Lauscher mit den blitzenden Pupillen, die sich von jedem ein Bild machten, und den unentwegt kreisenden breiten Schultern, die das Geschehen im Raum zu skandieren schienen" (75). Once again the harmony between the individual and the surroundings are central for his self-expression and the ability to communicate. Upon watching a group of construction workers in the city, he tries to establish a harmony "zwischen dem, was er verrichtete, und ihrem sehr gemächlichen Eins-nach-dem-anderen" (13), an attempt at attaining structure and order in the world, which thereby enables a systematic process of comprehension.

But the ability to comprehend and to make sense of his surroundings remains elusive for the narrator,[45] and at one point he discards all he has written, claiming: "Nicht bloß ungültig und nichtssagend war das tagsüber Geschriebene—es durfte auch nicht sein; zu schreiben war sträflich; die Anmaßung eines Kunstwerks, eines Buchs, der ärgste der Frevel, auf welchen, wie auf keine Sünde sonst, die Verdammnis stand" (71). The thought of consciously setting out to create a work of art, or even a book for that matter, is, he realizes, a questionable act at the end of the twentieth century. The narrator further doubts the entire business of writing:

> Was war seine, des Schriftstellers, Sache? Gab es in seinem Jahrhundert überhaupt noch solch eine Sache? Was für ein Mann ließ sich zum Beispiel benennen, dessen Taten oder Leiden danach schrien, nicht bloß berichtet, archiviert oder Stoff der Geschichtsbücher, sondern darüber hinaus überliefert zu werden in der Form eines Epos oder auch nur eines kleinen Lieds? (71–72)

Handke is here questioning the significance of being a writer and the action of writing in and of itself in a postmodern society. Can significance still be assigned to an individual's fate, as is the writer's task, so that it becomes worthy of an epic and thus being recorded for posterity? Are there still great actions or noble deeds that have a higher importance in a world in which relativism holds? Handke's rather solipsistic answer is yes. The narrator, faced with these daunting questions, formulates an answer whereby he elevates himself as a writer above society and humanity: "Schon indem ich, vor wievielen Jahren?, mich absonderte und beiseite-ging, um zu schreiben, habe ich meine Niederlage als Gesellschaftsmensch einbekannt; habe ich mich ausgeschlossen von den andern auf Lebenszeit" (73). That he as a writer will never belong to the people, reestablishes the position of the writer above the masses, one who possesses "eine Randexistenz" (65). This situation clearly presents the writer who tries to combine experience and perception, yet is removed from the center, with a fundamental dilemma. Gunther Pakendorf has defined this problem in linguistic terms, drawing on Roman Jakobson's theories of "contiguity disorder."[46] The writer's dilemma, in Jakobsonian terms then, is that "among people, there is a danger of contiguity disorder, the inability to combine things to a meaningful whole; in seclusion, there is the threat of similarity disorder, the inability to select and distinguish things in meaningful way" (82). Pakendorf sees the solution to this dilemma in the epiphany, namely the moment in which the writer/artist can transcend the here and now and through the "harmony of a mystical union" find a unity between word and perception and between the inner-world and the outer-world. This epiphany is embodied for Handke in the concept of the threshold and later in the category repetition, whereby repeated retrieval of objects (*die Wieder-Holung*) enables the perceiver not only to find meaning in the object but through narrative and story to find unity within the fragmentation of signifier and signified.

Unlike Fitzgerald's writer, Handke's protagonist ends his day with a feeling of optimism, a sense that he has found a unity in art and life, the catalyst being a conscious decision to narrate, *zu erzählen*, and by doing so to allow life to be represented as it is: "Im Zeichen der Erzählung habe ich angefangen! Weitertun. Sein lassen. Gelten lassen. Darstellen. Überliefern. Weiter den flüchtigsten der Stoffe bearbeiten, deinen Atem; dessen Handwerker sein" (90–91). This affirmation of life as source material for writing as well as the need and imperative to narrate life as it exists forms the basis for his series of three essays (*Versuche*) on storytelling.

Although these essays appear on the surface to have very little to do with storytelling per se, they each deal implicitly with the ability of a writer to narrate and the need to communicate and take up the dilemma faced by the writer in *Nachmittag eines Schriftstellers*. *Versuch über die Müdigkeit*, the first of these essays[47] is a meandering treatise on the different types and forms of existential tiredness. Here Handke reverts to perhaps the earliest form of narration and telling, namely the Socratic dialogue.[48] The entire essay consists of a series of short questions and somewhat more lengthy answers, all within the realm of the what he terms his "Sprach-Ich," his narrating-self, which renders a sense of self-questioning and answering.

However, it is this dialogic form that initiates and prompts thought and inevitably narration. Handke creates through this structure for both teller and audience and, in doing so, attempts to approximate the storytelling situation. From the outset, the narrator gives as his primary intention *das Erzählen*: "Ich will erzählen von den unterschiedlichen Weltbildern der verschiedenen Müdigkeiten" (14). *Müdigkeit* is defined differently depending on the different states of being which produce it, but quite often it is tied to linguistic questions and concerns, echoing some of the same issues that have been of concern to Handke since his earliest *Sprechstücke*. Indeed, the narrator clarifies that "Müdigkeit ist nicht mein Thema, sondern mein Problem" (23), inferring that the essay is more than just a discourse on a particular topic, rather it represents a fundamental question for him, the writer, namely how to transfer the visual image into words. As do many of his fictive protagonists, the narrator here is searching for *Empfindung*, or, as he has termed it in the past, a moment of true feeling. More importantly, though, he is searching for the ability to express this feeling in words.

Thus the *Versuch* of the title holds a dual meaning: on the one hand, it refers to the form of the prose work itself, an "Essay on Tiredness," as it has been translated. On the other hand, it also reflects the attempt of the writer/narrator to transform images into words: "Es soll mir genügen, den Bildern nachzugehen, die ich habe von meinem Problem, mich dann jeweils, wörtlich, ins Bild zu setzen und dieses mit der Sprache, samt seinen Schwingungen und Windungen, zu umzirkeln, möglichst herzlos" (23). This search for inspiration and the creative ability to transmute words and images is an underlying theme in all three essays, and in fact serves as the basis for the second essay, *Versuch über die Jukebox*.

In *Müdigkeit*, the narrator also presents his conception of reality, namely a world of small stories of which he is the chronicler. Throughout the essay, he does indeed tell numerous stories relating to the various types of tiredness he is describing. Most often these episodes come from his memories as a youth and are tied to his conception of the interconnectedness of life and art, his art being the ability to narrate and write. Storytelling is the only genuine means of relating these stories for it, as a form and method, "ursprünglich am meisten von Meinungen freien, weitherzigsten Weise zu reden [ist]" (29). It is the purity of storytelling and its unique ability to channel thought into narrative, the narrator continues, which makes it such a venerated form of expression. In one passage, he recounts the development of the different levels of his inner voice into a narrative voice, which allows this process, leading not only to the ability to narrate but also to an organic, innate level of communication:

> Ich habe dazu ein etwas grobes Bild von vier Verhältnisweisen meines Sprach-Ichs zur Welt: In der ersten bin ich stumm, schmerzhaft ausgeschlossen von den Vorgängen—in der zweiten geht das Stimmengewirr, das Gerede, von draußen, auf mein Inneres über, wobei ich aber noch immer gleich stumm, höchstens schreifähig bin—in der dritten kommt endlich Leben in mich, indem es da unwillkürlich, Satz um Satz, zu erzählen anhebt, ein gerichtetes Erzählen, an jemand Bestimmten meist, ein Kind, die Freunde—und in der vierten dann, wie ich es bisher am nachhaltigsten damals in der kläräugigen Müdigkeit erlebte, erzählt die Welt, unter Schweigen, vollkommen wortlos, sich selber, mir wie dem grauhaarigen Zuschauernachbarn da oder dem vorbeiwippenden Prachtweib dort (*Müdigkeit* 56).

This final conception of his "Sprach-Ich" represents a collective ideal based on many of the themes which Handke has dealt with in his works, for not only does it address the linguistic question of communication, postulating silence as a penultimate form of understanding, an extension of John Berger's notions of telling, but it also incorporates the romantic notions of an "All-Einheit" and an inwardly directed reflectiveness.[49] The narrators of all three essays are an embodiment of this philosophy, in that they search to find either within themselves or within nature a means of overcoming "das Untier 'Sprachlosigkeit'" (*Tag* 25), a vehicle appropriate for nature, but thwarting for the artist.

Handke's neoromantic tendencies, in which he seeks a greater communion with nature, began with the *Langsamer Heimkehr* trilogy in which the protagonist, as an outsider, seeks solace and understanding within nature and its natural forms. This theme is continued in Handke's second essay, *Versuch über die Jukebox*, wherein the narrator travels to an isolated region of Spain in order to find the peace and solitude necessary to write. His escape is not only from people and the world around him, but also from history, as the narrative time is the same as the actual time of its writing—during the fall of the Berlin Wall. This impetus to "escape history" is one which exemplifies Handke's view of the beguiling nature of the political. In *Nachmittag eines Schriftstellers*, the narrator remarks that news and current events are only means of distraction and that the writer should isolate him/herself from the outside world. In this way, Handke not only echoes the views of the apolitical writer, which he championed in his early essays, but he also places the writer in the long-standing German tradition of the outsider, removed from society, atop an Olympian perch, able to observe the surrounding world and to write and create, based on these images. In this context, the narrator's journey, superficially to set out to determine if there are any jukeboxes remaining in Spain and then to write an essay on them, becomes in typical Handkean fashion a journey of self-discovery. At times, the narrative becomes a meta-narrative in that he problematizes his own creative struggle, in turn writing a story about the process of writing an essay: another postmodern narrative about narrative.

What he finds and what serves as a source of inspiration throughout his journey are landscapes, both interior and exterior, which reveal to him a rhythm not unlike that heard from a jukebox, and provide him once again with the possibility to narrate.[50] And just as suddenly as one hears these rhythms, so too does one sense the rhythm of narration: "Und nun, auf seinem Wege-probieren ziellos in der Savanne, setzte in ihm auf einmal ein ganz anderer Rhythmus ein, kein wechselnder, sprunghafter, sondern ein einziger, gleichmäßiger, und vor allem einer, der, anstatt zu umzirkeln und zu umspielen, geradlining und vollkommen ernst in einem fort *in medias res* ging: der Rhythmus des Erzählens" (71). This rhythm of narration enables him once again to become a chronicler of events and experiences, ideally and ultimately leading to an epiphany of true feeling and creativity, which can only be described using the phraseology of his final essay, "ein geglückter Tag."

But it is not just the rhythms of music which serve to stimulate his creativity. Here as in many of his earlier works, the landscape becomes a reflection of his inner-self. His movement from the dry, arid plains of Spain to the moist, precipitous landscape at the finish where it has begun to snow and the beauty of winter has begun to show, mirrors his own struggle to be creative. His destination in Soria, Spain is significant not only for being a somewhat desolate area, but also as the home of the Spanish poet Antonio Machado. For Machado, the arid plains of the area served as a source of inspiration and as the subject of one of his greatest collections of poems, *Campos de Castilla* (*Landscapes of Castilla*). The irony that Handke is ostensibly searching for the last jukebox, the ultimate symbol of modern, mass culture in a small, rural village in central Spain is not lost on him. He recognizes a poetic source stronger than that of modern culture, namely the landscape: "Im Vorübergehen ein wenig in der Landschaft lesen zu können, war erdend, und er erfuhr, in Spanien sei die Geographie immer eine Dienerin der Geschichte gewesen, der Eroberungen und Grenzziehungen, und erst jetzt werde mehr auf die 'Botschaft der Orte' geachtet" (126). This appeal to heed the message of the landscape is a reflection of Handke's conception that the narratives of history should be absent from literature, but present in nature. The permanence of the countryside and the knowledge it holds of past histories should serve as a source book for understanding the narratives of history. Just as one reads a history text, so too should one "read" the landscape, so as to hear its narrative. In the end, he does not find the jukebox he had sought and must be satisfied with the fact that the only remaining jukebox in Spain is to be found in Andalusia. However, he does not leave disappointed but with the sense that he is just now, after this journey of self-discovery, beginning to understand geography and nature, an understanding of which will provide the material for him to write.

In the third and final essay on storytelling, *Versuch über den geglückten Tag*, Handke gives no formula for a successful day, but once again ties it inexorably with storytelling and creativity. An underlying motif in this essay is what he refers to as the "Linie der Schönheit und Anmut," a line in found in a painting by William Hogarth, but which, he feels, is symbolic of a larger concept in cultural thought. While recalling Schiller's eighteenth-century aesthetics on the one hand, Handke's conception of this *Linie* also comes to represent a twentieth-century striving for harmony and order in a fragmentary world. Just as he had earlier sought order through narrative constructs, so too does he now seek harmony in narration, a desire of producing a narrative of grand import. While in Paris, the narrator feels the need and urge to capture in words the images and feelings of the city which he senses: "Der Traum vom umfassenden, alldurchlässigen Buch, längst aus der Welt, längst ausgeträumt, mit einem Ruck war er wieder, oder 'erneut'? da, in der Tagwelt, und da, und da—brauchte bloß niedergeschrieben zu werden" (27). If he were able with one single word to somehow approximate the images he has in mind, he continues, so too would this be a successful day. But he realizes that conquering such linguistic challenges, which would be his conception of a successful day, is at best nothing more than a dream. Returning once again to the form of an inner Socratic dialogue as well as to his imaginary dialogue partner, "das zweite Ich," he ponders this very same problematic at the end of the essay, realizing this time, however, that such perfection in writing is a mere dream, "mit dem Unterschied, daß ich ihn nicht gehabt habe, sondern, in diesem Versuch hier, gemacht" (90–91). Once again, he acknowledges the advantage a postmodern writer has over his predecessors and their inability to overcome a "Sprachkrise": by having once again written an essay about writing an essay, he has succeeded in communicating his own conception of inner harmony as well as actually producing a written work, albeit a meta-narrative on the ability to achieve inner peace through successful narration.

If indeed Handke is, as Horst Steinmetz has argued, exemplary of a larger trend in Western Literature of a return to narrating and storytelling, one would perhaps wonder, based on Handke's three essays, if that return were a somewhat transmogrified return to formless, postmodern, meta-narratives. While these essays structurally give an indication that this may perhaps be the case, Handke's call for a new modernism seems to be saying that there is a bit more to narration than that. To be sure, he has no conception of what constitutes a successful day. However, he states that the impetus for him to write is an idea and the desire to "tell" this idea: "Aber eine Idee—wie ist sie erzählbar?", he asks (*Tag* 23). It is only narratable, he maintains, in the same way that modern life is understandable—through fragmentation, broken thoughts, and digressions.

If so, his essays and aesthetics argue for a modernism not unlike that which Benjamin called for in his analysis of storytelling as a means to exchange and communicate experiences. However, Handke's decided emphasis on personal realities and meta-narratives problematizing the creative process adds little to the conception of telling as a means of discourse and communication. Handke seems to be hoping for a return to narratives not only as a means of overcoming *Sprachlosigkeit*, but also as a bridge to harmony and peace, a theme he explores in greater depth together with Wenders in *Himmel über Berlin*. This program and aesthetic ideology is one he seeks to clarify with the concept of a "geglückter Tag," and one which best represents his own self-conception as a writer, namely as an epic storyteller.

But to be sure, Handke's embracing of the story has not resulted in a spate of "traditional" narratives. His texts are still highly personal, self-reflexive meta-narratives which more than anything reify the storytelling process. His most ambititous effort to date and one that represents the culmination of this metamorphosis (to use Handke's word) is his 1,000 page epic *Mein Jahr in der Niemandsbucht* (1994), a text subtitled "Ein Märchen aus den neuen Zeiten." The work opens with the confession of the narrator of a metamorphosis, without giving exact details to the nature of this transformation. Gradually over the course of the next 400 pages, the reader learns that the metamorphosis involved the necessity to narrate a story beginning, as it were, from scratch (379). Although the narrator had planned to spend a year in the *Niemandsbucht*, a space of isolation in which the narrator can passively observe his surroundings, he suddenly found himself faced with a linguistic crisis "eines Tages [ging] mir mitten in so einem Satz der Stoff aus. Und mit dem Schreibstoff der Lebensstoff" (385). The linguistic crisis had then manifested itself in an existential crisis, for when the writer's words run out, so to does the meaning of his existence. He finds the solution to this dilemma in the telling of the stories of seven of his friends, a portion which makes up 350 pages of Part III of the book. These acts of telling (seven in all, in true fairytale fashion) enable the narrator to overcome his existential crisis and to once again return to the task of writing his novel: a novel which never materializes within the logic of the text itself, whereas the preparations for and contemplations on writing it serve as the primary subject of the larger meta-narrative.

Later in the course of the narrative, still in search of the elusive task of writing, the narrator reflects on his predicament: "Und daß das vorgefaßte Registrieren, Berichten, Chronikherstellen, Draußenbleiben sich zu einer Erzählung verdreht hat, und eine in der Ich-Form, das kam aus der Erkenntnis, gleich schon am Anfang des Jahres, daß ich, der Schreiber, mit meinem Buch scheitern müßte, würde ich mich nicht wechselseitig selber hineinspielen . . . (und schon seit je tat es mir, dem Leser, gut, wenn in einem Buch solch ein Ich sich zu Wort meldete und die Sache beglaubigte, auch in sie eingriff)" (698–699). Here within the course of a fictionalized text, Handke delineates his narrative strategy as well as the change he has undergone in his conception of narrative structure. Whereas he had once hoped to be little more than the disembodied observer who merely observes and reports what he sees, he now realizes that these thoughts, observations and chronicles need form; and the form that he as a reader welcomes most is that of the chronicler, the teller, the narrative-I who gives shape to the events by turning it into "das althergebrachte zusammenhängende Erzählen" (699). Moreover, by utilizing a first-person narrator, the events take on meaning as well in that the narrator can attest to their authenticity.

But Handke and his meta-fictional narrator acknowledge the problems of the story in a postmodern and posthistorical society as well: "Manchmal kommt es mir vor, das Erzählen habe sich verbraucht" (700), whereas only stories of war seem to be the exempt.[51] But this conflict, between disengaged observing and active participation in the world—the source material for his narratives—and between the thought that the material for stories has been used up serves as the source of inspiration for his writing, or, at least, his desire to write. Although he may at times ponder the possibilities of new stories and the end of artistic inspiration ("War es denkbar, daß es heutzutage in der Welt nichts mehr zu erzählen gab, nur bloß noch einen Erzählzwang?" [702]), in the end, the narrator returns to the idea of the story as an end in itself, the only possibility for him, for the reader and for society: "Es ist meine Art der Teilnahme, und Teilnahme ist mir Musik genug, und die Erzählung ist die Musik der Teilnahme" (703). There is of course no answer to the questions that the narrator raises with regard to the story. But through his protracted musings on the potential of the story and the possibilities of writing, the narrator is able to accomplish his goal of overcoming his existential stasis and once more to actively participate in life and to write. Perhaps, too, the realm of the mythical and of the fairy-tale has supplanted the need for veracity and truth. When the story becomes the end in and of itself as opposed to the means to an end, as in his other "Märchen," *Die Abwesenheit* and *Lucie im Wald mit den Dingsda* (1999), then meaning is to be found in the act of telling as opposed to the subject of what is being told.

~ 3 ~

Cinema and the Narrative Tradition

In Chapters 1 and 2, the decline of narratives and literary storytelling was traced from modernist novels of the early twentieth century to postmodern writings of the mid-twentieth century fueled by a wave of anti-narratives manifested in the theories of the *nouveau roman*. The end of the twentieth century, however, has witnessed a rebirth in the use and telling of stories as narrative as well as a reevaluation of their importance in literary culture. The works of Peter Handke perhaps more than those of any other contemporary writer in the German speaking realm exemplify this shift in literary culture in that his writing has undergone a profound transformation since the 1960s. Whereas he once rejected narratives in the vein of the *nouveau roman* at the beginning of his career, his novels now embrace the story and literary narration. As a writer on the vanguard of the German literary establishment, Handke's new espousal of the story is symbolic; the once lamented loss of the story and its virtues, which Benjamin articulated in the early part of the century and postmodernist theorists have echoed, has been seemingly overcome. Moreover the renaissance that the literary story and traditional narratives are at present experiencing is paralleled in the cinema, a medium, which in the European tradition, has long been linked to literature and literary culture. Handke, too, has throughout his career shown an interest and affinity for the cinema, having collaborated on four films with Wim Wenders and having directed three films of his own.[1] Handke and Wenders most recent collaboration, *Der Himmel über Berlin* (*Wings of Desire*, 1986) is a culmination of both artists' reflections on the loss of the oral narrative tradition as well as a call for a new era of cinematic storytelling and narrative filmmaking. As such, it also represents a caesura of sorts in their respective oeuvres, in that it heralded the beginning of a stage in both their careers: in the case of Handke, his next five works would deal explicitly with the role of narration and its interrelationship to issues of time and place, and for Wenders, it began a similar period of examination but one that led more concretely to a series of films whose conception was based much more on an initial storyline than on an image or idea. Not surprisingly, literature and literary aesthetics played a major role both in the decline and rejection of cinematic stories in German cinema, but also in their rebirth.

In the European tradition of filmmaking, the overlap between literature and film is not unusual, for since the inception of cinema writers have been attracted to the medium and have often participated in a variety of cinematic projects.[2] As a result, there is a strong tradition of intertextuality between literature and film. In his study of this link, Joachim Paech argues that indeed film learned early on the art of narration from literature.[3] In the early 1900s, the film industry turned to literature in order to win over an audience for this new medium. As a result, film adopted structurally many literary techniques:

> [D]er Film mußte ein allgemeinverständliches Medium fiktionalen Erzählens werden und sich damit als Film und als Kino der Rolle von Literatur und Theater annähern; der Film fand sich in diese Rolle, indem er primär die Struktur literarischen Erzählens und zunächst auch szenischer Darstellung adaptierte und nur sekundär auch deren Inhalte, die ja auch vorher schon übernommen worden waren. (86)

Since the cinema adopted many of the same means of representation and narration as the novel and the theater, it too followed many of the same paths of the theater and paralleled its developments. Already by the turn of the century, as Frank Kermode has noted, there developed a sense that many of the tasks and functions once relegated to the novels could now be adopted by the cinema.[4] One of those tasks was the representational narration of reality. Whereas the novel was originally heralded as a literary form that, due to its length and ability to span time, could break the boundaries imposed by the theater, cinema, possessing the same qualities but also the advantage of visual imagery, was seen as an artistic medium that furthered the long-sought aesthetic goal of capturing reality and reproducing it in art. While photography advanced this goal tremendously in the nineteenth century, film was able to combine still images successively and in doing so visually tell a story. Consequently, the narrative construct that film initially appropriated was that of fictional storytelling. Whereas literature incorporated the framing narrative of the novella (*Rahmenerzählung*) as a means of approximating the oral narrative tradition,[5] early silent films also utilized the *Rahmenerzählung* to a similar end. The detective and criminal films as well as the more epic works of the silent cinema often began with introductory motifs that set the stage for the action to come and also functioned as a cinematic narrator. The most famous example is the narrative frame added to *Das Kabinet des Dr. Caligari*, which not only contextualized the story of Dr. Caligari as one being told by an inmate (and thereby changing the meaning of the film) but also called into question the reliability of the central figure.[6] As silent film lacked the ability to use voice-over narration, the use of such framing devices compensated for the lack of a narrator and thereby placed the film in a storytelling tradition not unlike that of a novella.[7]

With the discovery at the turn of the century of the ability to tell stories through images, the narrative cinema was born. Although there have always been experimental countertendencies, the dominant form of cinema became the narrative film.[8] Narrative film not only provides the audience with known structures and tropes, it is also the key element of its entertainment value. During the Weimar Republic, a host of filmmakers, photographers and artists began experimenting with the medium and, influenced by both Russian constructivist art as well as the Bauhaus school, called for an absolute cinema, one modeled not on literature but on the visual arts. In one of the most famous manifestos of absolute cinema, Walter Ruttmann argues that film must be conceived optically rather than theatrically, thus rejecting the dominant aesthetic of the time that films were staged literature or dramas.[9] Similarly, Hans Richter, another of the avant garde filmmakers of the 1920s, argued that at that time, "Es gibt noch keinen Film, nur eine perverse Abart photographierter Literatur."[10] The Absolute Film, he maintained, opened the eyes for the first time to the possibilities of the cinema: "Gegenstand, Bedeutung und Handlung sind bequeme Anpassungen an den Verdauungsschlaf im Parkett."[11] This rejection of narrative in favor of sound and image—or painting with the medium of time, as Ruttmann would refer to this method of cinema—would serve as the underlying principle for avant-garde and nonfiction filmmaking both in the Weimar Period as well as in the 1960s, when avant-garde filmmaking once again flourished in Germany after its total suppression during the National Socialist dictatorship. The theories and ideas of the Absolute Film would, however, continue to serve as an important counterpole to narrative filmmaking and perhaps not surprisingly, the first real rejection of the dominant aesthetic in the post-World War II era would come from a group of documentary and short filmmakers in Oberhausen who would not only be responsible for the new wave of nonfiction films in the 1960s, but also the birth of a new manner of nonnarrative filmmaking, the Young German Cinema.

In the post-World War II era, however, a number of European filmmakers and directors were exploring new methods and theories of the cinema, including the Italian neorealists and a group of young French filmmakers who heralded a *nouvelle vague*. The ideas these critics and directors espoused, especially in regard to the new found importance on "authorship" and the resulting concept of *auteur cinéma*, influenced the West German variation, the *Autorenfilm*. Common to these cinemas was a rejection of the dominant, narrative style and approach to film, which had become intricately connected to Hollywood, in favor of a more independent cinema which emphasized the signature of the individual director and his or her own vision and aesthetic. Likewise these filmmakers conceived of their films from a visual and optical standpoint as opposed to a narrative one and embraced and preferenced the image over the story. As a result, the so-called European "Art Film," which actually dated back to the earliest days of the cinema, established itself as both a countercinema and a vibrant alternative to narrative cinema for most of the latter half of the twentieth century. However, in recent years, the Art Film itself has been in decline, for both aesthetic and commercial reasons, and in many cases its death has been heralded, leaving the future of European cinema somewhat open.[12]

What has ironically resurfaced and come to overshadow many of the national, European cinemas, which themselves began as "protest" cinemas in reaction to the narrative traditions of their previous generations as well as to the commercialism of Hollywood cinema, has indeed been a new, narrative cinema characterized by films strong on story that utilize and at times play with conventional narrative structures. West German cinema in the latter half of the twentieth century has been no different. Whereas the Young German Cinema of the 1960s and the New German Cinema (NGC) of the 1970s and 1980s became synonymous with a German national cinema, the ideas, themes, constructs and even means of production have changed in the late 1980s and 1990s, as a new generation of filmmakers once again reject the cinema of their fathers and seek to establish a new aesthetic, one which is modeled on the dominant narrative cinema.

While the much studied NGC and its singular creation, the *Autorenfilm*,[13] came into being as a result of particular historical and cultural circumstances in the Federal Republic in the 1960s, it was in praxis also a manifestation of nonnarrative film theory and represented an alternative to the linear, story-driven cinema of both the Nationalist Socialist period as well as of the commercial Hollywood cinema. Since most of the New German filmmakers counted themselves among the political left, narrative cinema was thus rejected for both political and commercial reasons as it was associated with a bourgeois and capitalist means of production. In order to better understand the rebirth of narrative cinema within Germany in the 1980s and 1990s, it will be useful to trace the initial rejection of narrative cinema in the 1960s and 1970s, which led to the rise of the *Autorenkino* and the NGC of the 1970s and 1980s. While there have been many studies examining the death of the *Autorenfilm*,[14] I will examine the shift back to the story-driven cinema characterized by the popularity of the New German Comedy of the 1990s. Although many factors have contributed to this change, audience taste and the desire for narrative have played a large role.

Perhaps nowhere has this transformation been more dramatic than in the cinema of Wim Wenders, internationally the most well known of German filmmakers and one of the leading proponents of the NGC in the 1970s and 1980s. Wenders, an admirer of the French *nouvelle vague*, the movement which provided the impetus for many of the anti-narrative films in Europe in the last forty years, began his career as a theorist and avant-garde filmmaker.[15] However, since the late 1980s, Wenders, like Handke, has begun problematizing the use of stories in his works and has discussed their importance and value in numerous essays and interviews. His recent films have come to embrace storytelling as a necessary structuring element for the ordering of images and for the conception of his films. Chapter 4 will focus specifically on his transformation as reflective of what has become a central tenet for reestablishing the identity of the current German film industry, namely the return of narrative cinema.

Images and Narration

Since the invention of moving pictures, there has existed a close connection between literature and film, and within that, between narration and film. After the novelty of the moving image faded in the late 1890s and early 1900s, artists and filmmakers sought direction for the new medium, and literature seemed to be an appropriate choice. As Joachim Paech has shown, by 1907, some twelve years after the first motion picture exhibition, the film industry had already reached a crisis whereby it was forced to find an appropriate identity for this new medium within the culture industry (85). Whereas cinema had had its origins as a novelty in the variety shows, it soon reached the limits of this venue. In order to progress and compete with the theater (the more established and respected performance art), film had to expand in order to explore its own possibilities. The result was a redefinition of the cinema. As Paech writes: "Das Kino sollte zum 'Theater' werden, der Film zur 'Literatur,' damit das Kino als Medium bürgerlicher Wertvorstellungen fungieren konnte, die noch immer durch Literatur and Theater repräsentiert wurden" (90). As a form of entertainment shown in the Kintopps of traveling fairs, film was clearly counted amongst the lower art forms and certainly lacked the seriousness and austerity its competitors could offer.[16] If the cinema was to raise itself to a respectable art form, one worthy of reflecting the moral values of the bourgeoisie, then it needed to develop a structure and form which would enable it to tackle the themes and issues of the higher art forms. As a result, the cinema in essence sought to define itself as a theater for the nineteenth-century novel; visually it would take its cues from the theater, but thematically it would focus on the well known novels of the time. By filming classic novels whose plots were too complex or too expansive for the theater, the cinema similarly appropriated the role of purveyor of middle-class values. This meant, of course, borrowing from the narrative ideas of the novel, and more specifically, the epic storylines of the nineteenth-century realist novels. Consequently, like those novels before it, the popular cinema of the time took on the same role of portraying and reflecting society, from its triumphs to its misery, offering commentary and passing judgment. From this point on, cinema, like its literary predecessors, was associated with didacticism and the shaping of societal values, a role not unlike that which Benjamin assigns to the oral narrative tradition.

Unlike the drama, however, the silent film was unable to convey a message through text and dialogue and thus came to rely solely on the visual image and the effects of what Adorno had termed the cornerstone of modernist aesthetics, montage, to portray meaning.[17] It was at this point that the cinema developed along two divergent paths, which later would evolve into the narrative and nonnarrative cinematic traditions. As the nonnarrative, variety film began to lose its popularity, the film industry turned to narrative as a means of attracting a greater audience. Thomas Kuchenbuch, in his study of the history of narrative images,[18] maintains that the necessity to tell stories in early silent films arose from the predominance and familiarity of the audience with the interconnection between images and stories, a familiarity which stemmed from the picture books and picture novels (*Bilderbücher und Bilderromane*) of the nineteenth century.[19] When the originality and uniqueness of the early silent clips waned, filmmakers turned to the theater, a form of spectacle and narration familiar to most audiences, as a basis for their montage and storytelling techniques. Thus it came to be, Kuchenbuch maintains, that in the earliest montage films, actors entered the screen on the left and exited on the right, much as in the theater (99). This same actor would then enter from the same direction so as to indicate progression of place and linearity of time. Breaks in plot were indicated through discontinuities of spatial orientation and progression. By relying on theatrical techniques and aesthetics, film developed a narrative form not unlike that of the theater. Linearity, narrative progression and flow, as well as structural closure would become hallmarks of this style of narrative cinema, which, through the impact of Hollywood, would establish itself as the dominant form of filmmaking.

At the same time, this style and mode of film stood in opposition to the development of the other strand of cinematic aesthetics, the avant-garde and nonnarrative cinema, which sought to explore the possibilities and limitations of the medium. The avant-garde films of the 1920s and 1930s were less interested in relating a narrative and thus approached issues of reality and verisimilitude quite differently. By nature of its theoretical framework and more challenging ideology, nonnarrative cinema never achieved the same degree of success and popularity, as did the narrative cinema.[20] Nevertheless, in the early 1900s, many filmmakers in Germany experimented with this type of absolute or pure cinema, which utilized the constituent elements of the cinema (light and celluloid) and relied on nonrepresentational images.[21] These early absolute films and theories would inform many of the avant-garde movements in the latter half of the twentieth century and would be crucial for the European countercinema and the development of the Art Film in the 1950s. However, the fact that nonnarrative and experimental cinema would never achieve the dominance and popularity of the narrative cinema attests, in part, to the audience's desire for stories as well as to their importance on a larger scale as structuring principles within modern culture. Nevertheless, the impact and influence of the avant-garde should certainly not be discounted or underestimated, for such films have consistently served not only as a challenge to the dominant style but often as a source of inspiration for auteurist filmmakers. Not surprisingly, it was to nonnarrative cinema that West German filmmakers turned in the postwar era as a means of creating a new cinema to deal with issues of Germany's past as well as to distance itself from the established film industry under the National Socialist regime.

The *Autorenfilm* and the End of the Story

The rise of the private studio system in Hollywood as well as the devastating impact of the two World Wars on the national cinemas of Europe helped establish early on in this century the narrative "Hollywood" cinema as the dominant style of cinema.[22] This style of filmmaking is typically characterized by causality, linear narrative, and closure, which lend the film a certain theatricality in the Aristotelian sense.[23] The transparency and seamlessness of the film conceals the fact that it is actually a narrative construction, hence the viewer becomes caught up in the flow of the images that form the basis for the story and come together to simulate reality. Moreover, the illusion between fiction and reality is never broken in the Brechtian sense but maintained, so that the viewer, in the ideal case, forgets that she or he is in the cinema viewing a film. As such, the dominant cinema, as Christian Metz has defined it, can be characterized as story as opposed to discourse.[24] The dominant narrative cinema further avoids self-reflexivity, a tenet important for experimental and avant-garde film but one not in the realm of illusionary cinema that holds to the illusion of reality via the integrity of the story.

Another characteristic of the dominant cinema is a system of producers, studios, stars, and film genres, whereby the film becomes the product of a collaborative effort of groups of different people. Thus claims of "authorship" are relegated to a collective whole rather than to an individual, a fact which prompted Siegfried Kracauer to argue that film more than any other art form is most representative of a nation's mentality.[25] This mode of production was one of the primary elements of the dominant cinema that would be challenged in Europe after World War II, when filmmakers began to reject the studio system, to begin viewing the film as text and, conversely, to reassert claims of authorship. By rejecting a system of collaboration, these filmmakers asserted their desire for visual self-expression, an element that would allow for a much more personal style of film. These claims, together with a more general shift toward the self-referentiality of postmodern aesthetics, would result in the first major challenge to the dominant cinema in Europe in the 1960s. With this challenge, traditional narrative and means of storytelling within film would begin to be questioned, both structurally and contextually, as such structures were rejected as an artificial framework and artifice. Instead, filmmakers began to view the individual image as capable of narrating and "telling," an ideology manifested perhaps best in the films of the Italian neorealist Michelangelo Antonioni, an influence for many in the French *nouvelle vague* as well as for Wenders in the German context. Antonioni's use of extremely long shots of landscapes that functioned as symbols for the interior reality of his protagonists, shifted the focus of narrative from dialogue to image and created uniquely challenging films that often required the viewer to establish and construct meaning and narrative through association and visual rather than linguistic cues. Moreover, his use of close-ups of his protagonists allowed facial expressions and gestures to "narrate" visually as opposed to audibly.[26] Such a style of filmmaking was not only in marked contrast to the Hollywood films of the times, but also represented a break from the traditional narrative films being in produced in Europe as well.

The Germany film industry after World War II was ripe for change for, perhaps more so than in most other European cinemas after World War II, it was in ruins. The Allied forces controlled the output and releases in Germany with strict censorship (to avoid a resurgence of fascism), inundating the market with American films and keeping tight control on German film production.[27] When the German film industry finally did begin production anew, it lacked talent and direction, save for a few filmmakers who returned from exile. Most of the best talent had immigrated and those who remained were too intricately associated with Nazi film production to have credibility. Moreover, German films thematically avoided confronting the major issues of the postwar period: guilt, history, and responsibility. Instead, the films of the 1950s consisted for the most part of *Heimatfilme*, films which portrayed a fantasy world in which a pure, whole Germany was offered as a counterbalance to the grim reality of a country in tatters. Not surprisingly, these films functioned according to the dictums of the dominant cinema. As Anton Kaes has shown, the Heimat films offered above all a means of escape, which along with their unambiguous causality and traditional stories provided for the highly entertaining value of such films:

> Die immer wieder neu gefilmten Geschichten von Liebespaaren, die vor dem Horizont der deutschen Berge oder der deutschen Heide nach den üblichen Verwicklungen und Mißverständnissen zum obligatorischen Happy-End mit Musikbegleitung zusammenfinden, bieten ein Realitäts- und Geschichtsbild, das indirekt über Verdrängungen und Selbsttäuschungen ebenso wie über kollektive Wunschvorstellungen Aufschlüsse gibt. (*Deutschlandbilder* 22)

The constructs of these films were purely narrative; thematically, they depicted an idealized world of happiness and harmony and challenged none of the historical questions that would later be central to the process of *Vergangenheitsbewältigung* and would serve as a central theme in the films of the Young German Cinema and its successor, the much acclaimed NGC. Structurally, the Heimat film presented a linear narrative, with beginning, middle, and a happy end. As Kaes points out, the desire to come to terms with the reality of Germany's past and its history would be a major impetus for the next generation of young filmmakers to reject not only the themes of these films but their constructs as well (22). The link between narrative cinema and the repression of the past was established in large part due to the style of filmmaking in the 1950s, films which did not dare to confront Germany's very recent fascist past and opted instead for illusionary cinema.

Filmmakers in other European countries, however, were already beginning to experiment with new modes of representation and cinematic constructions by the 1950s, forms which challenged the classic Hollywood cinema and ushered in a new wave of the European "Art Film." In his study of postwar European cinema, Pierre Sorlin identifies the Italian neorealist cinema of the 1950s as representative of a major caesura in the dominance of the classic cinema. To be sure, the European cinema of the 1950s was still focused on entertainment, but beginning with Vittorio De Sica and Federico Fellini, there arose a crisis of the classical narrative style, which would inform the development of the cinemas in neighboring countries in the following decades (136). Sorlin goes on to state that part of this "crisis" arose from the decision of filmmakers like Fellini to begin emphasizing self-referentiality and to view film as "not just a fiction, but also a text, an audiovisual artifact which owes its qualities to its physical components (photographs and sounds)" (139). Fellini especially also began accentuating the visual component of his films and began including scenes by virtue of visual pleasure rather than for their contribution to the storyline. Such a conception of film is reminiscent of the theories of the avant-garde and especially of the Absolute Films of the 1920s. Moreover this new style of film, Sorlin shows, challenged the dominant cinema in three ways: it lacked a central narrative strand, included shots purely for the sake of visuality, and drew attention to its own artificiality (139). These three elements would form the underlying principle to all of the movements in the various European cinemas which attempted to create a counter-cinema. In effect, they represented a shift from narrative-driven film to image-driven film, celebrated their own self-referentiality and sought to break the illusionary nature of the dominant, entertaining form of the cinema.

Sorlin maintains, though, that this shift cannot be connected to any specific historical or political event in particular, but that in general, European film in the 1950s and 1960s began to challenge the classical style of filmmaking that had triumphed in Hollywood between the wars and had discarded formalist innovation and experimentation in the process (138–149). Due to its high entertainment value, however, these commercial films were successfully exported to Europe and became influential among filmmakers abroad. Thus an ironic aspect of the European counter-cinema was that the practitioners were well steeped in the Hollywood tradition and were, in fact, admirers of the American cinema of the 1930s and 1940s. This is especially true of the French and German directors of the 1960s and 1970s. François Truffaut often expressed his admiration for Hitchcock, whereas Rainer Werner Fassbinder has praised Douglas Sirk and Wenders both Nicholas Ray and Samuel Fuller.[28] Their admiration for Hollywood films (and the dominant cinema) manifested itself in the allusions and tricks they incorporated into their films in order to show their understanding and comprehension of genre cinema. So while they on the one hand rejected many of the formal narrative structures of Hollywood cinema, they praised certain directors whom they saw as film artisans, or *auteurs*, who were using the medium of film as a means of personal self-expression. Central to this method of filmmaking was the idea that the camera should have complete freedom, form was predominant over content, and image over narrative, so as to express the vision of the film artist and author.

Although the European directors of this time had very little in common per se, Sorlin shows that they did share a similar cultural background. Many of the young French directors wrote for the influential film journal *Cahiers du Cinéma*, whereas their German counterparts, like Alexander Kluge, often had university degrees, and as in the case of Kluge, were even associated with the literary establishment.[29] Of the second generation of postwar German filmmakers, such as Volker Schlöndorff, Fassbinder, and Wenders, many attended film school[30] or had worked extensively in the theater. Wenders, like Truffaut and Godard, also wrote film criticism for various cinema journals and newspapers and spent time in Paris during the 1960s visiting the Cinémathèque Française. What many of these filmmakers also shared was a similar aesthetic vision. Most of them as well, began their careers making short films which helped define the growing avant-garde scene of the 1950s and 60s.[31] Furthermore, making films was an extension of a love for the medium; and viewing film and writing about them were almost one and the same. And it was this shared passion for the cinema which formed the basis for development of the European Art Film

One of the first groups to consciously break from tradition were a number of French critics associated with André Bazin's *Cahiers du Cinéma* who began making films in the late 1950s and early 1960s in protest against the manneristic style of postwar French cinema. This "new wave," or *nouvelle vague*, of filmmaking emphasized the role of the director as artist and creator of the work, the auteur. Furthermore, it sought spontaneity and improvisation in direction, and flexibility and subtlety in cinematography.[32] Godard imagined an ideal cinema, in which everything was allowed, yet nothing but pure cinema was permitted. His first feature film, *À Bout de Souffle* (*Breathless*, 1959), was an embodiment of this style and method and as such, a call to cinematic revolution. The film also heralded the end of the linear story. What was remarkable about the film was, above all, its innovative use of the "jump cut," an abrupt cut in the narrative that calls attention to itself due to the obvious sharp break in time and space. The jump cut was instrumental in defining the films of the *nouvelle vague*, for it underscored the self-referential nature of the film. By introducing harsh cuts in the film, the filmmaker not only breaks the flow of the narrative, but also undercuts the cinematic illusion of reality that the dominant cinema so strongly strives to achieve. Godard's film, ostensibly a simple story of a criminal on the run from the police (such stories appropriated from Hollywood cinema where favored by many of the *nouvelle vague*), was initially over two hours in length. Rather than cut entire scenes or sequences as would normally be the case, Godard chose to edit, somewhat randomly, whatever he found boring without regard to narrative continuity, a technique which then became extremely popular within the new wave (Williams 381). What this did, in essence, was to reintroduce the idea of anti-illusionary devices to the cinema, techniques not uncommon in silent film, but ones opposed to the constructs of the dominant cinema.

Moreover, *Breathless* broke with tradition in that it no longer told a continuous, linear narrative. Instead Godard combines two distinct plots, reminiscent of the stories of the film noir. Critics have argued that that Godard's narrative technique of interweaving stories and images of Paris was necessitated by the fact that a single linear story would not allow Godard to develop what he in fact wished to show.[33] For Godard, the classic linear story was no longer useful when what he in fact wished to convey was itself not narratable. The conjecture that stories are no longer useful recalls the claims of the theorists of the *nouveau roman*, who similarly maintained that the telling of stories had become impossible. In fact, Robbe-Grillet, one of the primary exponents of the *nouveau roman*, collaborated on a number of these early films and has himself made several films in the tradition of the *nouvelle vague*. These films along with those on which he collaborated—especially the well known *L'Année dernière à Marienbad* (*Last Year at Marienbad* 1961)—are very hermetic and elusive and destroy the conventions of traditional narration to a degree that discerning a "story" becomes an impossible task.

The inability to narrate or the desire to abandon narration in the European cinema from the 1950s through the 1970s has been explained by theorists and critics in a number of ways. Alan Williams presents an argument similar to that made by many literary theorists of that time; namely, that films based on the classical model of linear narration "achieve a convincing coherence of their fictions by creating a unified place to which the events depicted all refer: the position of an ideal, disembodied spectator" (382). However, the unity of the dominant cinema is not to be found in the fictional worlds of the films of the *nouvelle vague*, for continuity would suggest a "veracity and coherence of what is represented," a claim which many of these films reject (383). Instead these films, much like their literary counterparts, sought an intentional disruption of teleological designs, the unity of a narratable reality being one of these. Furthermore, Williams cites a number of theorists who, following Lacan, argue that, above all, Godard's films seek to dissolve the unity of the viewing subject, an endeavor which ties in with the political nature of his films:

> Mainstream commercial films strengthen each spectator's sense of him-or herself as an isolated and unified subject, a process which has profound, ultimately political consequences. The (constructed) unity of the self purveyed by classic cinema narrative may be seen as reinforcing an individualism which forecloses the possibility of authentic solidarity with others. For this reason, many theorists argue that narrative cinema is the ideal vehicle of "bourgeois ideology," helping to maintain the boundaries which separate individuals from other individuals, classes from classes, nations from nations—regardless of a given work's subject matter. (383)

Williams notes further that Godard's films have been treated by critics as an attempt at creating a countercinema, a non-bourgeois cinema, which refuses to abide by the coherence of the narrative cinema. The dissolution of the subject and the splintering of the self were issues that were concomitant in the literature of the 1960s as well and visually, they were manifested in the deconstruction of narrative in the *nouvelle vague*.

By rejecting the coherence of the narrative cinema, this new wave of non-narrative cinema rejected bourgeois structures in much the same way as the *nouveau roman* rejected the bourgeois constructs of the nineteenth-century novel and its claims of unity and verisimilitude. Moreover, the *nouvelle vague* manifested itself as a generational conflict and rejection of the *cinéma de papa* just as the literary avant-garde renounced the establishment as part of the old guard.[34] In Germany, a group of like-minded avant-garde filmmakers similarly declared the death of the old cinema and the birth of the new in a 1962 manifesto signed at the Oberhausen short and experimental film festival. The "Oberhausener Manifest" was in itself both an ideological and a political document. Unlike the *nouvelle vague*, which had no manifesto per se, the Oberhausen group had specific goals and intentions for what they wished to actualize. Specifically, they argued that the future of the German film and film industry lay with the experimental short films, which had been praised and recognized at many international festivals and which spoke "eine neue Sprache des Films."[35] Moreover, this group of documentary and experimental short filmmakers acknowledged the advances made in other European cinemas: "Wie in anderen Ländern, so ist auch in Deutschland der Kurzfilm Schule und Experimentierfeld des Spielfilms geworden. Wir erklären unseren Anspruch, den neuen deutschen Spielfilm zu schaffen" (*Augenzeugen* 29). By basing their intentions on formalist constructs of the short film, itself an avant-garde genre, they rejected the claims of the dominant cinema. Moreover, in the spirit of the *nouvelle vague*, they called for greater freedom from cinematic conventions: "Freiheit von den brancheüblichen Konventionen. Freiheit von der Beeinflussung durch kommerzielle Partner. Freiheit von der Bevormundung durch Interessengruppen" (*Augenzeugen* 29). Not only did they reject the commercialization of the film industry, but they also affirmed their concrete formal and commercial ideas for the production of the new German film. In doing so, they called for a new means of film financing so as to liberate the German film from commercial concerns, thereby allowing a greater degree of experimentation and flexibility. Liberation from commercial concerns, however, also meant the release from the need to appease audiences thus necessarily making films that had narrative cohesion or that otherwise corresponded to the constraints of the dominant cinema.

What followed was a period of growth and experimentation in the German cinema unparalleled since the films of the Weimar Republic.[36] Of all the Oberhausen signers, Alexander Kluge was perhaps the most prolific filmmaker and theorist. His films challenged conventional notions of cinematic time, space and narration, and due to his background in law as well as his connections to the Frankfurter Schule, he made a number of highly political and controversial *Autorenfilme*.[37] Above all, though, Kluge's style established a radical break from the German film tradition and informed the type of formalistic structures that would characterize the Young German Cinema.[38] His films were more collages than traditional films and consisted of interviews, photographs, drawings, documentary footage, stories, thoughts, title cards, and commentary which were combined visually with a cinematographic verité that again avoided all conventions of the dominant cinema. His aesthetic is perhaps best described by his own much quoted statement: "Ich glaube, das ist der Kern: Der Film stellt sich im Kopf des Zuschauers zusammen, und er ist nicht ein Kunstwerk, das auf der Leinwand für sich lebt. Der Film muß deswegen mit Assoziationen arbeiten."[39] What Kluge argues for here is another kind of cinema that functions on a different plane of reference than that of the narrative cinema. In his prose writing, Kluge utilized a similar technique, whereby he often eliminated direct narration in and of itself. Rainer Lewandowski has described Kluge's rejection of narration in favor of documentation as one that requires the reader to be an observer whereby the author appropriates the role of collector who gathers documents, references and protocols (17–18). What Kluge rejects in such a process, both in his writings and is films, is the ordering principle of the story and narration. In the spirit of modernist aesthetics, Kluge rejects the story as a fictive device which obscures rather than reveals reality.[40]

Perhaps nowhere is this method of filmmaking better expressed than in Kluge's second full length feature film *Artisten in der Zirkuskuppel: ratlos* (*Artists under the Big Top: perplexed*, 1968). The film is a parable about the struggle of the artist to realize his/her artistic vision within a capitalist system, but also of the antagonistic relationship between commercial and artistic modes of filmmaking. Leni Peickert, the film's protagonist, dreams of creating a reform circus but lacks funding and support for her endeavors. Much like the young filmmakers of the 1950s and 1960s who themselves wished to reform the German cinema, Leni Peickert encounters a seemingly endless series of obstacles that she must overcome in order to create her new circus. Among the most interesting is her attempt at convincing her friend and mentor Dr. Busch, who questions the foundation of her very attempt: namely who wants to see such a circus? This was the very same question which plagued the Young German Filmmakers who were attempting to confront issues of Germany's past and to make challenging films which were documents of reality rather than mere narrative entertainment.[41] Aesthetically, this film is a pure manifestation of Kluge's theory: rather than present a straight-forward narrative about Leni's efforts, Kluge mixes the short episodes with still photos, intertitles, found footage, drawings and texts. The result is a film that, as Marc Silbermann has demonstrated, "no longer seeks unity in plot, character, and motivation but in the production of experience by the spectator who is willing to engage the film's structural challenge and sensuous associations."[42] By breaking down any unifying plot, there similarly lacks a unified subject in Kluge's film, a state that allows him to explore issues from a multivalent perspective. In doing so, he rejects the notion of a singular discourse and posits instead a polyphonic point of view, which explores and collects as opposed to structures and orders. Such an approach to filmmaking was important to the Young German Filmmakers especially in regard to their approach to history. In deconstructing narrative unity, Kluge in turn deconstructs history and the narrated history that had come to be the primary discourse of the period. To reject narrative and stories (*Geschichten*) was then to reject the narrative that was the immediate history (*Geschichte*) of postwar Germany, a topic Kluge explores in greater detail in his 1979 film *Die Patriotin*.[43]

Kluge's films were no doubt among the most demanding and experimental of the West German feature films of 1960s, and his groundbreaking efforts opened the door for the next generation of filmmakers to explore issues of historicity and the possibility of narratable subjects through structural and thematic innovation. Moreover, his films represented the most direct challenge to narrative cinema and offered the possibility of creating a new hybrid within the feature film, one that combined elements of both documentary and narrative filmmaking but with avantgarde sensibilities. Of course not all of the Young or even the New German Filmmakers chose to reject narrative or unified plots. Directors like Peter Schamoni or later, Fassbinder liked telling stories but still in a critical manner. In contrast to Kluge, however, they used personal stories to engage in larger issues of public history.

Unlike Godard's conception of an "anything goes" cinema, though, films of the Young German Cinema had very specific principles. In an essay published shortly after the Oberhausener Manifest, Kluge defines the demands and concerns of the filmmakers with regard to aesthetics and ideology. Besides increasing the international visibility of German film and lessening commercial demands, Kluge demands greater freedom in allowing film to deal with chosen themes: "der Film muß sich mit der sozialen Dokumentation, mit politischen Fragen, mit Bildungsfragen und mit filmischen Neuentwicklungen befassen können" (*Augenzeugen* 47). This reaffirmation of the didactic nature of film as well as its claim to political discourse are aspects that were integral to both the Young and New German Cinemas. Norbert Grob characterizes the development of the *Autorenkino* in conjunction with an increased political awareness and engagement as follows: "Die Autorenfilmer verstanden ihre Rolle als kritische Avantgarde. Sie wollten sich einmischen in den gesellschaftlich-politischen Kontext, und sie wollten ihre persönliche, subjektive Verantwortung beim Filmemachen gewährleistet sehen."[44] These subjective political ideologies were continued by the second wave of filmmakers as well. In 1979, most of the leading members of the NGC issued a declaration affirming much of what their predecessors had sought, but this time emphasizing the interdependence of narrative and nonnarrative film.[45] The *Hamburger Erklärung*, signed by Wenders, Herzog, Fassbinder, Schlöndorff and others, maintained that the strength of the German cinema lay in its diversity—a diversity which could not be legislated. Above all, though, the signers reaffirmed their solidarity: "Wir lassen uns nicht auseinanderdividieren: der Spielfilm nicht vom Dokumentarfilm; Filmemacher, die schon Filme gemacht haben, nicht vom Nachwuchs; Filme, die das Medium reflektieren (und das praktisch tun, indem sie experimentieren), nicht vom Erzähl- und Kinofilm" (*Augenzeugen* 32). This declaration that the self-referential, experimental film cannot be separated from the narrative and the feature film, reflects the strength of the *Autorenkino* at the height of its popularity. Moreover, it reflects the desire of these filmmakers to break the distinction between narrative and experimental film, whereby the nonnarrative *Autorenfilm* could (and would) become a model for the feature film.

In his article on postmodernism and the cinema, Thomas Elasesser has shown that there exists an aesthetic connection between the cinematic avant-garde of both the 1920s and in the 1950s and 1960s and the postmodern sensibilities of the NGC.[46] Both genres developed as a protest cinema against certain aesthetic and political principles, whereas in the case of the NGC it took the form of an oedipal reaction to the paternal politics and aesthetics. By the 1970s, the NGC had, like much of the contemporary literature, begun exploring a "new subjectivity," which, unique to the German tradition, combined elements of history with personal subjectivity. Consequently, this form of historicized subjectivity could only be represented by what Elsaesser has termed a "Kontinuität in der Diskontinuität" (317). Moreover, filmmakers sought to construct a political imaginary that deconstructed the history and politics of their "fathers," concepts they wished both to confront and ultimately reject. Such an approach, Elsaesser argues, best found expression in postmodern constructions, ones which mixed various modes of interpretation and representation, from high art to kitsch and from allegorical to realist narratives

(316). This pastiche of cinematic form and representation allowed New German filmmakers to realize their goal of mixing the narrative cinema with the avant-garde and the short, documentary film with the feature film. What resulted was a wave of highly personal films which broke from cinematic tradition and propelled German cinema into the vanguard of the European Art film.

The very elements that made the NGC unique, however, would in the end be its own downfall, as the documentary and experimental elements interwoven into narrative and feature films would alienate both audiences and governmental officials, who would later seek to reduce financing for what they thought was becoming a noncommercial cinema. Moreover, in the late 1980s and early 1990s, many young German filmmakers, the first generation of post-NGC directors, would reject the overt politicization of the German film and would seek, through a return to the narrative cinema, a shift film away from didacticism and back toward entertainment. After Fassbinder's death in 1982, Schlöndorff's departure for Hollywood, Herzog's interest in exotic locales and Margarethe von Trotta's self-imposed exile in Italy, the German film lost much of its political power and with it, its didactic nature. Wenders, however, despite a similar return to film narratives, would not relinquish the cinema's edifying and educative function, arguing instead that meaningful statements and messages could still be conveyed through stories, and not just through the utilization of documentary and nonnarrative forms.

The Death of the *Autorenfilm*[47]

In a 1996 article in the *New York Times Magazine*, Susan Sontag reminisces about the European Art Film and the cinephilia it spawned.[48] In lamenting the "decay of cinema," she sadly pronounces the end of the challenging and artistic era of European filmmaking that began in the 1950s and, with it, the love of movies as an art form that it produced. What has supplanted these Art Films of the past, she finds, is "bloated, derivative filmmaking, a brazen combinatory or recombinatory art," which is driven by commercial concerns rather than the aesthetics of modernist art (60). While her lambasting is at once directed at a postmodern aesthetic, it also establishes a dialectic inherent in recent film history, one that sets off "brilliance and poetry" against "commercial standards," as Sontag has characterized this issue (61). When innovative ideas took hold in Italy in the 1950s, what resulted was a "dazzling number of original, passionate films of the highest degree of seriousness" (61). These films, which Sontag so sorely misses, are in fact the films of the countercinema of the 1950s and 1960s.

Although many factors certainly contributed to the decline of the *Autorenkino* in Germany, including a drastic change in the means of production, cuts in governmental subsidies, and the conditions which originally necessitated the beginnings of the *Autorenkino*, one factor which cannot be overlooked is audience taste. Despite critical acclaim from abroad and then, belatedly, within Germany, the NGC was never a resounding success at the box office. By 1983, Kluge himself was exploring the psychology of the public in order to determine what appeals to an audience and what constitutes a spectator film. He published his ideas and a series of polemical essays in a collection tellingly entitled *Bestandsaufnahme: Utopie Film*. What he found was that market-oriented films relied on the structures of the narrative cinema, including recognizable stars and directors and were entertaining rather than issue-oriented films. While Kluge blamed the media to a large degree for lack of support and for promoting uncritical visual entertainment, the government was also echoing many of these sentiments. In October 1982, Interior Minister Friedrich Zimmermann (CSU) declared that German taxpayers had a right to *Unterhaltungskino*,[49] implying that since a large majority of films were financed by the government through the Kuratorium set up at the behest of the Oberhausener to subsidize noncommercial cinema, the public should have some say in the kinds of films being produced. This shift in government financing toward more commercially viable, spectator-oriented films, was a veiled attempt to diminish the *Autorenfilm* and revitalize the dominant narrative cinema. With the death of Fassbinder who was in many ways the driving force behind the NGC, the "state of things" within the German film industry was perhaps best summed up in Wenders's 1982 film of the same name, *Der Stand der Dinge*, which viewed the situation as a struggle between the aesthetics and vision of the film artist and the increasing commercial interests and production values of the studios and government financing agencies. An ideological struggle for the direction and future of the *Autorenfilm* and the German cinema as a whole was beginning to form, a struggle which would inevitably lead to the end of the *Autorenfilm* and the rebirth of the dominant cinema, a phenomenon that was not singular to Germany, but was evident across Europe.

In an essay on this debate and the decline and fall of, the "European Art Movie," Thomas Elsaesser pointed particularly to the flood of Hollywood films into the European market and Europe's attempt at resistance as a major factor. In the early 1990s, there were proposals in Europe to impose import quotas on American films, so as to preserve the integrity of the European national cinemas and the remnants of the *auteur cinéma*. As president of the European Film Academy at that time, Wenders himself called for tougher sanctions against American films, arguing that Hollywood films had become an addiction for European audiences (despite the fact that he himself has made a number of Hollywood financed films).[50] Nothing less than the survival of European filmmaking was at stake, Wenders claimed. However, Wenders's calls ran counter to the idea of a free market (something the European Union certainly fostered) and also posed the question—to some politicians at least—as to whether it was valid to create films financed by the government for a public that rejects them. Nevertheless there was great sympathy among filmmakers and artists throughout Europe to maintain a sense of national identity and integrity within European artistic production, something that could only be done, many maintained, only through government subsidies.

Elsaesser broke down the discussion about the need for subsidies into a series of sub-categories: the economic case, the cultural case, and the formal case (24). While the economic and cultural cases are very political in nature, yet nevertheless crucial for maintaining a sense of cultural identity, the formal case is quite different, for it gets to heart of the nature of the Art Film itself. Deferential to David Bordwell's analysis of the formal components of the Art Film, Elsaesser sets up a dialectic between the classical cinema and formalistic reactions to it by many auteur filmmakers. Typical for the dominant cinema, he outlines, are "character-centered causality, question-and-answer logic, problem-solving routines, deadline plot structures and a mutual cueing system of word, sound, and image" (24). *Auteurists* in the countercinema tradition employ narrative conventions that are self-conscious and strategic deviations from the norm. This paradigm then enables one to distinguish between the "norm" and any deviation thereof, the latter being traditionally termed an "Art Film". He argues further, however, that such deviations from the norm only underscore their own differences and as such confirm the hegemony of the dominant Hollywood cinema both economically as well as aesthetically, for the Art Film consciously works to break from the standards set up by the "norm" or dominant paradigm. Herein lies the essence of the formal case for subsidizing the countercinema Art Film, namely whether the artistic creativity that such non-hegemonic filmmaking fosters merits support on the basis that such works would never receive funding through commercial production venues. Although most cinéastes and critics would argue quite vehemently for this idea, the economic case against such financial support becomes a dominant factor against it.

Also central to the stylistic differences between the modes of filmmaking is the question of pacing and editing and its effect on narrative, which has a marked affect on audience taste and mass appeal. This issue is not unlike that which confronted novelists at the beginning of this century. As with the novel, a slow, detailed, expansive unfolding of the narrative is detrimental to traditional storytelling and subsequent tension created by the desire to follow the course of the plot. A standard complaint since the early days of the cinema has been that European films are too slow, especially for American tastes. This difference becomes quite obvious when considering any of the standard action-film fare generated regularly by Hollywood and comparing it to its subsidized European counterpart. The ubiquity of television and video editing in the U.S. (not to mention the influence of MTV and its own style of filming and editing) has only reinforced this trend toward fast-paced quick shot editing. European films, on the other hand, tend to be much slower, with longer shots and fewer quick edits, resulting from the fact that the European Art Film tends to be more character-based as opposed to its story-based American counterpart. To this end, Elsaesser gives as an example a recent documentary film made by Britain's Channel Four Films on the subject of the European Art entitled *Pictures of Europe*. When asked whether the fast-paced editing of American films was a positive or negative quality, the filmmakers interviewed for the documentary were of a split opinion. Not surprisingly, the two most Americanized of the European directors, Paul Verhoeven (*Basic Instinct, Show Girls*) and Jean-Jacques Annaud (*Big Blue, The Lover*) viewed such techniques as positive (24). David Puttnam and Pedro Almodóvar were more neutral, whereas Bertrand Tavernier, Liv Ullmann and Wenders, purveyors of the Art Film technique, preferred the slower pace of European films. Perhaps Paul Schrader best summarized the central problematic: "American movies are based on the assumption that life presents you with problems, while European films are based on the conviction that life confronts you with dilemmas—and while problems are something you solve, dilemmas cannot be solved, they're merely probed or investigated" (24). The distinction between problem-solving versus problem-probing can be extended to issues of narrative and storytelling: American films create storylines which, true to the nature of the tale, demand closure, while European films are more often character studies positing dilemmas that are not necessarily to be solved within a two-hour frame. American films thus follow an Aristotelian pattern of rising dramatic action, climax and resolution, whereas the Art Film, in true modernist fashion, seeks to break such imposed structures in order to reflect a more complex reality.[51]

Although this difference may be representative of European intellectual thought, it appears to be no longer reflective of the tastes of European audiences. Increasingly American comedies and thrillers are earning huge profits in Europe and in many cases forcing commercially minded European directors to rethink their approach to filmmaking. One of the most popular German films in recent years has been Katja von Garnier's final project for the Munich Hochschule für Film und Fernsehen (HFF), *Abgeschminkt!*, a comedy about two young women in search of love. In an interview with *Der Spiegel*, von Garnier attempts to account for the enormous success of the film: "Ist mir unerklärlich . . . Viele Frauen erkennen sich wieder, Männer können was lernen. Außerdem: Tempo, Tempo, Tempo" (214). What von Garnier learned very quickly is something she garnered from American cinema and certainly not from her predecessors at the HFF: namely, how to pace a film for success. Even more surprising is the fact that the film is only 55 minutes in length, something unheard of in both America, where studios have unwritten laws that with very few exceptions, feature films must be between 90 and 120 minutes, and Europe, where Art Films can often reach up to 4 hours in length (Bille August's 270 minute film *The Best Intentions* is a prime example, as well as Wenders's own *Until the End of the World*, which has also been released in its full five-hour version). Von Garnier admits that there was pressure to lengthen the film: "Kollegen wollten mich überzeugen, noch eine halbe Stunde dazudrehen, um den Film auf volle Kinolänge zu bringen. Ich habe abgelehnt, die Geschichte dauert 55 Minuten und Schluß" (214).

The idea that a given standard for the length of feature films even exists in Germany shows how much the conception of filmmaking, especially at the HFF has changed and how far the students have drifted from the ideas of the *Autorenfilm* in just twenty years. Von Garnier's construction of the film was obviously driven by story considerations; once the story had been told and reached its end, so too had the film. This in and of itself places the film more in line with the dominant, narrative-driven cinema than with the tradition of the European art film that one would normally expect from a German film academy. Furthermore, it stands in marked contrast to the approach Wenders took in creating his final project for the HFF some 20 years earlier. Wenders's conception of filmmaking at that time could not have been more different: "Filmmachen [war] für mich: daß man die Kamera irgendwo hinstellt und auf etwas ganz bestimmtes richtet und dann nichts mehr tut, sie nur laufen läßt" (*LB* 11). The original version, Wenders has stated, was three hours long, but was too long even for his own liking. However, length was not a consideration: "Dieser erste Film hat wirklich so lang sein dürfen, wie er wollte, das war mein Examensfilm an der Filmhochschule" (*LB* 12). Wenders was driven by the sheer joy of filmmaking and visual aesthetics, a central component of the *nouvelle vague*. Von Garnier, on the other hand, openly admits that she was simply orienting her film to the public. Furthermore she acknowledges that her generation is strongly influenced by American cinema, yet nonetheless steeped in the European filmmaking tradition: "Ideal wäre es doch, europäische Sensibilität mit amerikanischem Erzählkino zu verbinden" (214). Whereas Wenders views the American cinema as a reference point for his style as well, especially the cinema of Samuel Fuller and Nicholas Ray, he was also heavily influenced by the practitioners of the French *nouvelle vague*. For Wenders's early films, the European sensibility that von Garnier speaks of was a central component; the demands of narrative cinema were of secondary importance, and market orientation was of practically no concern. Clearly points of reference have changed as well as market orientation.

Nevertheless, Wenders, one of the last remaining practitioners of the ideals represented by the NGC, recognizes that the times have changed, as well as the conditions under which films are made. In a discussion on the future of the *Autorenfilm*, Wenders asserts that the situation at the beginning of the 1970s was much more conducive to the development of an alternative cinema than today. Specifically the creation of the *Förderrungssystem*, which provided easier access to governmental financing, eliminated the arduous process of production. Young directors today, like von Garnier, do not have that luxury. Furthermore, those filmmakers who were part of that earlier proliferation would be hard-pressed today, as Wenders himself readily admits: "Der Fassbinder, in den neunziger Jahren wäre der wahnsinning geworden, denn er hätte ja immer drei Jahre gebraucht, um einen Film zu finanzieren. Damals konnte er jedes Jahr vier oder fünf machen. Damals kam Ökonomisches zusammen mit einer Idee von Neubeginn, Neubeginn auch, was das Publikum betrifft" (Berg 46).

The New German Filmmakers were in many ways working from the standpoint of a cinematic *Stunde Null*. They had the privilege that no one was preceding them, for the National Socialist cinema and the Ufa-productions in the in the 1940s and 50s had in a sense been forgotten. However, today's filmmakers have a tradition behind them, and that they have chosen to reject the NGC style of cinema is understandable, Wenders maintains:

> Es gibt nichts Langweiligeres, als sich einfach in eine Tradition einzureihen, die von den Kinomachern der vorangegangenen Generation begründet wurde. . . . Der *Autorenfilm* von damals ist sicher ein auslaufendes Modell. Auch ich mache meine Filme heute nicht mehr allein, sondern arbeite mit Produzenten und Drehbuchautoren zusammen. Hollywood ist nicht zuletzt deshalb im Augenblick so stark, weil es die Gewaltenteilung der Aufgaben beim Film immer beibehalten hat. ("Zauber" 243)

Here Wenders's thinking echoes Kracauer's theory of cinema as a representative of a cultural mind-set. The division of labor within the filmmaking process, as Kracauer wrote some forty years earlier, is what makes cinema the most collaborative of arts and thus the most reflective of ideas within a cultural and artistic community. Thus the trend toward collective and interactive works reflects the desire of filmmakers to move away from the *Autorenfilm* as well as the means of production associated with it. Since *Der Himmel über Berlin*, Wenders too has collaborated with one or more screenwriters on all of his successive films. Schlöndorff continues to adapt literary works, using screenplays written by others. Within this collaborative framework, the role of the screenwriter is naturally strengthened, and the screenplay begins to serve as the narrative framework for the film, as opposed to images or issues, elements which drove many of the *Autorenfilme* of the 1970s and 1980s.

The New German Comedy and the Return of Narrative

While the future of the *Autorenfilm* is still being debated, there was a decided trend in Germany in the 1990s toward Hollywood-style comedies. These films, beginning with Doris Dörrie's 1986 box office success *Männer*, have achieved a domestic popularity that the *Autorenfilm* never reached, primarily by utilizing the elements of the classic narrative cinema. Sönke Wortmann's 1995 hit comedy, *Der bewegte Mann* about a man who moves in with a shy gay man after being kicked out of his apartment by his girlfriend, for instance, grossed over $40 million dollars in its first ten months making it the third most successful German film since 1980.[52] Moreover, Wortmann's follow-up films were equally successful and a general revitalization of the German film industry occurred in the 1990s, including the glamorization of the German film prize ceremonies.[53] Even Wenders has expressed an interest in trying his hand at comedy: "I have no more excuses. Comedy, I believe, is the toughest of all film genres. To make a comedy, a filmmaker must know his craft, because you have to follow a strict set of rules."[54] This new genre of German-comedy, "die neue deutsche Komödie," came as a bit of a surprise, for postwar German film had not garnered a reputation for its humor. What these new films had in common was their reliance on traditional elements of the classic cinema: causality, linear narrative, closure, and the most necessary element of all, a happy end. These principles are markedly different from the structures of the NGC, which were generally issue- or author-oriented.[55] Whereas the author-oriented film relied on the self-expression and personal vision of the filmmaker, the issue film dealt with social problems, controversial issues, or Germany's past. As a result, many of these films, and their respective filmmakers, were viewed by the German public as self-indulgent and indifferent to the audience's desires, a point that was very likely more viewer perception than reality, as many in the NGC were indeed concerned about reaching an audience rather than making films for their own satisfaction.

Part of the problem, von Garnier argues, is that, after the death of Fassbinder, German cinema lost its identity. She cited an incident as indicative of the position German film until recently held with the public. After the release of *Abgeschminkt!*, she and some friends spontaneously polled people on the street and those leaving the cinema to solicit their reactions to the film. They encountered a young couple who had a choice between her film and an American thriller.

Although the young woman wanted to see her film, the man exclaimed that she was crazy, that that was a German film, reiterating the stereotype that had come to be true even in Germany, namely that German films are long, difficult and sometimes boring ("Tempo" 214). Instead, they chose the American film. Von Garnier sees this as a problem against which young directors must continually fight.

By avoiding difficult themes and turning to comedy, a genre well established in Hollywood and one successfull in Germany as well, directors were able to find a niche for the German film once again by creating decidedly German comedies and once again developing a fixed set of actors and directors with recognizable names and faces.[56] Moreover, they began to recognize that cinema is a medium of the masses and in turn, have begun creating market-oriented films. Hark Bohm, another member of the NGC, agrees. When asked about the blossoming popularity of the German comedy, he gives a psychological explanation: "Dieses Volk taumelt von einem Extrem ins andere. Früher haben sich Kinogänger masochistisch in schwerblütigen Autorenfilmen gesuhlt. Heute lachen sie sich in Blödsinnskomödien kaputt."[57] Bohm recognizes as well, that the older generation of filmmakers (once, ironically, the young rebels) had become too removed from the masses: "Wir Alten wollten doch Elite sein, exklusiv und Hochkultur. Wir waren Ästheten und Romantiker wie Wim Wenders oder marxistische Pädagogen. Man machte Filme, um Thesen zu illustrieren. Die Zuschauer sollten im Kino lernen, bessere Menschen zu werden" ("'Gepäck'" 182). The problem was, the public soon tired of this enlightened, "elitist" approach to the cinema and rejected the German film as a whole.

Concomitant to this was a newfound emphasis on narrative and storytelling in the cinema. Dörrie, one of the most successful of contemporary German filmmakers who has made a number of commercially and critically successful comedies, attributes her stay in America to her approach to writing and filmmaking: "Ich kam von einem humanistischen Gymnasium, und dort hieß es, daß man Schreiben nicht lernen kann. Entweder ist man Goethe, oder man läßt es besser gleich. In Amerika herrscht die Auffassung, daß man alles lernen kann. Es war für mich eine unheimliche Befreiung, dort auf dem College all das weggefegt zu sehen. Da galt es nix, daß ich Latein und Altgriechisch gelernt hatte. Was zählte war, ob man gut erzählen kann. Das mußte ich erst mühsam lernen."[58] In the same interview, she describes her task as writer and filmmaker in remarkably similar terms to those of Handke, someone with whom she aesthetically, shares little: "als Geschichtenerzählerin fühle ich mich verpflichtet, über das, was ich hier sehe, zu erzählen, auch weil ich glaube, daß ich hier genauer beobachten kann als etwa in Amerika. All das, was meine Figuren durchmachen, bin ich zum Teil selber, auch in dieser schrecklichen deutschen Sehnsucht, jemand anders sein zu wollen, woanders leben zu wollen, im Süden am besten, wo man das wahre Leben vermutet." Her view of filmmaking is one based very much on the aesthetic of viewing and narrating; her figure, she readily admits, are based in part on herself as well as those in her immediate vicinity. As a filmmaker who come to the cinema from writing, she like many of her younger cinematic colleagues, views herself first and foremost as a storyteller who has an obligation to tell stories, ones which reflect the German "Alltag" as well as the mentality of the people.[59]

Although the popularity of the New German Comedy has at the end of the 1990s waned, due in part to overexposure and the overabundance of poor films, most of the current generation of filmmakers and directors seem to be relinquishing the didactic and even the aesthetic claims that the cinema of the 1960s, 1970s, and 1980s fought for and embraced. With the return to narrative cinema, there appears to be a shift toward the market-oriented, commercial fare so abundantly produced and exported by Hollywood at the expense of artistic vision. The ultimate irony is that this is the very same type of cinema that Wenders and many in the European market want to restrict so as to protect the European film industry. By succumbing to market demands and the temptations of commercial cinema, some directors have begun reestablishing the bourgeois cinema that Godard and Kluge originally sought to disrupt in favor of challenging artistic statements.

However, the *Autorenfilm* may not have breathed its last breath. Wenders and Schlöndorff continue to make European films that incorporate elements of the narrative cinema, yet are nonetheless true to the aesthetic ideals of the *Autorenfilm* and Schlöndorff took over control of the Babelsberg Studios in Berlin in the hopes of reestablishing Berlin as the prominent film center it once was. Moreover, there are signs that some young directors are willing to carry on in Wenders's foot steps and to combine story-driven cinema with artistry. In 1995, three young Berlin directors and producers founded X-Filme Creative Pool GmbH, a collective in the spirit of the Filmverlag der Autoren. Hoping to learn from the mistakes of the first generation of *Autorenfilmer*, the goal of X-Filme company is "der dritte Weg zwischen Kunst und Kommerz: schnelle, aktuelle, unberechenbare Filme, *Geschichten mit Handschrift und Haltung, anspruchvolles Kino für ein breites Publikum.*"[60] Whether or not "der Mittelweg bringt den Tod," as Kluge and Edgar Reitz once maintained in the title to one of their most compelling and political films, remains to be seen. What is for certain is that stories and narrative have made a comeback in contemporary German cinema in much the same way as in literature. With this return, writers and directors are attempting to come to terms with the possibilities and usefulness that stories as a literary and filmic trope afford.

If the *Autorenkino* and the Art Film as an aesthetic medium in general are to survive, there must be an attempt at finding a compromise between the demands of the audience and the vision of the filmmaker. Indeed, Hollywood films have also begun to change. More and more independent filmmakers are creating visually challenging films that combine elements of both the classic narrative film with the European Art Film. Wenders points this out as well: "was Inhalte und Formen angeht, finde ich die Kategorien 'europäischer Film' und 'amerikanischer Film' längst gequirlten Mist. In Amerika entstehen zahlreiche Filme, die nach allen Maßstäben europäisch wirken—und umgekehrt gilt das gleiche" (Zauber 243). However, this does not mean that the concept of national cinemas is no longer valid. Cinema, as an art form, still has its place and position within the world, and as Wenders maintains further, it is also crucial for establishing cultural identity: "Für die Zukunft Europas wird es sehr wichtig sein, daß Europa ein Bild von sich selbst entwirft. Es muß seine eigenen Mythen illustrieren. Bilder sind so wichtig für jedes Heimatgefühl, daß es ohne Bilder keine Idee von Europa geben wird" (243).

Wenders's conception of the cinema is crucial for understanding images, aesthetics, and narration. Myths and the feeling of place, elements important for establishing a cultural identity, can be portrayed in many ways, both visually and textually, and with narrative or through images. If cinema is to maintain its importance in contributing to a nation's artistic and cultural heritage, then it must continue to delineate between film as entertainment and the cinema as an art form. Although stories certainly do not signal the death of the *Autorenfilm*, as evidenced by any number of recent European films which have successfully combined narrative and visual aesthetics, focusing solely on commercial demands and viewer expectations, however, could lead to the death of the Art Film. Similarly, if the

German cinema is to establish a new identity, it will not be through copying the production standards of the mainstream Hollywood film. Instead, it will arise with new artists once again challenging the limits of medium and conceptions of what film and filmmaking is all about. This is what Wenders is attempting to do, not only in his function as president of the European Film Academy, but also with his recent films, which combine aspects of narrative cinema with the visual aesthetics of the Art Film.

~ 4 ~

Wim Wenders: a Cinematic Storyteller

Of all of the proponents of the New German Cinema (NGC), Wim Wenders has achieved the greatest international success and recognition.[1] In addition to having received numerous international film prizes and awards, he was named president of the European Film Academy in 1995. Like his friend and sometime collaborator Peter Handke, Wenders has evolved as an artist and a theorist. He has progressed from making films in the tradition of the *nouvelle vague* early on in his career, to making films in America for Hollywood studios, to finally returning to Germany and again making European films in more recent years. As such, he has continued to remain on the forefront of German cinema and, like Handke, his works echo many of the artistic discourses and shifts prevalent within his chosen medium. Although Wenders's earliest films were very much in the tradition of the anti-narrative cinema, his more recent works display a newfound advocacy of storytelling. Moreover, his theoretical writings expressly state the importance of stories for aesthetics. For this reason, I want to focus specifically on Wenders's transformation from a reluctant storyteller to a director who professes the absolute necessity of stories in the cinema and in society. For Wenders, stories serve a threefold purpose: first, they constitute a means of redemption for his protagonists, by imparting structure and meaning to their lives. Second, narratives create order and connections (*Zusammenhänge*) for the viewer which is important for a story's mimetic function and the ability of the visual image to portray reality. Third, in the best possible case, narratives posit both meaning and morality, for by their very nature, they establish causality and the denouement inherent in the art of storytelling not only carries a message but in the case of Wenders, is linked to an ethical stance.[2]

Wenders's cinematic career has in many ways paralleled Handke's, in that both early on embraced more radical, innovative techniques of representation, only to return to the more traditional form of narratives and stories in recent years. Their success and prominence has further made them influential in the course of German literature and film, as is evidenced by the abundance of secondary material on their works and their theories. By examining Wenders's aesthetics as well as comparing his early films with his most recent ones, a clear development and change in perspective can be seen. As with Handke, Wenders's recent works assert the need and value of the story in modern society as a means to order reality and impart meaning to the text.

Der ewige Erzähler

In a scene from Wenders's 1987 film *Der Himmel über Berlin*, the figure of an old man, a wanderer who inhabits the libraries and forgotten locales of Berlin, mourns the passing of time and the decline of the importance of storytelling in modern society. This figure, Homer, to whose inner thoughts the angels Damiel and Cassiel can attend, is the embodiment of the archetypal storyteller, the keeper of the epic, oral narrative tradition, whose own place and importance in the world has vanished. While sitting in the West Berlin *Staatsbibliothek*, he watches readers young and old sit silently alone, lost in contemplation and in reading, and laments his own demise as a result of the situation of the modern reader:

> Erzähle, Muse, vom Erzähler, dem an den Weltrand verschlagenen kindlichen Uralten und mache an ihn kenntlich den Jedermann. Meine Zuhörer sind mit der Zeit zu Lesern geworden, und sie sitzen nicht mehr im Kreis, sondern für sich, und einer weiß nichts vom anderen. (*Himmel* 30)

This direct reference to Lukàcs's and Benjamin's own theory of the decline of the oral tradition is actually prefigured at the beginning of the scene. Damiel and Cassiel, the two angel protagonists, are passing through the library listening to the thoughts of the readers, when they encounter someone studying a passage from Benjamin's *Über den Begriff der Geschichte* and the history of the ninth section, in which Benjamin likens Paul Klee's painting *Angelus Novus* to the angel of history. In this allegory, Benjamin imagines how the angel of history must appear: with its face turned toward the past, it is blown forcefully backwards into the future by the storm of progress, unable to close its wings, despite the mountain of wreckage—history—piled at his feet. The figure of Homer that Wenders and Handke (who wrote the angels' dialogues) created for the film is in many ways not unlike this angel of history, for he too is similarly being swept forward into the future by forces beyond his control. Despite his attempts, he is unable to awaken his listeners and impart to them through his storytelling, that which Benjamin would term wisdom or the epic side of truth,[3] much the same as the angel of history cannot stop the flow of progress and awaken the dead from the past, so as to once again make whole the wreckage thrown at his feet. Later in the film, Homer ponders his own importance and what meaning he still holds for humankind: "Soll ich jetzt aufgeben? Wenn ich aufgebe, dann wird die Menschheit ihren Erzähler verlieren. Und hat die Menschheit einmal ihren Erzähler verloren, so hat sie auch ihre Kindschaft verloren" (*Himmel* 57). Much as Benjamin believed, Wenders's fictive Homer postulates that should humankind lose its storyteller, not only will it have lost its childhood innocence, but also its source of truth and wisdom.[4]

This character in Wenders's thirteenth feature film is in many ways a summation and culmination of many of the ideas he has problematized not only in his earlier films but also in his theoretical writings, namely the importance of stories within the context of film and art. Furthermore, this is an issue which he has continued to deal with even in his most recent films, in which he actively calls for an examination of the importance of stories and decries their so-called "death." For Wenders, the story, in all its manifestations, is central to his aesthetic vision as well as to his conceptions of structuring narratives and film. In many of his films, stories have come to have a redeeming power, capable of saving his characters from a spiritual or existential malaise. Moreover it is the sheer beauty and joy of the visual story which is the driving force in his films and which serves as the impetus for the creation of his narratives. But his is also a different kind of story and narrating process. As Norbert Grob has noted, Wenders's trademark is an open form of cinema, which desists closure and relishes the "gaps" and free-roaming gaze.[5] Yet the story is nevertheless essential to his cinematic form for, as Grob correctly asserts, they do not so much propel the plot as keep it from falling apart (192).

For Wenders, the storyteller and stories themselves are inexorably linked to the cinema. In an essay discussing the inception of his films, he recounts the origin of the figure of Homer:

> In einer allerersten Version, die ich Peter Handke erzählt hatte, gab es die Person eines alten Erzengels, der in der Bibliothek lebt. Peter wußte nichts mit der Idee anzufangen, aber vor seinem Schreibtisch

hing an der Wand eine Reproduktion von Rembrandts *Homer*: ein sitzender alter Mann, der redet-aber zu wem? Ursprunglich spricht Homer auf dem Rembrandt-Gemälde zu einem Schüler, aber das Bild war in zwei Hälften zerschnitten und der Erzähler von seinem Zuhörer getrennt worden, so daß er jetzt alleine redet. Peter mochte dieses Gemälde sehr und hat meine Idee des Erzengels umgewandelt in den ewigen Dichter. Ich meinerseits wußte nicht, wie ich Homer in mein Drehbuch integrieren sollte. Endlich kamen wir darauf, daß Homer in der Bibliothek lebt und daß die Dialoge von Peter seine innere Stimme sind. Curt Bois [der Schauspieler, der Homer spielt] war weder Engel noch Mensch, sondern beides zugleich, denn er ist so alt wie das Kino. (*LB* 137)[6]

The metamorphosis of this figure from the original idea of the *ewiger Dichter* to the archetypal modern storyteller who speaks alone may have indeed been per chance (it was only chance that Handke's reproduction of Rembrandt's painting was not completely in tact), but it nevertheless corresponds ideologically with Wenders's conception of storytelling and narration. Even with his earliest films, Wenders struggled to convey an image and a story to the audience, and this vision of the storyteller-sage living in silence in modernism's temple of knowledge, the library, without an audience, symbolically reflects what Benjamin warned was happening to modern society, namely losing its capacity to share knowledge and experience. That Wenders chose Curt Bois, the German actor who, in 1987 at the age of 86, had been acting in film for almost 80 years, underscores his belief that the archetypal storyteller is as central to film as it is to literary narratives. This figure is one who continues to tell stories, either through literary or cinematic narrative, which have meaning and importance even if the audience who hears or sees them is diminishing or, in some cases, has even vanished. Indeed, Wenders dedicated the film to all former "angels," but especially to Yazujiro Ozu, François Truffaut and Andrei Tarkovsky, three of Wenders's cinematic idols who had recently died, but remained, to his mind, exemplary visual storytellers. His conception of the filmmaker as a storyteller is central to his understanding of the cinema as a form of communication on par with literature. The ability to express and convey a vision is, he believes, an artistic goal which the best of filmmakers are able to achieve, and it is one which, due to the unique nature of the cinema as a communal art form,[7] can in many ways preserve the storytelling tradition.

Wenders's Cinematic Aesthetics: Visual Storytelling

Wenders himself admits that he came late to appreciate the art of the story.[8] Nevertheless, his aesthetic view of filmmaking has long linked image and story, though for most of his career, the image was preeminent over story. From his earliest days as a filmmaker and a student, his inspiration for making films, and thus telling a story, has always been first and foremost an image. In the forward to a 1994 collection of photos and stories entitled *Einmal*, Wenders recounts not only the purpose behind the collection but also his *modus operandi*: "Jedes Photo, jedes 'EIN MAL' in der Zeit, ist auch der Beginn einer Geschichte, die anfängt mit 'Es war einmal. . . .' Jedes Photo ist auch die erste Einstellung eines Films" (14). Indeed, every photo in the volume has some story behind it, which Wenders recounts in short, poetic stories prefacing each photo or photo series. Often he shot more than one photo of a given image and in doing so, established a sort of story line. The process for creating a cinematic narrative is similar: with each successive click of the camera, the story moves forward thereby creating a montage; a collection of montages eventually leads to the outline of a film. From there, a narrative is created, or allowed to develop, from which the work emerges.

This approach to filmmaking is a central tenet in Wenders's concept of cinematic narrative and storytelling. Every person, every landscape, every object, and every image contains a story wanting to be told. It is then the task of the filmmaker to extract that story and through montage, dialogue, and music to create a narrative. This organic approach to filmmaking has informed Wenders's methodology and aesthetic designs since his early days as a film student and reveals much about his theory of narrative. In closing his forward to *Einmal*, Wenders borrows heavily from the receptionist theory of first-generation filmmakers of the Young German Cinema in the 1960's like Alexander Kluge and Jean-Marie Straub, who maintained that the actual story is created only in the mind of the viewer, and that it is the task of the viewer to order and impart meaning to the images with which s/he is confronted. With regard to photography, Wenders writes: "So wie wir im Moment des Photographierens verschwinden wollten hinaus in die Welt und hinein in die Dinge, so springen Welt und Dinge jetzt aus dem Photo heraus und herein in jeden Betrachter und wollen dort weiter wirken. 'DORT' erst entstehen die Geschichten, dort, im Auge des Betrachters" (16). What Wenders suggests is that the story begins in the eye of the beholder. His aim as an artist is to project himself into the object he is beholding, so as to capture it for others to "see" later. Once documented on film, these objects, all containing some story in waiting, then come alive for the viewer to enjoy and to use in order to develop a story using one's own imagination.

In many ways, Wenders's philosophy recalls that of the Realist film theorists Siegfried Kracauer and Béla Balázs, who maintained that film had the power to show the true reality of objects and in doing so, redeem their physical existence.[9] In fact, in answer to the question "Pourquoi Filmez-Vous?" posed by a French magazine, Wenders cites the only two quotes he remembers with regard to film theory, namely Balázs' contention that film above all art forms can show objects as they truly exist and Kracauer's redemption theory (although he attributes this to Balázs as well) (*LB* 9). Kracauer's stance was in reaction to criticism early in the century that modernization and technology had made it impossible for humankind to appreciate the natural world and thus see it unaffected. Cinema, with its ability to "record" reality, could then, better than any other medium, redeem reality from the destructive forces of technology. Wenders, too, believes in the innate power and force of objects and landscapes and has repeatedly expressed his concern about the direction and influence of technology on art. However, he parts company with Kracauer in that he distinguishes between the reality of images and the fabricated illusion of cinema, for cinematic images function much differently than the photograph. Whereas photographs are by nature still lifes, without dialogue, progressive action or character, film is able to traverse time and thus create not only character but story and narrative. Once a story line is imparted to the images, though, reality is no longer recorded; rather, a fictive progression of images and meaning emerges. However, the images can once again stake their claim to reality in the eyes and mind of the viewer.[10] In fact, some years after the release of *Paris, Texas*, Wenders recalled being asked if it were a true story: "Jetzt ist es eine," he responded, implying that not only is the concept of reality a subjective one, but that film has the power to create an alternative reality through the illusion of the visual experience (AS 12).

Wenders admits that he has always had problems with the idea of "stories" (*LB* 68). He began his career not as a filmmaker or photographer but as a painter, and moved on to film when he realized the limitations of painting with regard to the concept of time. Thus when he began making films, he saw himself less as storyteller than as a "Maler des Raums auf der Suche nach Zeit" (*LB* 68).[11] Space, cities, landscapes, and streets were the material that formed the basis for his films. The problem he then encountered arose with the editing of the images; any form of sequential editing created a form of montage and imparted meaning and thus the beginnings of a story. However, this process, he felt, is unnatural for, unlike the written word, images do not automatically gravitate toward forming stories; they must be "forced" into a story and this process is at best a laborious one. The danger then arises in the manipulation of these images, as it sometimes leads to the art of storytelling, while other times simply to *mißhandelte Bilder* in which the life of the image has been sucked out, like blood by a vampire (*LB* 71).

Nevertheless images do have the potential and ability to convey, via stories, a message, a meaning and a moral, all of which are very "fragile," yet essential for a public desirous of more than mere entertainment and suspense. Wenders has, in fact, articulated his profound belief in the power and importance of stories numerous times, arguing that, despite their fictive nature, they impart wisdom and truth, much in line with Benjamin's essays, as well as fill a basic need for human beings, as Reynolds Price has maintained:[12] "Geschichten geben den Leuten das Gefühl, daß es einen Sinn gibt, daß sich eine letzte Ordnung und Reihenfolge hinter der unglaublichen Verwirrung aller Erscheinungen verbirgt, die sie umgeben. Diese Ordnung wünschen sich die Menschen mehr als alles andere, ja ich würde beinahe sagen, daß die Vorstellung von Ordnung oder von Geschichte mit der Vorstellung von Gott zusammenhängt. Geschichten sind Gottesersatz. Oder umgekehrt" (*LB* 72). This need and desire for stories and the importance they play in society becomes crucial to Wenders's later understanding of cinema as art. In his later films, stories taken on an almost divine, redemptive power, which have the power to heal the lost and disenchanted. Furthermore, many of his characters are in search of their own poetic voice and a means of communication, often found through storytelling, which would help them gain a better understanding of themselves and the world, as well as reestablish some semblance of order in the world.

But as a filmmaker and an individual, Wenders has not always been an advocate of order or of stories. In a 1982 colloquium on narrative technique, Wenders's stated that the intrinsic nature of the classical story, with beginning, middle and end, is a fabrication and a lie within the context of a world in which entropy, not order, rules: "Geschichten . . . sind per definitionem

Lügengeschichten. Aber sie sind sehr, sehr wichtig als Überlebensform" (*LB* 71–72). By projecting the idea that order exists in the natural world, stories propagate a lie. Nevertheless they create *Zusammenhänge*, which help people overcome the fear of disorder and a lack of control (*LB* 72).[13] To this end, Wenders shares Kluge's emphasis on connection or *Zusammenhang*. In his 1979 film *Die Patriotin*, Kluge's protagonist Gabi Teichert is in search of such connections within German history, as she encounters and attempts to make sense of the multiplicity of voices attempting to construct Germany's historical narrative. For Kluge, the filmmaker's task is to create this connection through montage and the successive presentation of images. Although not favoring story per se, Kluge nevertheless feels that images must be mediated, otherwise one is left with pure documentation and a collection of images without meaning.[14] Roger Cook, in his reading of *Wings of Desire*, argues as well that part of the film's subtextual narrative of desire is a desire for connectedness. Damiel and Cassiel, condemned to a purely spiritual existence yearn for a sense of causality and connectedness rather then only being able to watch and allow things to happen. Damiel's increasing desire to "fall" is thus a longing for a personal story in which his life is imparted meaning through the structuring nature of narrative.[15]

The teleological need for stories has existed since antiquity with its great storyteller, Homer, and, as Wenders maintains, stories continue to be vital to mankind, for they accord a sense of purpose and thus the pretense, albeit a false one, that the individual is in control of the world (*LB* 59). The challenge of the director then is to take these collected images and impart to them order and meaning and thus establish a logic to the images. In accepting the Friedrich Wilhelm Murnau Prize from the city of Bielefeld, Wenders praised Murnau as a film giant and pioneer but, above all, as a great "Form-Erfinder, Erzähl-Pionier und Bild-Künstler des Kinos," or, in other words, the epitome of what it means to be a great director.

Given his inherent love of images and objects and his disdain for artificiality, it is perhaps surprising that Wenders has on numerous occasions turned to literary works as source material for his films. He has, in fact, filmed five novels and worked closely with three well respected writers.[16] He admits though that the part of filmmaking he despises most is the writing of the screenplay, whereas the preparation and the editing are the stages which are the most appealing (*AS* 237).

This underscores his conviction that the role of the director is primarily to create the images and then to establish logic and order. The creation of a storyline, or, as he would have it, the forcing of images into a story, is the most unnatural and tedious task, and, perhaps, the task of the writer. Excepting his first film, *Summer in the City* (1970), which was his final project for the Hochschule für Film und Fernsehen, Wenders's first major feature film was a literary adaptation, namely Peter Handke's *Die Angst des Tormanns beim Elfmeter* (*The Goalie's Anxiety at the Penalty Kick*, 1971). The impetus to film this short novel came from Wenders's observation that every sentence read like a camera shot (*AS* 246). Writing a screen play—and thus a storyline—involved for him little more than excerpting each sentence into an individual scene. At that time, writing and screenplays were for him "Neuland," as his short films and first feature were created completely on the basis of images and scenes, rather than from a concrete story board (*AS* 248). This was a natural approach to filmmaking for him as his entry into filmmaking came via painting and the visual arts. If Wenders's peers in the NGC represented early on a more literary and philosophical strand of the *Autorenfilm*,[17] Wenders was a practitioner of a painterly style, in which landscape and image were primary. Grob comments that Wenders's own emphasis on painting is inextricably connected to his understanding of the interconnectedness of film and reality: "Er sucht also sein Bekenntnis zur Malerei als Bestätigung seines Willens zur Dokumentation 'physischer Realität' zu nehmen" (*Wenders* 29), for painting has the ability to document reality perhaps better than any other cameraless art form. Thus the influence on Wenders of painters like Edward Hopper and photographers like Walker Evans has informed his own cinematic style. It is a style which Grob has likened to a *Pinselführung*, whereby it becomes important to decide "welcher Strich verzichtbar und welcher unverzichtbar ist, welcher stärker ausgeführt, welcher schwächer gezogen und welcher ganz neu entworfen werden muß, damit das Bild die gewünschten Wirkungen erzielt" (29). It is for this reason that Wenders has always preferred to work with one of the most accomplished and painterly of all cinematographers, Robby Müller and, for *Der Himmel über Berlin*, with the acclaimed camera man Henri Alekan.

Not until *Falsche Bewegung* (*Wrong Move*, 1975), his second collaboration with Handke, did Wenders seek to find a less restrictive approach to literature and screenplays.[18] He later recalled that at that time, the restrictions of a screenplay were still new to him, enabling him to view them more as an adventure than as a limitation, and further allowing a greater degree of freedom and experimentation (*AS* 249). Wenders has always alternated between making very structured, color films following a preset script and then very open, loosely constructed black and white films (*LB* 72–77). What draws him to the open black and white films, which are often improvised on the set and which generally do not have a preestablished ending when shooting begins, is the limitation of working with a rigid storyline and shooting schedule. On the other hand, he nevertheless returns to structured films, often works of literature, for they offer the freedom from having to create dialogue and a storyline, something Wenders professes to struggle with continually.[19]

His desire early on to film works of literature has less to do with the desire to create a national cinema, as Volker Schlöndorff is wont to do,[20] than with a repulsion to writing dialogue. During the making of *Im Lauf der Zeit* (*Kings of the Road*, 1976), for example, production was often stopped for Wenders to continue the screenplay, as the writing process was for him excruciating. Furthermore, he often begins work on his black and white films with little more than a rough sketch or a few working images in mind that suggest a film and/or a story. What this process once again underscores is the primacy of images in his overall conception of filmmaking. As with his photographs, his films were similarly so constructed that an image or an object formed the basis for the narrative rather than a sequence of events. For *Paris, Texas* (1984), for example, Wenders and Sam Shepard began simply with the image of a man walking through the desert as the starting point for the film (*LB* 85–87). The image was the foundation of the story and the narrative developed from this image. In two of his most personally frustrating films, *Der Scharlachroten Buchstabe* (*The Scarlet Letter*, 1972) and *Hammett* (1982), Wenders encountered a greater problem in which the narrative and the process of storytelling became more important than the images themselves, thus making it impossible for him to work. As Wenders explains it: "Zu der Geschichte kann ich sozusagen nur Vertrauen haben, indem ich zu den Dingen und zu den Personen Vertrauen haben darf, und dann entsteht vielleicht eine Geschichte. Also wenn es umgekehrt ist, wenn erst die Geschichte da ist und die Geschichte das Vertrauensverhältnis prädeterminiert, dann kann ich sozusagen nichts damit machen" (*AS* 65). This represents in many ways a decided contrast to the other practitioners of the *Autorenfilm*, who were decidedly more interested in presenting their vision though writing, editing, producing and directing and most often with a marked emphasis on narrative and dialogue. This difference was consistent with the fact that most of the other young directors of the 1960s and 1970s were concerned foremost with contemporary political issues as opposed to images surrounding the aesthetics of an inner-world, or what Grob has termed an "innere Empfindung" (28).[21] In many ways this interior aspect of Wenders's cinema reflects a cinematic version of the New Subjectivity, a literary movement in which Wenders's friend and collaborator Peter Handke was a main practitioner. The dialectic between the *innerer Empfindung* and the desire to redeem the outward physical reality of objects and landscapes represents a hallmark of Wenders films.[22] Although on the surface it may appear to be an irreconcilable contradiction, Grob sees the two as complementary: "Diese romantische Seite bei Wenders ist die komplementäre Ebene zur Lust am puren Beobachten. Seine ständige Beschwörung des Dokumentarischen, daß 'auf der Leinwand plötzlich etwas wahres oder Wirkliches' zu entdecken ist, weist nur auf die obere Hälfte seiner Filme. Darunter gibt es das Visionäre: das, was er in sich sieht" (28). Together they contain what becomes the film's dynamic and its narrative.

But despite his seeming aversion to stories before 1982, Wenders has continually problematized storytelling and, in numerous recent interviews, has stressed its importance and function within filmmaking.[23] In an interview from 1991 in which he discusses painting, photography and film, Wenders explicates what he sees as the inherent dilemma involved in filmmaking with regard to his methodology: namely the necessity to tell a story. Whereas his ideal method of filming would be to capture the moment of perception just as the eye does in the act of opening, the problem arises with the conflict between *das Sehenwollen* and *das Erzählenwollen* (*AS* 170). However, given that his earlier conception of "story" was not identical to the traditional idea of a narrative story, Wenders has been able to reconcile the two and demonstrate that they are in fact not that incompatible.

Wenders's view of filmmaking and storytelling was in many ways analogous to constructivist ideas of hermeneutics. The idea that the "meaning" of a work of art is buried within the work itself and is then to be constructed by the viewer/receiver from the system of cues implanted by the artist, as well as from the work's other elements, such as temporal and spatial representation, is central to the constructivist theory of interpretation. Neoformalist and constructivist ideas in film studies have become increasingly prominent within the last few decades.[24] Neoformalists have created an epistemological system which can help explain Wenders's methodology by analyzing a film's meaning in terms of its *suzhet* and *fabula*. The film's *suzhet*, sometimes likened to the plot, is the actual sequence of images presented in the film, whereas the *fabula*, or the story, is the series of events as constructed in the mind of the viewer, accounting for the gaps in the *suzhet* as well as arranging the events based on causality. As Wenders chose to work primarily with images and profess the primacy of the image over dialogue in his works, it is perhaps useful to think of his conception of "story" in terms of a *fabula*, that is, a story constructed from the visual chronology and from the cues imparted by the series of images presented in his films. Moreover, given that he nonetheless maintained that his films are constructed around a "story," albeit one quite different from the classical model of narrative cinema, viewing his films' structures in terms of a *suzhet* can help define the types of stories he created in his early films.

Wenders and the *nouvelle vague*

Wenders cinematic and artistic influences are manifold. Growing up, he was attracted to American rock-and-roll, Hollywood Westerns and gangster films as well as the typical influences a German upbringing and education of his time provided. He has likewise cited many sources of inspiration for his decision to become a filmmaker and has often stated that he came to the cinema through painting,[25] and thus considers his approach to images *malerisch*. Wenders originally wanted to follow in his family's tradition and study medicine in Freiburg.[26] Unhappy with the program there, he transferred after one year to Düsseldorf were he began studying humanities and also dabbled in painting. He was encouraged to apply to the Ecole des Beaux Arts in Paris, but, after being rejected, he moved to Paris anyway in 1966 to work as an apprentice with Johnny Friedländer, a Paris-based printmaker. While in Paris, Wenders spent many of his afternoons and evenings in the Cinémathèque Française, sometimes watching up to five films a day. It was here that Wenders (re)discovered his love for classic American and German cinema, and also came into contact with the French *nouvelle vague*. 1966 was also the year that Truffaut released one of Wenders's all-time favorite films, *Fahrenheit 451*, and Godard and many others were at a peak of artistic creativity.[27] Wenders, too, was at this time developing a sense for what would later become his own unique brand of visual aesthetics. He applied to film school in Paris, but after being unable to secure a place, he applied instead to the newly formed *Hochschule für Fernsehen und Film* (*HFF*) in Munich and became a member of its first graduating class. To support himself, he wrote film criticism for the *Süddeutsche Zeitung* and various film journals. Because of these early experiences, Kathe Geist has noted that Wenders's career more so than any of the other German directors of his generation, paralleled quite closely that of the *nouvelle vague*.[28] Like his French counterparts, he had studied art, spent hours watching and studying classic American cinema, wrote film criticism, and then served his apprenticeship in film school making experimental shorts and low-budget feature films. Although some critics have dismissed this influence on Wenders,[29] Wenders himself has in, retrospect, acknowledged its importance on his filmmaking: "The films of Godard, for example, up to *Made in the USA* and *Two or Three Things I Know about Her*, I saw and admired but with reservations. It's only now that I realize how much they really influenced me."[30] Not surprisingly, in Wenders's first feature film, *Summer in the City* (*Dedicated to the Kinks*), we see a clip from Godard's *Alphaville* on television; similarly, in one of Wenders's first essay films, the 1982 short *Chambre 666*, Godard is one of the directors interviewed about the future of the cinema and it was the French conception of narrative that would exert a strong influence on Wenders's own aesthetic once he began making feature films.

What Wenders learned from and admired about these films was not so much political discourse and critique, but more their stylistic innovations and freedom from tradition. Moreover, he developed a sense of the personal and the self-reflective, elements that typify the *nouvelle vague* and can also be found in his film criticism of that time. This personal and inward looking style was reminiscent of the *Neue Subjektivität*, a style that Peter Handke, his friend and soon to be collaborator, was exploring in greater depth in his literary works. In fact, one of their first collaborations was on a short film entitled simply, *3 amerikanische LP's*, a film which reflected their mutual love for American rock music. Music has been a central part of Wenders's life and filmmaking from the beginning, and rock-in-roll, as he has often stated, saved his life. But music was something more than just a passion and a love for Wenders, it was an artistic form, an ordering principle. The structuring principle Wenders and Handke used for *3 amerikanische LP's* was the same used by Peter Fonda in *Easy Rider*, a film which Wenders greatly admired and reviewed for *Filmkritik*. What he praised about the film was the fact that the songs were not merely part of the soundtrack, but served as a functional part of the film: "Sie illustrieren nicht einfach die Bilder des Films, die Bilder handeln vielmehr von ihnen" (*EP* 41).[31] As Geist notes, rock music was at first pure form rather than narrative for Wenders, for, like many Europeans, he did not fully understand the texts; thus the music was elevated to a primary level. In fact, his 1969 short, *Alabama: 2000 Light Years*, was, as he has stated, quite simply a film about the difference between Bob Dylan's version of *All Along the Watchtower* and Jimi Hendrix's. The music was fundamentally the story; it was the narrative (*LB* 110).

This ordering principle and concept of narration also formed the basis for his first feature film, *Summer in the City (Dedicated to the Kinks)*, a film which develops little of a storyline per se, opting instead to present a series of impressionistic sounds and images. Ostensibly the film is loosely centered around a man who has been released from prison and who tries to pick up his life again in Munich. Overburdened by former acquaintances and obligations, he decides to flee (in many ways an updated version of Döblin's *Berlin Alexanderplatz* and sharing a similar use of collage and montage), driving first rather aimlessly around Munich, staying awhile with friends, then fleeing again. He finally ends up in Amsterdam after a short stay in Berlin, but he never quite really finds his way or a sense of *Heimat*. Thematically, the film represents many of the same features as the literature of the 1960s and 1970s—isolation, political and social estrangement, disillusionment, and detachment. Structurally, it was an exercise in open-ended filmmaking, something relatively new to German cinema at that time, but a style that was being developed in the aftermath of the Oberhausen Manifesto. Norbert Grob has perhaps best summarized the atmosphere of the film:

> Wenders's Strategie in *Summer in the City* lautet: nichts zusammenfassen oder raffen; nichts abkürzen, beschleunigen oder gar auslassen; nie so tun, als sei das, was man zu erzählen habe, unter Kontrolle; nichts dramaturgisch überhöhen; jedes Geschehen voll und ganz für sich lassen, damit es sich nicht einfügt als Baustein für etwas anderes, sondern hervorsticht als Ereignis. (*Wenders* 172)

This conviction to allow the slow unfolding of events, not to hurry them, not to slow them, and not to edit them, represents a fundamental aspect of Wenders's cinema: namely the belief in the primacy of images. Wenders's early films are thus never story-driven; rarely does one find fast-paced editing or motifs which serve only to move the plot forward. His films are first and foremost *image*-driven, whereby the importance of the image or the spontaneous event supersedes the artifice of traditional narrative. In reflecting on his story-telling method, Wenders stated in the commentary to another essay film, the 1982 *Reverse Angle—New York City*, a film primarily about narrative constructs: "Man sollte meinen, daß ich nach zehn Spielfilmen das als meinen Beruf verstehen sollte: Geschichten in Bildern erzählen. Ich habe das allerdings nie wirklich richtig glauben wollen. Vielleicht weil mir im Grunde Bilder immer mehr bedeutet haben als Geschichten, ja, Geschichten mitunter nicht mehr als ein Vorwand waren, um Bilder zu finden" (*LB* 32).

Because Wenders's own cinematic aesthetic was in his early years greatly informed by the French *nouvelle vague*, his early films, too, were characterized by loose yet realistic plot structures and somewhat existential thematics.[32] Moreover, because of the shortage of money to finance the pictures, the French filmmakers of the late 1950s and 1960s often used handheld cameras and portable equipment that allowed for a greater measure of spontaneity. These techniques appealed to many of the young German directors of the 1970s, and as a result, their films had a similar atmosphere. In fact, in Wenders's film reviews from that time, he singles out these very elements in the works he praises.[33] His 1970 review of Rudolf Thome's *Rote Sonne*, for example, reflects many of his own views and practices with regard to filmmaking. It is the film's *Haltung* and *Einstellung*, as opposed to its story or plot, that Wenders emphasizes. The story itself just seems to progress without any direction or concern. However, this enables the film to portray its characters as they are, realistically and without being artificially forced into a storyline: "[Die Leute] reden unverfroren in ihrer jeweiligen Situation. Sie sind immer nur gerade da präsent, wo sie sind. Sie wissen noch nicht, wie es weiter geht: der Film läßt sich auf ihre Geschichte ein, er drängt sich ihnen nicht auf" (*EP* 55). For Wenders, the story of a film, then, is one which arises out of a situation—rather than situations being created to fit a storyline—the underlying tenet to his style of visual storytelling.

Thematically Wenders's objective as writer/director throughout the 1970s was to present characters and situations as realistically as possible. To this end his objection to stories and plot can be likened to that of many postwar writers and advocates of the *nouveau roman*, who similarly viewed "story" as an artifice and an artificial framework that was forced onto reality. Just as these writers attempted to portray their characters without these artifices, so, too, does Wenders's aspire to show his characters and inevitably to show their stories. In a review from 1976 of Robert Altman's *Nashville*, a film which established Altman's unique brand of filmmaking involving the interweaving of various stories told simultaneously, Wenders praises the film, not for its complex storytelling technique, but for its ability to teach the viewer how to see and hear, two elements which form the foundation of the cinema.[34] Altman's method of storytelling, combining numerous stories with over 20 different lead figures, creates a new kind of story, Wenders argues:

> [D]iese Art, eine Geschichte zu erzählen, befreit alle 24 Figuren von den Zwängen, die sonst die "Story" den Schauspieler auferlegt, in denen die Personen sich nämlich mehr nach der Dramaturgie zu richten haben als nach dem, was in ihnen an Potential steckt, sich selber auzustrahlen, unvermittelt ihre Präsenz DARZUSTELLEN. In *Nashville* können das 23 Schauspieler tun: befreit von einer Story-Dramaturgie und damit frei für die Geschichte, können sie alle ihre Fähigkeiten ausbreiten, LEBENDIG zu sein, obwohl sie natürlich etwas SPIELEN. (111, *emphasis Wenders*)

This same style and method of filmmaking, with an emphasis on realistic characterization and loose, free-form structures, would be Wenders's guiding principle throughout the 1970s and would reach its high-point with his three-hour 1976 film *Im Lauf der Zeit*, a film for which he would receive the director's prize at Cannes and one which would also close a specific period in his work.[35] This period is perhaps best characterized by Wenders's exploration of the road-movie, a genre with a long cinematic tradition that was revitalized through the literature of the American beat poets, a group which was enormously popular and influential in the 1960s in Germany. Characteristic of these films is the disillusioned, male protagonist on a journey along a desolate landscape in search of some phenomenon or inner truth. From the images of landscapes, countrysides and cities, Wenders extracts stories in these films in much the same way Handke attempts to read history from landscapes in his novels. *Im Lauf der Zeit* is then in many ways a culmination of this style and a period of filmmaking which came to an end with

Wenders's trip to America and his experiences and disillusionment with the American film industry while making *Hammett*. His life-long fascination with America would ultimately end in disappointment, primarily due to the different ideologies and aesthetics of Germany and the U.S., aspects which were tied to fundamentally differing philosophies of stories and narrative. Ironically, instead of strengthening his aversion to narrative, this experience would lead him to reevaluate that stance and move toward narrative filmmaking within a European context.

Todesboten: Stories and Film

In 1977, Wenders received a telegram from Francis Ford Coppola, asking if he would be interested in directing a film based on the life of detective novelist Dashiell Hammett. Coppola had a vision of reestablishing the old Hollywood studio system, whereby a group of actors and directors would be contracted to work exclusively for his newly formed American Zoetrope studio. Coppola was hoping to engage Wenders as part of this system. For Wenders, this meant not only the opportunity to work in Hollywood, a lifelong dream, but also a chance to follow in the footsteps of his German cinematic idols, F.W. Murnau and Fritz Lang, who had decades before become famed German Hollywood directors.[36] Wenders agreed to the project, but inevitably, the experience would be a disaster. Wenders's style and method of filmmaking was in almost complete opposition to Hollywood's. Moreover, in America, Wenders no longer had the complete control afforded him by the production standards of the *Autorenkino*. Disagreements with the producers and with Coppola would result in the film actually being shot twice, with three different scripts and numerous rewrites. In the end, the film would take over five years to complete, before its final release in 1982 to a rather mediocre reception. During the long, arduous process, however, Wenders had the opportunity to make two other more personal films which reflected much more than *Hammett* ever could, his own ideology and views on cinema: *Nick's Film: Lightning over Water* (1980), an homage and quasi-documentary on Nicholas Ray, a dying friend and idol of Wenders, and *Der Stand der Dinge* (*The State of Things*, 1981), a piercing commentary on the nature of filmmaking.

The State of Things is on the one hand a thematic reflection of Wenders's own frustrations while making *Hammett*, but more than that, it is an exploration of the differences between American and European cinema and of the nature of stories in film. Wenders began working on the film while waiting to shoot the second version of *Hammett*. Before flying back to the U.S., he stopped in Portugal to visit an actress-friend who was also waiting to complete a film. While there, Wenders stumbled across a hotel that had been damaged by a recent storm, and the sight of the deserted hotel and the dramatic coastline of Portugal became the inspiration for the film:

> Dort sagte ich mir: es ist alles vorhanden, um einen Film zu machen. Der Ozean, ein großartiger Ort, der westliche Punkt von Europa, sozusagen der nächste zu Amerika. Ich wollte einen Film machen, ausgehend von meiner eigenen Situation zwischen den Kontinenten, und von dieser Angst sprechen, von der Angst, einen Film in Amerika zu machen. (*LB* 127)

Once again, an image and a situation served as the basis for constructing a film, this time a personal commentary about the nature of the American and European film industries.

The State of Things begins by using a favorite motif of the *nouvelle vague*: the film within a film.[37] Friedrich Munro, a Swiss-born director (a figure based partly on Wenders and partly on Murnau)[38] who for the past ten years has been making films in America, is in Portugal shooting a remake of a postapocalyptic science-fiction film with the financial backing of an American producer. Work on the film, *The Survivors*, comes to a complete halt when the crew runs out of film stock and money, and are forced to wait for further financing in order to finish the film. At a dinner party for the cast and crew, Munro gives a speech about filmmaking in which he points out that all of what they are doing is fiction, the essence of the cinema. Moreover, he maintains "stories only exist in stories, whereas life goes by in the course of time without the need to turn out stories."[39] Munro repeatedly recites this to himself and considers its implications. Back in his hotel room, he writes this phrase down but, significantly, changes the last part to "without the need to turn into stories." What Munro is commenting on is not only his style of European filmmaking but also Wenders': life exists as is, without the necessity for the structuring principle of stories. Filmmaking is about visualizing life, as it is, in the course of time.

But it is this very philosophy which has engulfed Munro's project in financial difficulty. Unable to reach his American producer by phone, Munro decides to travel to Los Angeles to speak with him personally. Once there, he finds that Gordon, his producer, has mysteriously vanished. Wenders then shifts the direction of the film toward one of his favorite genres, the detective film, giving in, perhaps, to his desire to make his own detective film in America. Gordon, it turns out, had been financing films using laundered money and is now on the run from his creditors (a rather pointed jab at Hollywood's financing practices). By chance, Munro finds Gordon, a caricature of the "ugly American," riding in a motor-home with his bodyguard, stopping at every fast-food restaurant they find. When Munro asks for the remainder of the money for the film, Gordon retorts angrily that he never should have agreed to finance a black and white film in the first place. Moreover, he had shown excerpts of the film to his loan sharks who, first, could not understand what was wrong with the color and, second, demanded to know wherein lay the story. They were willing to put up $100,000 if the film only had a story. Gordon then outlines the problem for Munro:

> If I would have shot that same film, with an American director and an American cast, in color, I'm sittin' on top of the world in six months. The same story, all you had to do is just . . . You gotta have a story, Friedrich. The same old story I keep telling you: without a story, you're dead. You can't build a movie without a story. You ever try building a house without walls? It's the same. You can't build a house without walls. A movie's gotta have walls, Friedrich.

Munro, like Wenders before him, had hit a brick wall: Hollywood's demand for stories. The flexibility and artistic freedom afforded filmmakers in Europe is absent in Hollywood. Whereas the *Autorenfilm* was financed to a large degree through government sources and funds and thus had the relative freedom to be artistically creative, Hollywood films were and are market-driven and must cater to the tastes of an audience who demands structure.[40] In essence, the dominant cinema demands stories, artifices, and walls to structure reality. Munro protests this conception, arguing that life can be depicted between the walls:

> MUNRO: Why walls? The space between the characters can carry the load. The space between people.
>
> GORDON: No. You're talking about reality. Fuck reality, Friedrich. When are you going to wake up? Cinema's not about life going by. People don't want to see that.

MUNRO: I've made ten movies, Gordon. Over ten times. There were several times when it was the same story I was saying. In the beginning it was easy, because I just went from shot to shot. But now in the morning, I'm scared. Now I know how to tell stories. And inevitably as the story moves in, life sneaks out. . . . Everything gets pressured into images. Mechanized images. Death. That's all a story is carrying. All stories are about death. *Totesboten.*[41]

Wenders's indictment of Hollywood's rejection of reality is an indication of his persistence in emphasizing the visual as well as his view of the organic nature of stories. His films were up to this point still an attempt at filming "life in the course of time," as Munro believed. In fact, this belief is perhaps best depicted in the final shot of the film: Munro takes leave from Gordon and as the two are departing in a parking lot, Gordon is shot by two figures in a car. Friedrich then picks up his video camera and begins "shooting" the escaping car: reality captured on film, without a story, a symbol of what he stands for. However, Munro too is shot and killed while filming his executioners.

Kolker and Beicken suggest that Wenders intentionally killed off both men, symbols of the opposing poles of the cinematic tradition, in the hopes of establishing a compromise about filmmaking.[42] In doing so, they argue, Wenders turns to the cinema for redemption and renewal and in the process discovers that the only hope for redemption would be in "yielding to the recognizable cinematic conventions of redemption" (112). To be redeemed in and by the cinema, however, requires redemption *through* the cinema by means of a renewal of the very pattern of love and death that form the basis of the cinema: its stories. Indeed Wenders's next projects would reveal a different perspective on the nature and portent of stories, one that professes a newfound belief in the power of human redemption through narrative and its ability to convey both history and morality.

After his American experience in the 1980s Wenders explores the possibility of finding the self with personal narrative, thus emphasizing the interconnectedness of identity and story. Beginning with *Paris, Texas* (1984) and continuing through his Berlin films and up to his 1995 film *Lisbon Story*, Wenders demonstrated a new found understanding and appreciation for stories. When asked about the conclusion of *Until the End of the World* (1991), in which the power of words and stories is extolled, Wenders recognizes his profound change: "In a strange way, I think I would've been more amazed than anybody else to hear what the narrator says at the end of the film if I had heard that myself a few years ago. I must've come around."[43] This is not to say, however, that Wenders has totally switched positions. Instead, he has come to the realization that both story and image can co-exist and, rather than being detrimental to one another, they can actually be complimentary. This conclusion, advocated in his most recent films, represents not just a restitution of stories and storytelling, but also a reaffirmation of the cinema and the power of images in conjunction with and no longer in opposition to narrative. The development of his films from image-dominated to story-dominated narratives, and finally to a harmonious co-existence of the two, represents in many ways a coming together of the ideas of the *Autorenkino* and the commercial necessity required for filmmaking today—in many ways an attempted synthesis of the European Art Film with the dominant, "classical" film style. Although he has come under attack for this new approach, he continues to advocate the importance of stories not only for the cinema, but for society as a whole.

Storytelling and the Power of Redemption

In retrospect Wenders has described *The State of Things* as a film which was very much a product of its time and his situation.[44] The thesis of the film, as Rauh has formulated it, was "die Unmöglichkeit von Geschichten" (85), a thesis that was itself a contradiction, for Wenders chose to present this idea via a fictive story. As such, the film is perhaps best understood as a product of frustration working in the confining environment of Hollywood. Indeed, Wenders has since admitted that his views about stories are no longer in line with those postulated in *The State of Things*. In a 1988 interview for a project entitled *Schreiben für den Film: Das Drehbuch als eine andere Art des Erzählens*, Wenders acknowledged the contradiction inherent in the figure of Munro and stated that the film was in fact a turning point for him ideologically as a director:

> Ich tu mich schwer mit den Mauern in den anderen Filmen, das stimmt schon. Aber wie gesagt, Friedrich ist widerlegt worden. . . . Um sich die Zwischenräume vorstellen zu können, um sie auch definieren zu können, dazu braucht man Mauern. Nach *Stand der Dinge* dachte ich: jetzt oder nie. Entweder du schaffst es, diese These wirklich zu widerlegen mit dem, was du aus diesem Film

gelernt hast, oder du hast keine rechte Zukunft mit dem Filmmachen. Deshalb habe ich versucht, *Paris, Texas* ganz radikal nach einer Geschichte zu machen. (*AS* 257)

By giving in to the *Mauern*, to structures, that is, to stories, Wenders refutes his thesis on the impossibility of stories. At the same time, he rejects the claim of the *Autorenkino* to portray reality through its own visual aesthetic, by accepting the need for more definite narrative structures, a principle which was fundamentally renounced by the signers of the Oberhausen Manifesto who sought freedom from the strictures of conventional narrative filmmaking.

This turning point for Wenders could also be seen as a turning point for the NGC as a whole. Fassbinder had died in 1982 shortly before the premiere of *State of Things*; Werner Herzog, another leading exponent, had become less and less concerned with the principles of the movement and more interested in the political causes of many oppressed native peoples and in turn emphasized cinematic themes as opposed to form. Volker Schlöndorff, whose Oscar for his adaptation of Günter Grass's *Der Blechtrommel* represented at once the pinnacle of success for the NGC as well as a restitution of postwar German cinema as a whole, had himself begun work in Hollywood, leaving Wenders as one of the last internationally successful representative of the ideals of the *Autorenkino*.[45] Thus Wenders decision to make a film based on a story, and one made in America dealing quite directly with stories and narratives, was a blow to the objectives of the Oberhausen Manifesto. Nevertheless, or perhaps as a result, this film, *Paris, Texas*, was Wenders's first resounding success, winning the Golden Palm at the 1984 Cannes Film Festival.

Kolker and Beicken argue that in addition to Wenders's methodological crisis, he also faced at this time an aesthetic one; namely, a paradigmatic shift from modernist to postmodern tropes, "from the concept of art as a clarifying and redemptive mediation of history to the idea of art as spectacle that vacates history and dissolves valued commodities" (111). While this certainly was true of the theoretical and philosophical discourses of the early 1980s, it does not appear to get at the essence of *Paris, Texas*, a film which restores narrative structures into its overall framework and in doing so, postulates these devices as a means of personal redemption and a purveyor of history. Unlike many postmodern films which sought to open readings of the text to a multiplicity of meaning, *Paris, Texas* nullifies this and other postmodern tropes in favor of thematic unity and compositional closure via a search for truth and redemption. Through the protagonist's search to reclaim his identity—an act which is possible only once he is able to tell his own story—the film posits the idea that personal history is grounded in the ability of an individual to address and convey that reality and thus lay claim to the past and one's own history. Moreover, the film begins an exploration on Wenders's part, one that would continue into his next films, into the possibility of restored interpersonal communication as a means of reintegrating the isolated and alienated individual into society. The outsiders of his previous films would now express a desire to take part in a community whereby they can establish meaningful relationships and explore love and ethical values. Whereas Kolker and Beicken argue that Wenders experienced a methodological crisis at this time in which he succumbs to the paradoxes of the postmodern, his cinematic subjects reject the alienating ramifications of the postmodern condition and seek refuge in developing a greater sense of community and shared experience. And having a narratable history, a story, is their entry into this community and, as these films posit further, their key to happiness.

With *Paris, Texas* one of Wenders's favorite themes, the quest, is explored from anew. Ostensibly, the film centers around the character of Travis, a figure like many of Wenders's other protagonists, the wanderer. Most of Wenders's films are populated with such characters who are on a journey or a quest, in search of some inner or metaphysical truth (as is the case with Wilhelm Meister in *Falsche Bewegung*, as well as with Bruno and Robert in *Im Lauf der Zeit*) or are attempting to distance themselves from society (as with Hans in *Summer in the City* and Bloch in *Tormann*). One of Wenders's favorite archetypes is the Homeric wanderer, a figure who is sometimes on a journey home, and other times on a journey of self-discovery, much as Handke's protagonists seek inner-revelations and self-understanding.[46] Travis is a figure in the same vein; once again, Wenders's starting point for the film was not a preconceived story, but an image—the image of a man walking through the desert without memory. Moreover, Wenders and Sam Shepard decided to work on the film without an aesthetic model, specifically, not with Walker Evans or Edward Hopper in mind, two of the strongest American influences for him: "Mehr Bezug zum Kino, so lautet unser Grundsatz. Wir wollten uns der Landschaft aussetzen" (*LB* 130). However, Wenders nonetheless structured the film in the end around a concrete story line, thus accepting the walls around his images and foregoing an open-ended form.

While Travis is in many ways a reconfiguration of the typical Wenders's protagonist, he differs from the others in certain aspects as well. When the film opens, we see him walking through the desert, unable to speak and unable to remember. He is an extreme outsider, an individual whose estrangement from society has reached the point of total isolation and has resulted in an inability to communicate past or present. Travis' linguistic and communicative seclusion is reminiscent of Kaspar Hauser, the mythologized figure of German literature and culture, whose predicament was treated by Handke in the late 1960s, as well as by Herzog in his 1975 film *Jeder für sich und Gott gegen alle*. Unlike Wenders's other isolated protagonists, however, Travis slowly begins to reintegrate into the world. While Wenders had in other films previously treated the theme of a character's rejection of society, this time he begins with a figure who has reached the limits of estrangement and is then concerned with the process of inclusion and resocialization. The film moves very slowly in depicting this process, reaching a climax after two hours. However, the fact that Wenders chooses to follow the classical pattern of story development—introduction, ascending action, climax and resolution—suggests that he is clearly working in the traditional context of narration.

But Wenders's conscious decision to work with structuring principles and narrative is not limited just to the film's framework. Thematically, the film postulates the necessity of narrative as a means of reclaiming the past as well as of establishing connections and positing meaning. In fact, Wenders's viewpoint after the experience of *Hammett* and *State of Things* had changed drastically. In a 1982 interview, shortly before beginning work on *Paris, Texas*, Wenders delineates this new ideology:

> [I]m Kino will Geschichten-Erzählen auch ein Wiedererkennen provozieren und durch die Form eine Ordnung in die Kakophonie von Eindrücken bringen. Das Bedürfnis für Geschichten, seit Homer, den ich jetzt lese, ist doch auch: zu hören, daß man Zusammenhänge herstellen kann. Es gibt ein Bedürfnis nach Zusammenhängen, weil die Menschen ja eigentlich wenig Zusammenhängendes erleben. . . . Deshalb denke ich, daß das Bedürfnis nach Geschichten eher größer wird, weil es da jemand gibt, der erzählt, der das ordnet und die Idee reinbringt. (*LB* 59)

The desire now to bring order to the cacophony of impressions stands in marked contrast to his early desire to present life in the course of time, without connection, as one would experience it. Furthermore, the need for connections and the need for someone to establish them through storytelling, *Geschichten-Erzählen*, suggests a shift from a personal, inwardly reflective vision to an audience-oriented approach to filmmaking. This shift is significant, for it represents a change in Wenders's understanding of his role as filmmaker and artist. By creating stories and establishing connections, the filmmaker is no longer presenting a series of unconnected images and impressions, rather through the very nature of a created structure, the artist is imposing meaning on these images and with this meaning, comes a message, a truth. Although this "truth" may in fact be representative of a multiplicity of truths, it is nonetheless an attempt at reestablishing order in a world which is seemingly dissolving from a lack of cohesiveness. Thus Travis' journey and his struggle to regain his sense of language and memory is at once a struggle to reimpose order and meaning into his life and his world as well as a struggle for restitution of his own history, a struggle which is possible only through story, his own narrative.

The climax of the film comes when Travis encounters his ex-wife, Jane, who is working in a peep show. Although Travis has regained his ability to speak and to remember, he is still unable to communicate on an interpersonal level. Thus he confronts Jane in her booth, where she is unable to see him but can hear his voice. He begins to tell her a story, a story in the third person about a couple he knew. The narrative is in actuality his own history, reformulated as a story. While telling her this tale, he is unable to face her and look at her directly. Kathe Geist has argued that this configuration functions both spatially and thematically as a confessional for Travis, in that he is able to confess his "sins" to Jane in hopes of redemption for his past abusiveness (121). Jane, too, then tells him of her anxiety and fear, but as Geist points out, it is only Travis who is redeemed, not Jane, for she must function in another role, that of Madonna and redeemer, rather than as the redeemed.[47]

Indeed, Geist maintains that "Christian theology and family ideology" are central to the film's story. Travis does achieve a redemption of sorts; he is removed from his emotional burden and in a sense pardoned of his sins. But beyond that, the recognition of and reconciliation with his own past through narrative is established as a trope which Wenders would continue to exploit. Travis' story reestablishes order and meaning to his life and allows him to break from his self-imposed isolation and estrangement from society. Furthermore, the act of storytelling enables him to reintegrate himself into society. Although he is still emotionally unable to handle direct interpersonal relationships, he is saved and redeemed by the power of narrative and is able to rejoin, both physically and linguistically, his community of family and friends.

Wenders develops a similar theme in his 1991 film *Until the End of the World*, in which narrative once again functions as a means of redemption and the reestablishment of social discourse. An underlying theme to this film is one that has been of concern to Wenders for many years, namely, the ubiquity of images. The modern, technological society has become inundated with visual images and as a result, has in many cases forced the estrangement of the individual from society, resulting in diminishing human contact. Whereas Benjamin postulated the increased isolation of the individual through the rise of the novel, Wenders echoes this concern for modern society by arguing that now visual technology poses a threat to communication and interpersonal contact. He explores this theme in *Until the End of the World*, a futuristic road-movie set at the end of the year 1999. The film follows Sam Faber, a somewhat mysterious figure who has traveled the world with a special device collecting images which can then be digitized and electronically transmitted to the brain. The device will allow his blind mother to "see" the world electronically and the images he has captured on his journey through the direct transferral of brain waves. Toward the end of the film, while in the Australian desert, both Sam and Claire (who has followed and fallen in love with him on his journey) discover a unique feature of this device: by reversing the operation of the machine, they are able to see their dreams played out in front of them on a video screen. The images are mesmerizing and they soon become addicted to watching their dreams, or in other terms, become addicted to the electronic image. Wenders portrays this as a metaphor for the dangers inherent in the overwhelming flood of unmediated images in modern society. Sam and Claire's relationship has broken down and both have become isolated from the world and each other. Their only concern is with the reality of the video screen; thus an artificial visual reality has supplanted their own.

Claire is eventually saved by her husband Eugene, a writer who also serves as the film's narrator through a voice-over commentary, a device Wenders uses for the first time in this film. In doing so, Wenders establishes a connection between narration and writing. At one point, Eugene comments that his manuscript was lost and with it the inspiration for his writing. He turns instead to Claire's and Sam's story and begins writing a new novel in the best Handkean tradition, by basing it on his own experiences, and by incorporating those of his wife and her lover as well. As such, the film engages in a self-reflexive dialogue; it becomes clear that the film we are seeing and that Eugene is narrating is in fact the story of his novel. The emphasis on literature through this character supports one of the film's subtexts; namely, the power of words and literature over the visual image. Eugene attempts to help Claire once again (he has "saved" her many times throughout the film already), but says in the voice-over: "I didn't know the cure for the disease of images. All I knew was how to write. But I believed in the magic and healing power of words and of stories."[48] Eugene denies Claire her portable video monitor and gives her instead his manuscript, which is nothing more than her own story. Upon reading his novel, she is "cured" of her addiction, and, like Travis before her, through the narration of her own story and history, she is able to reestablish contact with society and the outside world.

Wenders sees a certain similarity between the ending of his film and the closing scene of Truffaut's *Fahrenheit 451*, a scene which Wenders has called his favorite in film history (*AS* 197). At the close of Truffaut's film, a number of characters in a futuristic totalitarian society are standing in a forest reciting the narratives of books they have memorized, in an attempt to keep literature, which has been banned, alive. The difference, Wenders notes, is that "in terms of a story line, in *Fahrenheit 451* books become evil, and in our film it is images . . . [I]n our film Eugene tells Claire her story and that cures her" (Donohue 13). Her "cure" is the restoration of her sense of reality through the healing power of the literary story. The final scene of the film, an intertextual reference to Truffaut's ending, shows Claire standing in the desert reading Eugene's book, her story: a clear symbol that the written word has the power, as does film, to redeem reality.

For Wenders, though, this metaphor is to be carried one step further: it is not just the written word, but stories themselves which have the capacity to deliver us from drowning in images. This idea is an interesting reversal of Kracauer's postulate that film has the power to redeem reality.[49] Moreover, it is a marked change from his earlier belief in the primacy of images. In his "Reden über

Deutschland" from around this time, Wenders emphasizes this new ideology quite dramatically, reiterating as well the need for form and structure:

> Wenn die Welt der Bilder auch aus allen Fugen gerät, und wenn sich über den Fortschritt und die Technik die Bilder immer mehr verselbständigt haben, so daß sie jetzt schon aus der Kontrolle geraten sind und demnächst noch so viel mehr geraten werden, so gibt es doch auch eine andere Kultur, die Gegenkultur, in der sich nichts geändert hat und in der sich nichts ändern wird: das Geschichtenerzählen, das Schreiben und Lesen, das *Wort*. Ich glaube nicht an vieles in der Bibel, aber doch, inbrünstig, an diesen ersten Satz: 'Am Anfang war das Wort.' Ich glaube auch nicht, daß es einmal heißen wird: 'Am Ende war das Bild . . . ' Das Wort wird bleiben. (*AS* 197)

Interestingly, Wenders recognizes that in our society reading, writing and storytelling have become the *Gegenkultur*, while film and images are in the forefront and thus considered the primary *Kultur*. But this belief in the permanence of the written word seems at first paradoxical for an artist who himself works in the realm of images. However, Wenders changed conception of the cinema must here be taken into consideration. Filmmaking is not unlike writing in that both are a form of storytelling, a way of sharing human experience (*LB* 60). What Wenders is in fact arguing is that it is only *unmediated* images which pose this danger, that is to say, images that are unstructured and unnarrated. As a filmmaker, Wenders is not arguing against images per se, but against the abuse of images. What threatens both writing and filmmaking (and what threatened Claire) is not the rise of a visual culture itself, but the loss of the art of visual storytelling.

"Vidioten" and the Ubiquity of Images

But is cinema really the keeper of the storytelling tradition? Wenders's answer seems to be a definite maybe, for the cinema too is in danger of dying out and succumbing to new forms of media and technology. At the 1982 Cannes Film Festival, Wenders made a short film, *Chambre 666*, in which he set up a camera in his hotel room and asked a number of directors (from Godard and Antonioni to Steven Spielberg and Susan Seidelmann) to enter at their leisure and discuss the future of the cinema. Specifically, Wenders posed the following question: "Ist das Kino eine Sprache, die uns verlorengeht, eine Kunst, die schon im Untergang begriffen ist?"

(*LB* 36) His concern for the future of the cinema was manifold, but primarily he noted that more and more films were being produced as if premade for television and thus cultivating a television-like aesthetic. Furthermore, a large number of these films were no longer based on "reality" but on experiences from other films "als ob 'Das Leben' keinen Stoff für Geschichten mehr hergäbe" (*LB* 35). Wenders seemed, at that time, in 1982, to be standing in the line of film theorists like Benjamin and Kracauer, who maintained that film should redeem physical reality. But in a postmodern, technological age it is, for Wenders, the ubiquity of images which paradoxically threatens the very existence of the cinema.[50] Some ten years later, in 1991, Wenders articulated this fear in his "Reden über Deutschland," basing his argumentation primarily on Benjamin's famous essay "Das Kunstwerk im Zeitalter seiner technischen Reproduzierbarkeit." With the advent of the reproducibility and changeability of images, Wenders argued, "die Bilder haben sich immer mehr von einer Wirklichkeit entfernt und haben schon fast nichts mehr mit ihr zu tun . . . Zuviel Bilder schaffen Verlust der Realität" (*AS* 196–97). The flood of images present in modern society represents a threat not only to the cinema and the classic art of storytelling, but also to reality itself.

This situation was one with which Wenders has since attempted to come to terms and it is also one that he has problematized in recent feature films and shorter, essay films.[51] Technological innovations and the development of new forms of media are inevitable and Wenders has come to recognize that they do not necessarily threaten the existence of older forms of communication. His 1989 essay film *Notebook on Cities and Clothes*, a documentary primarily about the Japanese fashion designer Yohji Yamamoto, included a digressive discourse on the advantages and disadvantages of film and video. At the beginning of the film, Wenders shoots a number of scenes simultaneously on film and video, deconstructing both media and, in doing so, allowing the viewer to compare both 35mm film stock and video images. The voice-over commentary (Wenders's own) poses questions about identity, and how we as humans create our identity. For Wenders, part of this process has, in modern society, been connected with the photographic image. But so much has changed since its inception:

> Vor allem die Bilder, die Bilder um uns herum verändern und vervielfältigen sich mit rasender Geschwindigkeit, seit jener Explosion, die die elektronischen Bilder freigesetzt hat, die nun

allüberall die Fotografie ersetzen. Wir haben gelernt, dem fotographischen Bild zu vertrauen, können wir dem elektronischen Bild trauen? (*AS* 104)

The film then sets out to explore the possibilities of film, for Wenders akin to the photographic image, and video, the electronic image which threatens the purity and aesthetic beauty of the filmic image.

To Wenders surprise, he found that the video image was not the "monster" he had originally thought. At times, he noted, using a video camera to follow Yamamoto as he prepared for a fashion show was even preferable as it was less intrusive: "Die Sprache der Videokamera war nicht 'klassisch,' eher 'effizient' oder 'nützlich.' Zu meinem Entsetzen waren die Videobilder mitunter sogar 'richtiger,' so als ob sie besseren Zugang zu den Dingen vor der Kamera hätten" (*AS* 109). Reluctantly, he feels he must get used to new technology. In fact, with regard to the question he posed in Cannes to his fellow filmmakers about the death of the cinema, Wenders has stated that above all Antonioni's answer intrigued him the most:

> [Antonioni] meinte: Das Kino mit den großen Leinwänden und großen Geschichten, das muß man wohl halt aufgeben, aber man soll nicht klein beigeben. Man soll nicht so sang- und klanglos das Ende des Kinos einläuten. Das Bedürfnis für Bilder-Erzählungen wird weiter wachsen. Man muß sich mit den neuen Medien vertraut machen und versuchen, ihnen Form zu geben . . . ." (*LB* 63)

Indeed, Wenders has taken this advice to heart, having since experimented with HDTV (High Definition TV) in *Until the End of the World*. What Wenders's resistance to technology shows is his love for the cinema as an art form and as a cultural institution, a theme that he has portrayed throughout all of his films with their many references and homages to past filmmakers, actors and even to the old cinema houses themselves. What Wenders still objects to, however, is the use of video images without meaning and order, an objection that he articulated more specifically in his 1995 film *Lisbon Story*.

Lisbon Story, a film commissioned by the city of Lisbon when it was selected to be the cultural capital of Europe in 1994, is a continuation of Wenders's *State of Things*, in that it resurrects two of Wenders's alter-egos, Philip Winter, a multifaceted character from many of Wenders's films, and Friedrich Munro, the European film director protagonist in *State of Things*. Among other things, the film deals with the ubiquity and abuse of images and finds Wenders coming down once again in favor of film and filmmaking over the annoying video-idiots or *Vidioten* who are destroying the purity of images. As he did in the earlier of the two films, Wenders constructs the film around a somewhat whimsical mystery story. Winter, now a soundman for Munro, receives a postcard from Munro, who is once again in Portugal, asking him to come and work on the film Munro is making in Lisbon. Upon arrival in the city, Winter finds that Munro has mysteriously vanished, and armed with his recording equipment, Winter sets out into the city to find the director.

The film, originally conceived as an essay film about the city, became a film which tells about the city through sound and image. At one point, Winter demonstrates his sound techniques to some local children by having them sit in another room and listen to the story he will tell through pure sound. He then makes up a story about a vegetarian cowboy who springs into the water after being attacked by a lion while fixing a meal. Winter tells the story entirely through artificial sound, illustrating the magic of filmmaking to the children. This scene is symbolic of the entire film as a whole, for it demonstrates the ability to tell a story through means other than the narrative voice, the underlying premise of the film.

Eventually, Winter tracks down Munro, who is holed up in a small automobile on the edge of the city. He learns that Munro originally began making a sepia tone film using a hand-cranked camera (*Kurbelkiste*), but gave up the idea over concerns about the over-commercialization of images and films. Images, Munro maintains, are too often used to sell products and as a result, have become tainted. The only "pure" images left are those which are "unseen." He therefore began making a film using a camera strapped to his back which records images unseen by the human eye. He had voluntarily removed himself from society in order to come closer to the city and become one with its being. Winter rejects Munro's thesis and chastises him for his folly. He argues that Munro must make films from the heart, that is, with all of his senses. Seeing comes not just from the eyes but from the soul and the senses. Winter argues that sight and insight can come only from the true act of seeing, one that is passionately felt as opposed to the cold mechanical approach Munro has been taking.

This plea for feeling and emotion when seeing and creating an artistic work is once again reflected in the film through literature. While looking for Munro, Winter finds the apartment where he has been living and discovers a book by the great Portuguese poet Fernando Pessoa. Winter is struck specifically by Pessoa's twenty-first English sonnet, a poem about the senses, postulating sight as touched thought.[52] As Wenders is wont to do, he uses literature as a leitmotif and allows it to convey the message of his film, namely that true vision and the true act of seeing comes from giving form to the passions of the senses. This form, as the film makes quite clear, is none other than the story. Stories once again form an integral part of the film, not only within the context of the narrative but also given the suprastructure of the film: *Lisbon Story* itself tells the story of a filmmaker's attempt to tell a story.

In this regard, *Lisbon Story* is summarily symbolic of Wenders's own transformation from an inimical narrator to a storyteller. The film also stands as a critique of Marxist ideas of filmmaking, an ideology not unlike Godard's criticism of the capitalist appropriation of the image. In reaction to the commercialization of images, many filmmakers, like Godard, rejected traditional forms of filmmaking and sought instead new means of achieving a cinema verité, a struggle embodied in Munro's exaggerated attempt at creating a film from "unseen" images. Wenders own early style of filmmaking was heavily influenced by this movement, although never to the point of deconstructing images of popular culture, a favored technique in Godard's anti-cinema. With *Lisbon Story*, Wenders has made a film pleading for emotional filmmaking by contrasting Munro's concrete, absolutist ideas of avant-garde filmmaking with Winter's passionate, involved approach. Whereas Munro has isolated himself from society, Winter has become involved in the sights and sounds of the city and has even fallen in love with the singer of the Portuguese band Madredeus. He actively seeks to become part of the city so as to experience its rhythm. After viewing a clip from Munro's original film, Winter encounters an old man wearing a hat who appeared in one of Munro's scenes. He asks the man to sit down and recount his life story, which Winter records. Here Wenders echoes the thesis he offered in the Foreword to his collection of photographs, *Einmal*, namely, that individual images have an associated story which must be told. Munro, like Godard in many of his films, is concerned with the image itself and not with associated stories or meanings. Thus Winter, like the "new" Wenders, becomes irritated with a group of children who follow him around and videotape him. The images they are recording have no meaning, no story, and thus only contribute to the abundance of unmediated images. They have succumbed to the idiocy of video technology and have become video-idiots, or, as Winter expresses it in German, *Vidioten*. What these images lack, like those Munro has been taking with his backstrapped camera, is the heart and soul of the artist, a person who can impose logic on the images by giving them meaning through story. Or in the words of Pessoa, which Winter repeatedly quotes, "Thought was born blind, but Thought knows what seeing is." Through seeing, the object touched by thought and the senses stands real in memory. Thus Wenders acknowledges once and for all that images themselves do not create a "Verlust der Realität" (*AS* 197), only storyless and meaningless images do. Stories created with passion and with the senses give meaning to the images and as such can then redeem physical reality.

The Morality Plays: *Der Himmel über Berlin* and *In weiter Ferne, so nah!*

Wenders's two-part cycle on Berlin and angels, *Der Himmel über Berlin* (*Wings of Desire*, 1986) and *In weiter Ferne, so nah!* (*Far Away, So Close!*, 1992), represents respectively one of Wenders's most critically acclaimed films and one of his biggest disasters, both critically and financially. While *Himmel über Berlin* was hailed as Wenders's return to Germany and the European style of filmmaking after a long sojourn in America, *In weiter Ferne* was criticized as being trite and overly moralizing. Moreover, since cinematic sequels are so closely linked with Hollywood, it came as a disappointment to many that Wenders would even consider making a sequel to a film as aesthetically accomplished as *Himmel über Berlin*. Nevertheless, despite their differences, these two films represent a culmination of Wenders's ideas on storytelling and the cinema.

As discussed earlier, one of the key figures in *Himmel über Berlin* is Homer, the archetypal storyteller who mourns the decline of the oral narrative tradition. Homer's lament recalls in many ways Benjamin's description of the reader of a novel, who, more so than any other reader, is isolated from society and other individuals. Once isolated, an effective exchange of ideas and of human experience dies out. The importance of storytelling and of storytellers, as Homer tells us later, is to keep alive the childlike nature of the human spirit which, when gone, leads to war, misery, and destruction:

> Die Welt scheint zu verdämmern, doch ich erzähle, wie am Anfang, in meinem Singsang, der mich aufrechterhält, durch die Erzählung verschont von den Wirren der Jetztzeit und geschont für die Zukunft. . . . Meine Helden sind nicht mehr die Krieger und Könige, sondern die Dinge des Friedens, eins so gut wie das andere. . . . Aber noch niemandem ist es gelungen, ein Epos des Friedens anzustimmen. Was ist denn am Frieden, daß er nicht auf die Dauer begeistert und daß sich von ihm kaum zu erzählen läßt? (*Himmel* 56)

In this soliloquy, Homer mourns the changes in modern society yet notes that his song as changed as well: his heroes are no longer the warriors and kings of epics of the past, rather the modern storyteller's heroes are bringers of peace, an idea that Wenders will develop in the sequel. The tragedy, he states, is that no one has yet been able to write an epic of peace, a reference of course to the tradition of the bellicose oral heroic epics of antiquity. Nevertheless, Homer cannot allow himself to stop telling stories, for the consequences would be dire: "Wenn ich aufgebe, dann wird die Menschheit ihren Erzähler verlieren. Und hat die Menschheit einmal ihren Erzähler verloren, so hat sie auch ihre Kindschaft verloren" (57).

This *Kindschaf*" and naiveté, which the storyteller preserves and imparts to humanity, are central motifs in the film. Both Damiel and Cassiel (the two angels) possess a childlike wonderment about the world, and, not coincidentally, only children can see and hear the angels. Edward Plater, in his article on the storyteller in *Himmel über Berlin*, has shown that not only is the childlike a characteristic of the storyteller but also of the angels, and in particular of Damiel. Plater sees Damiel as the future incarnation of the storyteller, whose task it will be to "reveal through himself the childlike quality in Everyman" (16), as Homer has charged the storyteller to do. For only the storyteller is capable of saving humanity from the misery and despair of the modern world by transporting the listener into a wondrous and childlike world. The connection between Damiel as angel and storyteller is made clear from the beginning of the film, when we see a hand writing the poem that is being recited through an off voice, namely Handke's *Lied vom Kindsein*, a poem that extols the innocence and wonder of childhood. The viewer soon realizes that the hand that is writing and reciting the poem is that of Damiel.

In the "sequel" to *Himmel über Berlin*, *In weiter Ferne, so nah!* (although Wenders prefers not to see it as a sequel), Cassiel chooses to join Damiel and to "fall" to earth, whereby he proceeds to experience first-hand the misery and despair as well as the greed and corruption of modern society. He then devotes, and finally sacrifices, his life to an act of "goodness," a good deed to help somehow his friends and—on a symbolically larger scale—humankind, by foiling an illegal arms smuggling ring. His role takes on, at times, a certain Faustian element, for at the height of his despair, we see him wandering the streets of Berlin trying to make sense of his life. He is intent on doing a good deed and somehow rectifying the trouble he has inadvertently created for himself and his friends. Although this subplot is at times ludicrous and overly moralizing, it nonetheless achieves a sense of closure and further fulfills one of Benjamin's requirements for a "real story": namely, that it contain something useful—a moral, if not simply practical advice.[53]

The moral that Wenders adds to *In weiter Ferne, so nah!* represents not only his belief in the importance and usefulness of stories, but also reflects his attempt at combining elements of the *Autorenkino* with the narrative cinema. Wenders has a message to convey in this film; unfortunately, he does it with a somewhat heavy hand: despite the misery and despair in modern society, there is still hope and a sense of morality left in the world. Acts of peace and harmony can still be committed so as to improve the lot of humankind. Thematically, the message or moral of the story is in line with Wenders's newfound sense of Christianity at that time.[54] But structurally, Wenders experiments with a means of incorporating story and image and didacticism and aesthetics into film. The problem, as most critics would have, is that he attempts to incorporate too many elements of the classic Hollywood cinema (gangsters, intrigue, explosions, suspenseful climax and a happy end) and too few of the visual aesthetics and too little of the experimentation that is typical of the *Autorenfilm* and that made *Himmel über Berlin* such a success.

But Damiel and Homer are not the only storytellers populating Berlin. Peter Falk, playing both himself and his familiar role of Columbo, portrays another angel fallen to earth who acts as a teacher and mentor for the other angels. Like every good storyteller, Falk acts as a keeper of tradition who passes his skill on to Damiel. His role as a storyteller, and the importance and usefulness of stories in general, is underscored in a scene from *In weiter Ferne, so nah!*, in which Damiel and Cassiel, having become deeply entangled in the weapons smuggling ring, enlist the help of Falk in an attempt to put an end to the ring. At one point Falk asks Damiel if there is anything he can do to help. "Do you know a good story?" Damiel asks. And of course he does, and the story he "tells" evolves into playing the role of an actor—his famous role of Columbo—who is in the process of filming a movie, a nod on Wenders's part to his own medium's contribution to the storytelling process. Many of the other minors characters serve as prototypical storytellers in the film as well. As Wenders has always held music and song texts in high regard, it comes as no surprise to find one of his favorite musicians, Nick Cave, who is a writer as well who half-sings, half-narrates his musical compositions, appear in a scene toward the end of the film. While giving a concert in a Berlin night club, the viewer listens in through the angels to Cave's thoughts as he complains about having to go on stage and tell another story. However, he does in fact go back on stage and introduces his encore, the song "From Here to Eternity" (an interesting reference to Wenders's next film *Until the End of the World*, which he was working on simultaneously) by telling the audience exactly what he had promised himself he would not: "I'm gonna tell you about a girl" (*Himmel* 155). He then proceeds to tell a story via music and song as a somewhat reluctant storyteller. That both an actor and a rock musician are considered by Wenders and Handke as storytellers is a reflection of their well known love for rock-and-roll and American culture. But the true hope for the survival and continuance of the storytelling tradition lies not in the realms of pop music or American cultural institutions but in the cinema.

    For Wenders, the storyteller is not limited to the teller of oral tales. Plater has noted that *Himmel über Berlin* both begins and ends with a close-up of Damiel writing, and upon closer reflection we realize that he has been writing the entire time his own story, closing with the account of a man and woman, a love story, an "epic of peace," as it were, which Homer had hoped would one day be written (23). Thus Damiel is established in the film as an angel, a storyteller and a writer, a thematic construction not unlike that of *Until the End of the World* which similarly involves a narrator who is at once a writer. At the end of *Himmel über Berlin*, we once again see that, as with Damiel, the text being written at the opening and closing of the film was indeed the film that we are seeing and that he is narrating; that is, in both films the narrator serves as both storyteller and creator. This alignment of angels with writers and filmmakers represents the interplay which Wenders himself sees between storytelling and artistic creation.

The epic of peace that Homer so wishes to be written finally materializes both fictionally and historically in *In weiter Ferne, so nah!*. Part of the subplot about the arms smugglers involves an old chauffeur, played by Heinz Rühmann, a veteran actor of German films from the 1930s through the 1950s. In flashbacks to the Second World War, his role in abetting a wealthy family comes out as well as his desire to atone once again for the past. By assisting at a crucial point in the scheme to foil the plot, he too is able to commit a moral act to help humankind, and in doing so, help write the epic of peace. In addition, Mikhal Gorbachev makes a cameo appearance, in which the viewer sees him sitting at his desk in contemplation. Through the eavesdropping of the angels, the viewer hears that he is thinking about world peace. Wenders's reference here is, of course, to the fact that Gorbachev was instrumental in bringing about the fall of the Berlin Wall, and with it an end to the cold war.

Wenders belief in the power of storytelling and of the cinema, though, is perhaps best revealed in his dedication of *Himmel über Berlin*: "Allen ehemaligen Engeln gewidmet, vor allem aber Yazujiro, François und Andrej" (170), three great storytellers of the cinema, now departed, for whom Wenders has professed the highest admiration, namely Ozu, Truffaut, and Tarkovsky. These three filmmakers represent the ideal of what cinematic storytelling can be: a combination of aesthetics, visual beauty and a story. Although Wenders may have rejected narrative constructs early in his career, he has now come to accept and praise them wholeheartedly. However, he has not relinquished his commitment to visual aesthetics or to the power of the image, one that is expressed in *Lisbon Story* and through the camera work of his recent collaboration with Antonioni, *Jenseits der Wolken* (1995). Moreover, the moral and aesthetic nature of many of his films is not only in line with Benjamin's conception of the didacticism of the oral narrative, but also reflective of the mandates of the Oberhausener, who similarly saw an edifying function to film. As such, Wenders has perhaps better than any of his other colleagues in the NGC come to terms with the demands of commercial cinema while maintaining his vision as an artist. Perhaps he himself has best summarized his philosophy as a filmmaker in a postmodern society confronted with ever increasing new forms of technology, when he stated: "Als Filmemacher habe ich herausgefunden, daß es für mich nur eine Möglichkeit gab, zu verhindern, daß meine Bilder von der Flut all der anderen mitgerissen wurden, daß sie dem Konkurrenzkampf und dem übermächtigen Geist der Kommerzialisierung zum Opfer fielen: Ich mußte eine Geschichte erzählen" (*AS* 121).

~ Conclusion ~
Towards a New Narrative: German Literature and Film at the End of the Twentieth Century

Reynolds Price has maintained that "the simple companionship of the narrative transaction [and] the union of the teller and the told" have been a vital part of society since the beginning of recorded time (26). At the beginning of the twenty-first century, this need is no less prevalent; in fact, given the lack of cultural and aesthetic order and the dissolution of notions of truth in a postmodern society, the desire for a locuter of meaning and a means of structuring reality through causal relationships make the story once again an attractive medium for both artist and writer. The pattern in recent German literature and film toward the reexploration of traditional narratives can, I would argue, be read as a reflection of the tendency in society to come to terms with the ramifications of the postmodern condition.

In literature, many contemporary German writers have in recent years come to argue that the possibilities explored through the experimental anti-narratives in the 1960s are exhausted. As discussed in Chapter 1, there has been, at the end of the twentieth century, a decided trend toward the restitution of narrative, of stories and of the storyteller. Perhaps nowhere has the power of storytelling been more evident in German literature than in four recent novels, which have received both popular and critical acclaim: Patrick Süskind's *Das Parfum* (1985), Uwe Timm's *Die Entdeckung der Currywurst* (1993), Robert Schneider's *Schlafes Bruder* (1994) and Sten Nadolny's *Selim, oder die Gabe der Rede* (1994). These texts not only embrace storytelling as an important means of communication and narrative discourse, but exemplify how storytelling is central to the questions of historicity and identity discussed in the preceding chapters. Each uses the story and the storytelling act differently yet decidedly, and all four works reaffirm this tendency in literature which espouses the need for order, meaning and a sense of connection in the world, a need which is best filled by the story. Nevertheless, these authors are aware of certain postmodern sensibilities and as such these works do not represent a return to nineteenth-century style narration; rather, they embrace the story and utilize to their own end the discourses of the postmodern to offer a new narrative literature that allows for the coexistence of the story and elements central to postmodern aesthetics.

The more traditional or conventional of these novels with regard to narrative style and storytelling are Schneider's surprise best-seller *Schlafes Bruder* and Süskind's *Das Parfum*. Schneider's debut novel has become somewhat infamous as a result of its publishing history. The manuscript was initially rejected by some 36 publishers, before Reclam-Leipzig opted to publish it. Since then, Schneider has received numerous literary awards and the novel has been translated into most major languages, filmed, and turned into both an opera and a ballet. The story, though, is remarkably similar in language, theme and structure to Süskind's controversial bestseller *Das Parfum*, one of the first of the more recent German narrative novels to enjoy both international critical and commercial success. Not surprisingly, the two novels use the same narrative technique, one based strongly on the constructs of the nineteenth-century historical novel, a genre which Patrick O'Neill argues is concerned largely with presenting and telling a believable story and one which Thomas Mann, some fifty years earlier, proclaimed to be the successor of the epic, itself the inheritor of the oral narrative tradition.[1] Yet both novels are very contemporary and display a self-consciousness not found in the nineteenth-century novel.

Das Parfum, the story of a olfactorial genius and *Schlafes Bruder*, the story of an aural genius, both rely on traditional elements of storytelling in their conveyance of the plot: linear chronology, defined temporal and spatial indicators, unambiguous causality, and an omniscient narrator who relies heavily on the preterit as well as other rhetorical devices commonly associated with the oral narrative tradition.[2] Both novels are also peculiarly in the tradition of the Schelmenroman or picarequese novel in that they episodically recount, from the unusual birth to the ceremonial death, the story of a genial figure who by an odd twist of fate is endowed with a sensory gift enabling his survival in the harsh environment into which he is born: in the case of Elias Alder an acute sense of hearing and musicality, with Jean-Baptiste Grenouille a heightened sense of smell. Süskind's and Schneider's novels also bring to mind another classic German Schelmenroman of the twentieth-century, Günter Grass's *Die Blechtrommel*, a novel centered around its self-proclaimed clairaudient (*hellhörig*) protagonist

Oskar Matzerath and a novel which itself relied heavily on narration and storytelling.

What separates Grass's novel from Süskind's and Schneider's is the distinct unreliability of Grass's narrator, a narrative situation which O'Neill argues elevates the level of discourse of the narrative above that of the story being told, a construct typical of postmodern novels.[3] The narrators in *Das Parfum* and *Schlafes Bruder* are true chroniclers of the events they are relating; they never offer any hint of unreliability, rather demonstrate at all times not only confidence in their knowledge but also an awareness of their audience. For instance, early on in both novels, the narrators introduce characters who figure only in the initial stages of the story. Whereas modernist and even postmodernist novels would be unconcerned with the disappearance of such characters, the narrators here, fully aware of the coming course of events as well as of the necessity of veracity, acknowledge the departure of the figures and offer a brief account of the remainder of the characters' lives, purely, they maintain, for the benefit of the reader.[4] Such a device, the acknowledgment of the audience, is again a classic storytelling device, used to lend authenticity to the story, but also to engage the reader, by imparting concern for all those who populate the tale. As one critic has commented about the narrator in *Schlafes Bruder*:

> Ungeübte Leser werden beispielsweise vom allwissenden Erzähler, wie ihn Schneider einführt, behutsam an der Hand genommen. Da erzählt einer mit großer Übersicht, gibt auf der ersten Seite unmißverständlich zu erkennen, wohin seine Handlung steuern wird, redet—als hätte es die Zweifel der modernen Literatur nie gegeben—permanent von seinem "Helden," kommentiert, wertet und spricht mit seinem Leser, als gäbe es Thomas Manns ironischen Umgang mit dieser fiktionalen Übereinkunft nicht. (Moritz 16–17)

Such a technique is of course popular among readers (leading in part to the success of the novel) but equally unpopular among critics. Süskind's use of a similar technique led many critics to argue that the novel lacked originality and that it is, at best, a paradigm of postmodern pastiche.[5] Regardless, what is clear is that the narrative structure and technique of both novels borrows from the tradition of the nineteenth-century realist novel.

But *Das Parfum* and *Schlafes Bruder* differ from *Die Blechtrommel* in another important aspect, namely in the historical referentiality of their narratives and symbolism. Whereas Grass is an avowed admirer of early modern literature, both Süskind and Schneider chose to follow the constructs of the Romantic novel (as Judith Ryan has also noted), creating protagonists who, besides showing aspects of the Romantic *Genie*, also have a heightened sense of their own individuality, experience a decisive epiphany early on in life, and find refuge and redemption in nature. Although Süskind has been sharply criticized for his appropriation of Romantic and neoromantic symbolism, his use of nineteenth-century narrative techniques led in part to the novel's great success and a similar style helped Schneider's novel achieve critical and commercial acclaim as well.[6] Their choice of the Romantic novel as a referential basis is, I would maintain, not coincidental, for the poetics of the Romantic story underline the importance and indeed glorify the naive storyteller (*Erzähler*). In fact, Schneider's novel corresponds in many ways to the quintessential nineteenth-century German literary genre, the novella, for Elias Alder's story is quite simply in Goethean fashion "eine sich ereignete, unerhörte Begebenheit."

As discussed previously, the novella, besides being a highly readable and story-driven genre, has among all literary genres been viewed as a form which best approximates the storytelling tradition.[7] Peter Brooks' argument that the novella attempts to reconstruct storytelling situations by introducing a second level of narration allows such works a greater sense of authenticity within the tale being told. Moreover, he argues, the Romantic writer felt attracted to oral communication because of a profound desire to transmit a sense of experience and knowledge to the reader, a tenet central to storytelling and many new narratives.

This desire to communicate a sense of shared experience forms the basis for many of Uwe Timm's recent works, especially his 1993 novella *Die Entdeckung der Currywurst*. Timm has outlined his views of literature and literary aesthetics in the *Poetikvorlesungen* that he gave in 1991/1992 at the Paderborner Universität.[8] Here, Timm clearly counts himself among writers who value the experiential nature of writing. A fundamental aspect of his works and thus his poetics is what he terms "sprechende Situationen," that is individual situations which give meaning to a larger context or complex of actions. His narratives are splintered into multiple layers of stories, wherein the single situation, which may indeed be an object, a gesture, or an image, are laden with meaning which then in turn impart meaning to the actual situation being described. This meaning, he argues, oscillates according to mood and interest of the reader. In this way, Timm acknowledges the postmodern conundrum of finding or placing meaning in a text, yet argues for non-stasis, whereby meaning can still be had and found, not in the larger grand meta-narratives, but on a subjective level in the everyday and in the situational (66, 69).

A prime example of his methodology is his novella *Die Entdeckung der Currywurst*, a veritable Chinese box of narrative frames. Timm designates the story "eine Novelle" for two reasons: first, it is in the truest sense of the word a "kleine Neuigkeit," namely a literary excursus on the "Entdeckung der Currywurst." Secondly, however, because of the genre's intricate link to storytelling and listening, a connection, Timm is want to point out, dating back to Boccaccio's *Decamerone*.[9] Whereas the underlying structural principle informing the *Decamerone* was the telling of and listening to stories, so too does Timm's fictional narrator cajole Lena Brückner into revealing the origins of the currywurst. The driving force behind the narration is the interplay between Lena and the narrator: Lena wants to tell her life story, a long story, one much more suited to a novel than a novella, while the narrator wishes only to learn the origins of her culinary invention. He finds himself compelled then to intrude continually on her storytelling so as to limit her digressions. Not only does this make for an interesting narrative, it also lends a degree of naturalness and authenticity to the narrative situation.

Through the interplay of reality and narration, Timm weaves a tale of courage, resistance and inventiveness set against the backdrop of Hamburg in the last days of World War II. For Timm, reality is confirmed and authenticated through the act of narration; that which is told and can be told is "das Wirkliche": "das ist die Magie, die das Erzählen von Geschichten auch bei den sogenannten primitiven Völkern hat" (*Erzählen* 105). Thus Timm negates Adorno's dictum that today's reality "läßt sich nicht mehr erzählen" by arguing that "das Wirkliche" exists only if it can be narrated and told. In fact, Timm argues that theories which maintain "daß das Erzählte nicht wirklich sei, sondern erzählt" are not only boring but unproductive (115). Every reader, he argues, knows that that which is told is not reality, but fiction. Moreover the demands in the 1960s for meta-narratives and its corollary "man müsse das Erzählen erzählen," have castrated storytelling (115).

In this regard, Timm rejects the meta-narratives of postmodern fiction in which the narrative quite often is concerned primarily with the narrative act itself. But this does not mean that Timm is advocating only naïve or empty narrative, for he distinguishes between literary narration and day-to-day storytelling, and thus between *Trivialliteratur* and higher forms of narration, based on the strength and quality of the language. Herein lies the difference between literary narrative and a narrative act with no other function than to advance the plot. Literary narrative, he argues, is a *Sprachreservoir*, which challenges and changes our conceived notions of language thus elevating it above the level of *Trivialkunst* (*Erzählen* 54).

This power inherent in language and the relationship between storytelling and the establishment of community—another important aspect of narrative for Timm—is explored further in Sten Nadolny's 1994 novel *Selim, oder die Gabe der Rede*, a novel that deals with the power of oral storytelling as well as the interrelationship between stories and community and stories and identity. Selim, a Turkish migrant worker living in Germany, has the natural gift of speech and the ability to tell stories as a means of entertainment, as a method of establishing authority (amongst fellow Turks) and as a means of placating others in situations of conflict. Within the novel, Selim is constructed as an oppositional figure to the German Alexander, a former soldier who, after a series of personal failures, becomes infatuated with the gift of speech and rhetorical skills. Alexander befriends Selim precisely because of the latter's oratorical abilities and sets off to improve his own skills with the goal of opening a *Redeschule* to train others in the gift of speech.

As hagiography, the novel is not unlike Handke's *Die Wiederholung* in that it explores the notion of identity as being intricately linked to a narratable history. Alexander, the narrator (in both the first and third person), creates his own history as well as that of Selim through the act of writing the novel. Nadolny, who maintains that the figure of Selim was actually based on a Turkish friend who possessed the same gift of oration,[10] wished to write a nonfictional account of this person as a means of better understanding Germany as a multicultural society. That Nadolny chose to do so in a novel is telling, for the novel plays with notions of narration and storytelling on a number of levels. On the one hand, it is involved in the construction of the identity of its protagonist, Selim, in a manner reminiscent of Christa Wolf's *Nachdenken über Christa T.* and Handke's *Die Wiederholung*, two other highly proclaimed novels which posit the notion that one's identity exists only when given a narratable form. On the other hand, Nadolny's novel glorifies Selim the storyteller, portraying him as a figure who is able to survive, live, and, in the true manner of the storyteller, share experience and convey wisdom to his listeners. This gift of speech, Nadolny implies, is a gift that appears to be dying in the Western world yet remains alive in Eastern cultures where the storyteller is still venerated. Although Nadolny's construction and portrayal of the Orient runs the great risk of becoming overly stereotypic (as a number of critics have pointed out[11]), it nonetheless underscores an aspect of Wittstock's argument, that the German literary culture is in danger of losing its ability to construct engaging and skillful narrative.[12]

The high regard Nadolny holds for storytelling is revealed at one point in the novel, in which Alexander is asked by a *Wirtschaftsinstitut* in Kiel to hold a talk on "narrative economy" (404). Alexander, in many ways Nadolny's alter-ego, considers how best to approach the subject and asks himself rhetorically: "Wie soll ich anfangen? Am besten mit einer 'Es-war-einmal' Geschichte" (407), implying that the Märchen, i.e., oral narrative, is the best means of conveying his thoughts about narrative and rhetoric as well as narrative economy. Moreover, some weeks before preparing his talk, Alexander views Claude Lanzmann's nine-hour documentary film *Shoah*, which offers personal testimony to the Holocaust through individual narratives. Alexander is intrigued by the film for he claims that first-person, oral narratives have a claim to authenticity stronger than documentary photos: "Unmenschlichkeit ist weder durch grausige Beweise noch durch Zahlen schon fühlbar. Sie wird es nur als Geschichte" (407).[13]

Alexander's conflation of history and narrative forces him to consider the question of objectivity and subjectivity in narrative and the issue of authenticity in storytelling.[14] He postulates, for instance, that *Wahrheit* and *Erfindung* are inseparable and, quoting a Celtic saying, that truth should never ruin a good story, a maxim to which Selim, his storytelling friend, held tightly. Alexander thus dismisses the ability (or inability) to separate truth from fiction as inconsequential to the narrative act, postulating instead the communicative act as superior to claims of truth and reality. If the story becomes representative of a greater truth (as is the case of many of Selim's stories) then its correspondence to fact is of lesser importance. In this way, Nadolny (through Alexander) seems to be offering an answer to the postmodern dilemma whereby truth and reality are no longer absolute and thus lose their normative categories. When narratives and stories appropriate symbolic meaning and become representative of a larger whole, then the question of the (in)ability to narrate "reality" becomes secondary. The author and storyteller no longer need to be concerned with issues of veracity and authenticity, for s/he is dealing in the symbolic and allegorical and positing truths which are to be interpreted and applied to an exterior reality.

But this conflict between story and reality had been a life-long problem for Alexander (and thus symbolically for the German literary tradition as a whole) and was one which he attempted to rectify with his *Redeschule*. He realized that analytic discourse has failed him personally and, to a larger extent Germany symbolically, whereas narrative discourse has served Selim well. Here too Nadolny runs a great risk of stereotyping Eastern and Western culture by positing storytelling and narrative exchange as characteristic of non-Western societies and as an alternative to the Platonic, Anglo-Saxon tradition of analysis. Whereas Alexander, like Germany in many of its institutions, was failed by the enlightened tradition of logical discourse, Selim, and many non-Western cultures as well, has been spared the burden and turmoil of history.

Nadolny further expounds on these ideas in his collection of *Poetikvorlesungen* which he held in Munich, *Das Erzählen und die guten Absichten*. In his thoughts and comments on writing collected there, Nadolny shares with Uwe Timm a number of convictions with regard to the function of narrative literature, convictions which in fact serve as the basis for most of the new narrative literature. First, they both contend, stories are crucial to human existence by virtue of their ability to establish order, causality and impart meaning (57f). Here, Timm and Nadolny follow in the line of many narratologists and writers who maintain that stories are a means of ordering reality; a world lacking stories and their inherent structuring principles, so the argument goes, is a world without order. Second, both agree further that the writer must not only convey his/her own version of reality, but must do so in a playful manner, like that of an entertainer, or a *Gaukler*, thereby emphasizing the entertainment value of narrative and stories. Critics hold, however, that it is exactly in this regard that literature runs the risk of losing its value and seriousness, for story-driven narratives are more closely linked to *Trivialliteratur* than serious literature. Both Timm and Nadolny though emphasize an important aspect of narrative storytelling that many critics too often overlook, namely that the art of storytelling lies as much in how the tale is told and in the language used to tell it as in the content of the story. Finally, both Nadolny and Timm share the view that literature holds the power of resistance, a *Widerstandsform*, as Timm has termed it, through which they distinguish between engaged literature and *Trivialliteratur*.

Nevertheless, despite the intent of these writers, there remain two exterior forces strongly contesting and controlling the future of German literature: the critics and the readers. Readers, it seems, besides desiring a more readable and entertaining literature, are also demanding of a more "authentic" literature, one which Wittstock posits is more reflective of day-to-day life and one which thus seemingly speaks to the myth of real-life and "das wirkliche Leben."[15] Peculiarly, neither Nadolny's or Schneider's recent successes speak to the "Alltagsrealität" of the average reader, although both write in a highly readable style. On the other hand, Bernhard Schlink's *Der Vorleser* and Ingo Schulze's *Simple Stories* do and as a result became bestsellers. Critics, however, have in most cases been more demanding. As the literary critic of *Die Welt* has pointed out, there are very few laws left today in the German publishing world, but one still remains: "Wer mit seinem Debüt Erfolg hatte, geht mit dem zweiten Buch baden."[16] This was indeed the case with Schneider's second novel, *Die Luftgängerin* (1998), which has, according to the author's own calculation, received two positive reviews among the 85 which have appeared so far.[17] The question for many critics, though, is whether much of this new narrative literature is just "tale(s) full of sound and fury . . . signifying nothing," or whether there is greater import and depth to these novels. For Timm, the tale and the art of telling is certainly an end in and of itself. *Die Entdeckung der Currywurst* celebrates Lena Brückner, the naïve storyteller, who recounts not only the origin of her culinary dish but also the spirit of her resiliency. Similarly, Nadolny's Selim is a glorification of the storyteller that has been lost in Western culture (as Alexander sees it) but remains an important cultural figure in other societies. Süskind's and Schneider's novels thus hearken back to an epoch in which the omniscient teller of tales still commanded the authorial voice that was lost with the rise of the modernist novel.

Whatever the literary merits of Schneider's second novel may or may not be, the critical reception the novel has received reveals one thing: entertaining, readable narratives even in a highly literate language like Schneider's, though perhaps commercially successful, still face high critical standards—and for good reason. Still, such standards should not exclude traditional narrative and methods of storytelling, for as is apparent from recent works of German language fiction, discriminating literature need not preclude storytelling, thus demonstrating that the story and discourse may once again coexist on an equal plane. In fact, Wittstock's judgment of Süskind's *Das Parfum* echoes this very line of thought: "Mit welcher Virtuosität es Süskind darüber hinaus versteht, dies alles in eine sprachlich brillante, traditionsgesättigte, ungemein fesselnde erzählerische Form zu bringen, macht sein Buch zu einem hervorragenden Beleg für die These, daß es sehr wohl möglich ist, Literatur und Unterhaltung, hohe ästhetische Ansprüche und Lust bei der Lektüre zum gegenseitigen Vorteil zu verschmelzen" (140).

This shift in narrative aesthetic is however not limited to literature. German cinema has at the end of the century undergone a similar transformation and has witnessed an unparalleled rise in the use of narrative and storytelling structures in the late 1980s and 1990s. Interesting, both critics and audiences alike have been more receptive of the trend toward a new cinematic narrative than have their literary counterparts. The acceptance of these new films has in fact led to a new identity for the German cinema, one that perhaps would not have been possible without the dual support of audiences and critics. After the relative domestic success of the Neue deutsche Komödie in the 1990s, German filmmakers began to seek greater depth and to create challenging films that tackled broader societal issues yet at the same time remain true to the narrative style that they admire. Like their literary counterparts, they do not view traditional narrative and stylistic innovation or "depth" and entertainment as incompatible. Their attempts at reconciling two poles which have traditionally been distinct (at least in the NGC) has led to a certain division within the German cinema along generational lines, as the filmmakers of the NGC feel their legacy has been neglected and that commercialized "entertainment" has supplanted meaningful, engaged cinematic works.

Upon the awarding of the 2000 German Film Prize, Helma Sanders-Brahms, one of the more prominent among the New German filmmakers of the 1970s and 1980s, issued a statement claiming that German film is "öde" and that "[d]er deutsche Film funktionert nicht mehr."[18] Her reasoning was that there lacked a tradition from one generation of filmmakers to the next in Germany, and that younger filmmakers continually reject and dismiss their predecessors and their body of work: "Heute will uns niemand mehr. Deutschland legt seine Filmemacher ab wie andere Hemden. Das passiert jeder Generation. . . . In Deutschland gibt es kein Nebeneinander von Generationen. Die Nachfolger schaffen ihre Vorgänger ab. Das deutsche Kino könnte existieren, gäbe es ein Neben- und Mitander, eine Koexistenz der Filmemacher-Generationen."[19] Although her pessimism may be little more than a veiled critique of the inundation of German film comedies of the previous decade as well as an expression of her own frustration in securing financing for her more serious projects, Sanders-Brahms statement nonetheless draws renewed attention to the notion of a German national cinema. Her contention that German film "funktioniert nicht mehr" not only implies that German film has a particular function to play but also that there is a body of work which can be characterized as peculiarly German and which distinguishes itself from the cinema of its neighboring countries. At a time when European cultures and economies are adjusting to integration within the European Union, the future of national cinemas is naturally called into question. Although some critics have feared the coming of a "Euro-pudding," that is, films co-financed by several European states and lacking in cultural specificity,[20] others have warned against the total subsuming of European film by Hollywood and the in-roads made by the increasingly international Hollywood studios. This debate is crucial for the new narrative cinema in Germany, for if it is to maintain a distinct identity, then German narrative films must somehow distance themselves from the notion of Hollywood films all the while utilizing some of the structural elements inherent in the dominant cinema.

In recent years, however, much discussion has taken place on European identity in general and the degree to which countries currently designated as "European" share common traditions, culture or even social goals.[21] The only consensus one finds is, first, that European identity posits a tradition rooted in Judeo-Christian ethics and Enlightenment ideas of freedom and democracy[22] and, second, that with regard to film, European cinema defines itself primarily in opposition to Hollywood's dominant narrative tradition. Thus European national cinemas can be said to share these two loosely defined commonalities and little else. Whereas there has been a move afoot on the political stage toward what Susan Sontag has called the "Europeanisation . . . of Europe itself," the question of Europe's cultural identity remains uncertain.[23] Whereas Europe was once about expansion, it is now about retrenchment, as waves of nationalism together with a rejection of the Euro and sometimes of the European Union itself reflects attempts in various corners of the continent to redefine their own identity vis-à-vis Europe. As a result, Europe has been split into unifiers and Eurosceptics, the later fearing an ever greater loss of cultural autonomy and identity.

Within the cinema one finds a unique tendency: collectively, most European filmmakers feel they share a common aesthetic; individually, however, they continue to make films which reflect a specific cultural identity. In his analysis of national cinemas, Andrew Higson argues that an imaginary coherence within a given national cinema is a necessity which, in its cultural specificity, helps form a unique identity reflective of a national consciousness. In fact, it is this real or imaginary coherence which Sanders-Brahms has argued is lacking in German cinema today, one that would set it off from the cinemas of France or Spain and England. For New German Filmmakers in the 1960s and 1970s as well as for the critics who helped define the NGC, questions of historicity, complicity and collective guilt served as central textual discourses which defined, at least thematically, the German art film that was the NGC. Together with the issue of a divided Germany, these issues also reflected the larger *Kulturpolitik* of the Federal Republic for some forty years.

But beginning in the 1980s, a young generation of filmmakers rejected the politicized, issue-oriented film that was the mainstay of the NGC and opted instead for situation comedies and a new narrative filmmaking, whereby many German films were no longer representative of an oppositional cinema rather were fashioned on the dominant Hollywood cinema.[24] Both critics and German movie-goers alike, though, have since cooled on the new German comedy and at the turn of the century, German cinema once again finds itself in a crisis: is this new trend toward narrative filmmaking the death of "German" cinema or can a new identity be formed using the constructs of the dominant cinema but focusing on issues and themes that are peculiarly German? One film has stood out as a possible signal for a new direction in German cinema: Tom Tykwer's *Lola rennt*. Seldom has a German film been such a popular success while receiving praise in the German press: the *Frankfuter Allgemeine Zeitung* called it "Kino in seinen mitreissendsten Momenten,"[25] while the *Süddeutsche Zeitung* went even further, saying: "ganz sicher vermittelt [der Film] erstmal das Gefuehl, hier werde ein neues Kapitel der deutschen Filmgeschichte aufgeschlagen . . . Also darf man sagen: So sieht der Film aus, von dem das deutsche Kino all die Jahre getraeumt hat."[26] Even the venerable *epd-film* had only the highest praise, saying that *Lola rennt* and Hans-Christian Schmid's *23* were: "zwei Filme, die einen neuen Aufbruch im deutschen Kino markieren, den man gar nicht hoch genug einschätzen kann."[27]

What critics praised most about Tykwer's film was its cinematic playfulness, for it used the medium of film to its fullest extent, from editing to cinematography to self-reflexivity, but it was also, as the critic for the FAZ termed it, "zielbetont und Bewegung pur." What critics seemed to overlook, though, was that more than anything else, the film is about storytelling and the possibilities of storytelling in the wake of postmodernist aesthetics. The film's plot, essentially nothing more than a short thriller dealing with a low-level Mafia wannabe who loses 100,000DM and needs to replace it in twenty minutes, is told three times in which differing endings are probed. The film purposely and playfully engages in a retelling of the same story, each different in its expression of the will of the protagonists. Gone is the authorial narrator who determines the direction of the story and gone too is the powerful driving force of narratives of old: fate. In its place is the simple will of the individual and the ability to change the outcome of a story to create the happy end that is desired. Such a conceit reflects an understanding on the director's part of the dominance of the inner logic of the story (not surprisingly Tykwer studied philosophy before beginning his film career). Whereas a primary rule in storytelling is that the story has an intrinsic logic that drives its path, the modernist (and later postmodern) rupture of the story led in part to its demise in the twentieth century. Tykwer, however, resuscitates the storytelling act by acknowledging the postmodern rejection of the authorial voice and instead supplanting it with a multivalent structure. Each segment represents possibilities of a story, all possible, yet none laying claim to the truth or "reality."[28] Instead, the viewer is left with choices and possibilities rather than an attempt at representing reality through a linear narrative. It is in fact the variations within each story which becomes the supratext and the true narrative of film.

Such a narrative construction has become increasingly more popular in the cinema in the last few years. In an attempt at reconciling the uninventive uses of traditional narration and storytelling in Hollywood cinema, filmmakers have begun problematizing the act of narration itself by cutting and rearranging the narrative itself, thus forcing the viewer to reconstruct the story at hand. This technique not only draws greater attention to the story itself and the act of narration, but it opens up greater narrative and thematic possibilities. Martin Rubin has termed this style and trend in filmmaking "neonarrative" or "permutational cinema," a trend he maintains that is the most striking innovation in filmmaking in recent film history.[29] Its origins lie interestingly both in the innovative Hollywood films of the 1940s and 1950s (from Orson Welles' *Citizen Kane* to film noir) and in the European countercinema of the 1960s and 70s (Alain Resnais' *Hiroshima mon amour* and the films of Luis Buñuel) as well as Akira Kurosawa's *Rashomon*. Fundamental to the neonarrative film is "the notion of gamelike, permutational rearrangement, where the narrative is broken down into a series of modular, non-linear units, rather than coalescing into an inevitable, transparent flow." Unlike the countercinema and avant-garde films which similarly deconstructed narrative, neonarrative films amplify the story rather than deconstruct the limitations and contradictions within the logic of the story.

But Tykwer's film represents a further breakthrough for German film and its cinematic identity in that it recognizes and references classics of the Art Film as well as milestones in German film history and thus consciously places itself within a tradition of German filmmaking both old and new. The construction of the film and its retelling of the same event recalls and is indebted to Akira Kurosawa's 1950 masterpiece *Rashomon*, which itself tells the same tale three times, but from different perspectives. While *Lola rennt* clearly explores different terrain than *Rashomon*, it does share the earlier film's kinetic editing and visual aesthetics. Moreover, the two films share the idea of the unstable nature of truth, a topic Manny and Lola discuss repeatedly in the bed scenes between the main narratives. Tykwer also clearly references *Die Blechtrommel*'s Oskar Matzerath and his uncanny glass-shattering scream, which allows him to alter and take control of events that seem to be slipping from his grips. Lola, in similar fashion, lets out a glass shattering scream in the third episode in which she attempts to recover the money through her luck with roulette at a local casino. Her scream not only shatters the clock in the casino (à la Oskar) but also seems to influence the roll of the ball on the roulette wheel and she comes away a winner. Such a reference is small but significant, for it recognizes a classic of postwar German cinema and the first German film to have won an Oscar for Best Foreign Film. As such, Tykwer seems to be heralding rather than rejecting his "elders" who were pathbreakers before him, but also placing his film in the cinematic tradition of the Art Film.

But perhaps the most important signifier within the film in this regard is the lead character's name: Lola. By choosing "Lola," Tykwer consciously conjures up figures from Germany's cinematic past: from Marlene Dietrich's Lola Lola in *The Blue Angel* to Barbara Sukowa's Lola in Fassbinder's 1981 film of the same name. Whereas Dietrich's Lola in many ways came to embody Weimar cinema, Fassbinder used Lola to embody his critique of postwar Germany in Part II of his BRD-trilogy. Moreover, the statuette for the German Film Prize was recently named "Lola" in recognition of this most German cinematic name. Thus Tykwer uses the name once again to call forth a German identity, but now one embodied by a postwall, postmodern, postpunk Berlin. His heroine, the city and his film are embellished with pop cultural referents, from comic books and music, to televisions and telephone cards, reflecting the director's desire not only to look back on German cinematic history, but also to look around and reflect the reality of modern-day Berlin. And by doing so, he has also given the *Autorenfilm* a new respectability. Whereas *Autorenfilm* was once the pride of German cinema, it has of late, as both Sanders-Brahms and Wim Wenders agree, become a *Schimpfwort*, symbolizing a filmmaker who is out-of-touch and out-of-date.[30]

But with the success of *Lola rennt* as well as several other films from Tykwer's X-Filme Creative Pool—the production and now distribution company he formed with Wolfgang Becker, Dani Levy and Stefan Arendt—a host of young filmmakers are rediscovering the concept of the "Autorenfilm." With recent films like Peter Lichtefeld's *Zugvögel*, Sebastian Schipper's *Absolute Giganten*, and Fatih Akin's *Kurz und Schmerzlos*, the *Autorenfilm* seems to be making a comeback. But this time, the writer-filmmakers are not creating anti-narratives that attempt to explore and deconstruct the narratives of guilt, neocolonialism or cold-war politics like their predecessors. Instead, unlike the previous generation of *Autorenfilmer*, this generation is making films that not only reflect the everyday reality of the average film-goer but that also celebrate the pluralism of regions within Germany and its multicultural society, much like their literary counterparts are doing within the new narrative novel. Thus it's not surprising to find films like *Absolute Giganten* and *Kurz und Schmerzlos* that take place not only in a particular region (North Germany) but in a particular city (Hamburg) and particular neighborhoods (Altona and Ottensen). Such films—and in this case, especially *Kurz und Schmerzlos* with its three protagonists, a Serb, a Greek and a Turk—also celebrate the diversity within Germany and through that diversity help redefine German identity and the identity of German film.

Moreover, this younger generation of *Autorenfilmer* are drawn toward genre cinema and as such, capitalize on the constructs of popular cinema. Lichtefeld's *Zugvögel*, for instance, expands on the classic road movie, in that its protagonist sets off to a remote corner of Finland to take part in an International Train Timetable Contest. While underway, though, he becomes a murder suspect and is chased by the police across Scandinavia. The film then takes on classic elements of a Krimi, another beloved genre of German culture. Similarly, the tension that *Lola rennt* creates is not unlike that in Fred Zinnemann's 1952 film *High Noon*, in which the hero is racing against the clock, and we as viewers anxiously await the outcome. In this way both of these recent German films reference classic genre cinema, yet imbue them with elements that are distinctly German.

Collectively, such films help reestablish a German cinematic identity that draws on the strengths of popular cinema, yet recognizes and pays homage to a cinematic tradition and particularly to Germany's cinematic heritage. While Sanders-Brahms laments the discarding of previous generations of filmmakers, it is also important for younger generations to set themselves apart from their predecessors. However, recent films indicate that young German filmmakers are not only aware of their predecessors, but willing to recognize them and "coexist" with them, as Sanders-Brahms had hoped. Moreover, these films depict an attempt at redefining German cinema both thematically, through a celebration of Germany's diversity within a larger European context and artistically and aesthetically, through a recognition of the European Art Film, and an embracing of genre cinema. These films are successful in their attempt at conveying one artist's vision in the tradition of the *Autorenfilm*, but utilizing the constructs of the story and linear narrative.

The resurgence of narratives and storytelling in literature and film comes after a long period of experimentation and attempts at achieving a more profound mode of expression in European art. The search for expression, of both the self and the external world, will not, of course, cease. Nor is the return to stories an end to the crisis of narration and narrative possibilities. Whereas the histories of literature and film are marked with change and as dialectic imperatives have often been a driving force in the development of the creative arts, the use of stories and narratives could very well be rejected again in favor of new modes of expression. The legacy of the avant-garde and the experimental movements brought forth in the 1960s seem, at present, to be in question. However, the dominant paradigms in art are generally challenged by movements stemming from the avant-garde and other nontraditional forms of expression. How this challenge will be manifested in the future remains to be seen. Until then, there exists a wide array of possibilities afforded by the story for writers and filmmakers to incorporate and utilize. Already new forms of literary and cinematic expression which synthesize the populist aspects of storytelling and the already well established postmodernist tropes have gained wider acceptance. At present, the full extent of the possibilities afforded by such neonarratives has yet to be exhausted.

~ NOTES ~

Introduction Notes

1 "Letter from the Editor: On looking back two years, and 1,000," *New York Times Magazine*, 5 Dec. 1999, 28.
2 Steiner, "Look Who's Modern Now," *New York Times Book Review*, 10 Oct. 1999, 18–19.
3 Frank Kermode cites both the debate between Theodore Dreiser and Ford Maddox Ford as well as that between Henry James and Arnold Bennett as examples in Britain in the early 1900s of the disagreement over the function of narrative and its relationship to reality. Dreiser criticized Ford for not telling stories in a way in which the world was easily recognizable, whereas Bennett was much more direct in his critique of James: by dismissing the latter's foray into modernist techniques and stating outright that the greatest novelists ignored technique altogether, he maintained that a writer should instead concentrate on the uncomplicated presentation of reality. The counterarguments of course maintained that this trivialized the art of literature itself by making it merely representational as opposed to aesthetic. This debate was not singular to Britain, for in Germany as well the issue of the possibilities of the novel was similarly debated and in fact formed the basis for the crisis of narration and of the novel as a form of expression in the first half of the century. See Kermode, *The Art of Telling: Essays on Fiction*, 15–17.
4 Thomas Medicus writing in the *Frankfurter Rundschau* notes with regard to the international success of Schlink's *Der Vorleser*: "Die Anerkennung durch die amerikanischen Leser ist vermutlich der transatlantischen Form seiner Prosa geschuldet: deren melancholischer Realismus kommt dank luzider Schnörkellosigkeit und einem gewissen suspense amerikanischen Erzähltraditionen sehr nahe." Medicus, "Populäres Sprachrohr der Katharsis: Warum der Schirftsteller Bernhard Schlink bei uns und auch anderswo so erfolgreich ist," *Frankfurter Rundschau* 16 Feb. 2000, on-line.
5 Horst Steinmetz, "Die Rückkehr des Erzählers. Seine alte neue Funktion in der modernen Medienwelt." *Funktion und Funktionswandel der Literatur im Geistes- und Gesellschaftsleben.* (Bern: Lang, 1989): 67–82.
6 See especially Paul Ricoeur's three volume study *Time and Narrative*. Section II, Part IV of Vol. 3 focuses on the "Poetics of Narrative" and includes a discussion of Hegel's *Lectures on the Philosophy of World History* and the question of the relationship between narrative and reality.
7 Wittstock refers to this as one of five "helige Kühe [des deutschen] Kulturbetriebs," against which contemporary writers must struggle. *Leselust: Wie unterhaltsam ist die neue deutsche Literartur?* 26–27.
8 Keith Bullivant, *Realism Today: Aspects of the Contemporary West German Novel.* (Leamington Spa, U.K.: Berg, 1987.) Writers and critics as diverse as Brecht, Broch, Döblin and Erich Kahler all developed anti-realist theories of the novel in the 1920s, ideas which served as the basis for Adorno's and, to some extent, Robbe-Grillet's writings in the 1950s and 1960s.

9   See Ricouer's *Time and Narrative*. Vol. 2. (Chicago: U of Chicago P, 1985) and Lyotard's seminal essay *The Postmodern Condition: A Report on Knowledge*, Geoff Bennington and Brian Massumi, trans. (Minneapolis: U of Minnesota P, 1984).
10 Patrick O'Neill, *Acts of Narrative: Textual Strategies in Modern German Fiction*. (Toronto: U of Toronto, 1996).
11 See here also Keith Bullivant's contribution on the death and rebirth of narration in Vol. 12 of *Hansers Sozialgeschichte der deutschen Literatur* (Munich: Hanser, 1980).
12 Uwe Timm. "'Das Erzählen muß wie Sand im Getriebe sein': Ein Gespräch mit Uwe Timm." Interview with David Coury and Herman DeVries. *Focus on Literatur* 2.1 (1995): 102–112.
13 This is especially true of Handke. While most literary scholars see his transformations as a reflection of a writer who is continually on the forefront of the German literary scene, others, especially writers like Milo Dor, view him as an opportunistic writer, who masterfully cultivates this image. See Dor, "Wie Peter Handke Peter Handke wurde," *Auf dem falschen Dampfer* (Wien: Zsolnay, 1988). However one chooses to view this issue, both his admirers and his detractors agree that his work is a fairly accurate reflection of current trends in German literature and thus a study of his works serves as an excellent indicator of broader issues within the context of the German literary establishment. One such typical assessment serves as a good example: "Mit einer genialen Intuition für kontrapunktisches Timing deklarierte Handke alle paar Jahre literaturtheoretische Positionen, die er kurz darauf mit seinem eigenen Werk widerlegte," Thomas Rothschild, "Österreichische Literatur," in: *Hansers Sozialgeschichte der deutschen Literatur*, Vol. 12, 679.
14 Richard Firda's Twayne monograph gives an excellent overview of his work, as does Jerome Klinkowitz and James Knowlton's analysis of Handke as a postmodern writer. In German, Manfred Durzak's monograph gives extensive analyses of Handke's prose as do Peter Pütz's and Raimund Fellinger's collection of essays.
15 For an excellent analysis of structuralist and formalist film theory, see Edward Brannigan's and David Bordwell's work on theories of cinematic narrative discourse. Similarly, Christian Metz' works remain the standard semiotic studies of cinema. My concern is less with the examining of narrative constructs effecting the conveyance of story to the viewer than with how films of the late 1980s and 1990s—after the much heralded death of the New German Cinema—represent a shift back toward the dominant cinema.
16 See especially Thomas Elsaesser, *New German Cinema* (New Brunswick, NJ: Rutgers, 1989), Eric Rentschler, *West German Film in the Course of Time* (Bedford Hills: Redgrave, 1984), Timothy Corrigan, *New German Cinema: The Displaced Image* (Austin: U of Texas P, 1983), Marc Silbermann, *German Cinema: Texts in Context* (Detroit: Wayne State UP, 1995) and Julia Knight, *Women and the New German Cinema* (London: Verso, 1992).
17 From Tales of Graz 2000: http://www.graz.tales.org.
18 "New Ideas Flourish in an Old Venue: The Return of the Literary Salon," *This Week in Germany*, 17. Dec 1999.
19 Jörg Magenau, "Die neue Lust am Erzählen," *Deutschland: Zeitschrift für Politik, Kultur, Wirtschaft und Wissenschaft* (Okt/Nov 2000): 29.
20 On this issue, see Wittstock's *Leselust: Wie unterhaltsam ist die neue deutsche Literatur?* (Munich: Luchterhand, 1995).

Chapter 1 Notes

1   See, for example, Ruth H. Finnegan, *Limba Stories and Storytelling* (Oxford: Clarendon, 1967); Roger D. Abrahams, *The Man-of-Words in the West Indies: Performance and the Emergence of Creole Culture* (Baltimore: Johns Hopkins UP, 1983); Cristopher Nash, ed., *Narrative in Culture: the Uses of Storytelling in the Sciences, Philosophy, and Literature* (New York: Routledge, 1990).

2   Reynolds Price, *A Palpable God* (New York: Atheneum, 1978): 3.
3   The official declartion can be found on the web site of the Nobel Academy: http://www.nobel.se.
4   Grass's speech is available in German, English and Swedish on the web site of the Nobel Academy: http://www.nobel.se.
5   Roemer states further that our need to make connections may be why storytelling and mathematics share many common words: "tell" being derived from the Anglo-Saxon *tellan*, meaning "to tell" or "to count"; and "tale" being derived from *talu*, meaning both "speech" and "figure." The fact that characters are also referred to as "figures" and that a synonym for "tell" is "recount" further underlines this relationship. Micheal Roemer, *Telling Stories: Postmodernism and the Invalidation of Traditional Narrative* (Lanham, MD: Rowman and Littlefield, 1995): 388n1. The story's ability to establish connections will be explored in detail later in this chapter, as it is an important aspect in the argument for the importance of stories.
6   Here Price refers to Erich Kahler's study *The Inward Turn of Narrative*, which suggests that the basis of the modern novel and its turn away from the audience is to be found much earlier, namely, in the novels in and leading up to the eighteenth century. Kahler's study ends with an analysis of Laurence Sterne's *Tristram Shandy*, a "decisive work" which "anticipates the modern novel, all of whose devices and strategies may be found within it" (7). Thus, exactly when the relationship between teller and audience begins to break down in literature is difficult to ascertain. Kahler. *The Inward Turn of Narrative*. Richard and Clara Winston, trans. (Princeton, NJ: Princeton UP, 1973).
7   Price's essay prefaces a collection of translations of biblical stories, thus his argumentation that the act of communication between teller and reader is a mutual one is based primarily on the assumption that the writer/teller was indeed actively seeking an audience and conversely the reader is "moved" by what is being told. This, I believe, is a valid argumentation for non-religious narratives as well, as many writers have expressed the desire to reach or move their readers, especially in the formative stages of the novel, but also in the twentieth century.
8   For an interesting discussion of the development of storytelling in antiquity, see John Harrell, *Origins and Early Traditions of Storytelling* (Kensington, CA: York House, 1983) which traces the origins and functions of storytelling in Sumerian and early and late Greek culture. Roemer's study *Telling Stories*, also provides an excellent in-depth analysis of what constitutes a story and defines the structures inherent in narrative literature.
9   This is the very argument that Wittstock makes regarding contemporary German literature. One of the cardinal rules of artistic production in the latter half of the twentieth century, he feels, has been the incessant striving for something "new." Wittstock, *Leselust: Wie unterhaltsam ist die neue deutsche Literatur?*, 26f. In the context of German literary production, this led to the demise of narration and the branding of the story as obsolete. See my discussion of this in the final chapter.
10 See here my discussion in the Introduction of Patrick O'Neill's contention that "modernist texts focus on the relationship between story and discourse, postmodernist texts treat the discourse as the story," *Acts of Narrative*, 7.
11 Especially germane to this discussion are the following essays: Alfred Döblin, "Bemerkungen zum Roman," *Aufsätze zur Literatur* (Olten: Walter-Verlag, 1963): 19–23; Thomas Mann, "Die Kunst des Romans," *Gesammelte Werke*, vol. 11 (Berlin: Aufbau, 1965): 457–471; Robert Musil, "Die Krise des Romans," *Gesammelte Werke*, vol. 8 (Reinbek: rowohlt, 1978): 1408–1412.
12 M.E. Humble, "Lion Feuchtwanger's Erfolg: The Problems of a Weimar Realist." *Weimar Germany: Writers and Politics*, Alan Bance, ed. (Edinburgh: Scottish U P, 1982): 65.
13 See for example Döblin's collection of essays on the novel, all of which establish a connection between the novel and society. Similarly, but from a decidedly different viewpoint, Hermann Hesse's "Beim Lesen eines Romans" (VII 402–408) laments the "Niedergang" of

the art of narration due to young writers' carelessness of description. He further calls for greater accuracy and attention to detail in narration so as to present a more realistic portrait of life and the characters' experiences, an idea that Peter Handke would reiterate some twenty-five years later when a renewed debate on the situation of the novel arose. I will discuss this later in this chapter.

14 Mann quotes a passage from Schopenhauer which is echoed in a later work by Mann's friend and colleague at Princeton, Erich Kahler. Kahler's study *Die Verinnerung des Erzählens* (1957) traces this process from the earliest forms of narrative in antiquity through Sterne's *Tristam Shandy*, but oddly mentions neither Mann's essay nor Schopenhauer's discussion, even though Schopenhauer views *Tristam Shandy* as a caesura within the development of narrative fiction as well. Lukàcs makes a similar argument in his *Theorie des Romans* and comments in the "Vorwort"—written in 1962 some forty-five years after its initial publication—that Mann had enthusiastically read upon its appearance.

15 A similar thesis forms the basis of Frank Kermode's *The Sense of an Ending*, in which he maintains that no other literary trope has had so much effect on world literature than the apocalypse and no work since the Bible has been able to achieve closure as a result. His discussion of the apocalypse as a metaphor for literary closure has interesting parallels to Benjamin's discussion in "Der Erzähler" of death as the ultimate goal and driving force of the novel. See Kermode, *The Sense of an Ending: Studies in the Theory of Fiction* (New York: Oxford UP, 1967).

16 Alfred Döblin, "Der Bau des epischen Werks," *Aufsätze zur Literatur*: 103–132.

17 Werner Welzig, in his compendium to the twentieth-century German novel, notes that this term was analogous to the concept of anti-theater in that it not only expressed a polemic, but dissatisfaction with modern literature. See especially his introduction: Werner Welzig, *Der deutsche Roman im 20. Jahrhundert*. (Stuttgart, Kröner, 1970): 1–10.

18 See also Döblin's essays "Bemerkungen zum Roman" (19–23) and "Die Romane von Franz Kafka" (283–286) in *Aufsätze zur Literatur* for a further discussion of this idea.

19 Theodore Ziolkowski, *Dimensions of the Modern Novel* (Princeton, NJ: Princeton UP, 1969): 137.

20 Handke is an excellent example of this. As a practitioner of the so-called New Sensibility, his works tend to be very experientially based and combine autobiography with fictional narration. In fact, his return to stories and storytelling, as discussed in the next chapter, was in many ways enabled by this combination, also a type of "selbsterlebte Realität," as Welzig would have it. See Chapter 2 for a more detailed discussion.

21 See Döblin's 1913 essay "An Romanautoren und ihre Kritiker," in: *Aufsätze zur Literatur* (Olten: Walter-Verlag, 1963) and Adorno's 1954 essay "Standort des Erzählers im zeitgenössischen Roman," *Noten zur Literatur* (Frankfurt: Suhrkamp, 1958).

22 Kayser makes interesting reference to Benjamin's conception of the "Einzelleser," the isolated reader of novels, suggesting in some ways a connection between the inwardness of the modern novel and the isolation of the modern reader.

23 See note 6.

24 As was discussed earlier in this chapter, Benjamin saw the dissemination of information as an integral part in the decline of storytelling as well: "Wenn die Kunst des Erzählens selten geworden ist, so hat die Verbreitung der Information einen entscheidenden Anteil an diesem Sachverhalt" (II.2 444). In fact, he feels that the growth of information as a form of communication brings about a crisis in the novel, for information demands comprehension and shuns ambiguity.

25 Döblin, "Epilog," *Aufsätze zur Literatur* (Olten: Walter-Verlag, 1963): 383–399; Benjamin, "Krisis des Romans," *Gesammelte Schriften*, Vol 3.1 (Frankfurt: Suhrkamp, 1980): 230–236.

26 Andreas Huyssen makes an important distinction between modernist and avant-garde writers. Too often, he writes, American critics and theorists especially tend to use the terms

interchangeably. While he does note certain similarities between avant-garde and modernist writers and artists—especially in regard to language experimentation—the differences, he notes, cannot be overlooked. While I certainly do not want to use them interchangeably here, I would argue that whatever experimentation and rejection of stories and narratives there was by modernist writers, such tendencies were even more pronounced amongst the avant-gardists. See Huyssen, "The Search for Tradition: Avantgarde and Postmodernism in the 1970s," in *After the Great Divide: Modernism, Mass Culture, Postmodernism* (Bloomington, IN: Indiana UP, 1986): 162–163.

27 Frank Kermode, *The Art of Telling: Essays on Fiction* (Cambridge, MA: Harvard UP, 1983): 8–23.

28 For an excellent overview of this period, especially with regard to the avant-garde, see Stephaine Baron's *"Degenerate Art": The Fate of the Avant-Garde in Nazi Germany* (Los Angeles: Los Angeles County Museum of Art, 1991).

29 This is especially true for the postwar avant-garde and for Handke in particular. Handke's essay "Zur Tagung der Gruppe 47 in USA" reflects this very issue. Hugh Rorrison sees this as a major impetus for the *Grazer Gruppe*, a group which he defines as a "literary pressure group rather than a school," and for Handke in particular: "As Handke saw it, the novels of the 'Gruppe 47' had come to work in terms of conditioned responses to hackneyed stimuli—Hitler, Auschwitz, Berlin, napalm—which left him cold. Handke's assertiveness at this time was symptomatic of a generation that was immune to the sense of collective guilt that had preoccupied postwar German, and to a lesser extent Austrian literature, and was about to articulate its frustrations and aspirations in the Student Movement...." (254). See Rorrison, "The '*Grazer Gruppe*', Peter Handke and Wolfgang Bauer," in: Alan Best and Hans Wolfschütz, eds. *Modern Austrian Writing*, (London: Wolf, 1980): 252–266.

30 Hans Meyer and Wolfgang Emrich have debated the origins and efficacy of these various terms and terminologies. Although much debate has arisen as to the validity of these characterizations, I think it useful to assume that a certain rejection on the part of young writers of the linguistic and literary heritage of the Nazis existed, which later extended to the realm of literary narration and storytelling. See Meyer, *Zur deutschen Literatur der Zeit* (Reinbek: rowohlt, 1967): 300–320 as well as Emrich's definition of "Nullpunkt" in *Kulturpolitisches Wörterbuch: Bundesrepublik Deutschland/Deutsche Demokratische Republik im Vergleich*, Wolfgang R. Langenbucher, Ralf Rytlewski and Bernd Weyergraf eds. (Stuttgart: Metzler, 1983) for a discussion of the terminology.

31 See for example Wolfgang Borchert's "Das ist unser Manifest," *Das Gesamtwerk* (Reinbek: Rowohlt, 1959) as an example of the latter and Ernst Cassirer's *The Myth of the State* (New Haven: Yale UP, 1946) as exemplary of the former.

32 For a thorough discussion of the ramifications of Adorno's essay on German literary production, see Keith Bullivant and Klaus Briegleb's "Die Krise des Erzählens—'1968' und danach," in *Hansers Sozialgeschichte der deutschen Literatur*, Vol. 12, 302–310. This essay also provides an excellent in-depth analysis of the cultural and social aspects of the narration crisis as well as the debate over the dichotomy between art and experience.

33 He is careful to point out that the *nouveau roman* is not a theory but an exploration. He identifies a commonality among like-minded writers who reject the rigidly defined constructs of the literary establishment, primarily with regard to character, narrative and description (134–135).

34 In his programmatic essay "Ich bin ein Bewohner des Elfenbeinturms," Handke proclaims "Kleist, Flaubert, Dostojewski, Kafka, Faulkner, Robbe-Grillet haben mein Bewußtsein von der Welt geändert" (20). These influences are strikingly similar to Robbe-Grillet's own conception of the evolution of the novel through the writings of many of these same authors. See "New Novel, New Man" in *For a New Novel*. Firda, in his monograph on Handke, also makes

this connection stating that influences from both Robbe-Grillet's and Nathalie Sarraute's theoretical works are evident in the early stages of Handke's writing. See Firda, 50, 144.

35 Another interesting similarity is the rhetorical nature of these essays. Both take a defensive stance toward the establishment; Robbe-Grillet defending his style and ideas in the face of critical opposition and Handke offering a sort of apology in which he defends his remarks at the Princeton meeting of the Gruppe 47. In both cases, the authors define what they represent by deconstructing the criticism of their previous works.

36 See especially his early play *Kaspar* as well as his so-called *Sprechstücke*, which problematized the function and degradation of language in modern society. Handke belongs in a long line of Austrian writers concerned with this problematic. In this regard, however, he demonstrates an even greater affinity with Ionesco and Beckett, and the tradition of absurdist theater. See Nicholas Hern, *Peter Handke: Theater and Anti-theater* (London: Oswald Wolff, 1971).

37 In her essay "Nathalie Sarraute and the Novel," Susan Sontag argues that Robbe-Grillet and Sarraute actually belong to a "second wave" of avant-garde writers, the first occurring in the 1940s and being led by the likes of Maurice Blanchot, Georges Bataille, and Pierre Klossowski: *Against Interpretation* (New York: Anchor, 1990): 104.

38 Ibid, 102.

39 See primarily Barthes' influential 1968 essay "The Death of the Author" in: *Image—Music—Text*. trans. Stephen Heath. (New York, Hill and Wang, 1977): 142–148.

40 Literally hundreds of books have been written on this topic and address the basic tenets of both postmodern and poststructuralist theories. None deal specifically with the issue of storytelling and the death of the storyteller, but this issue is a corollary to the central discourse of both theories. Excellent summaries can be found in English and German. In German, Wolfgang Welsch's *Unsere postmoderne Moderne* (Weinheim: Acta humaniora, 1988) as well as his *Wege aus der Moderne* (Weinheim: Acta humaniora, 1988) summarize many of the cogent points. In English, David Harvey's *The Condition of Postmodernity: an Enquiry into the Origins of Cultural Change* (Cambridge, MA: Blackwell, 1989), Linda Hutcheon, *The Poetics of Postmodernism* (New York, Routledge, 1988), Charles Jencks, ed. *The Post-Modern Reader* (New York: St. Martin's, 1992), and Thomas Docherty, ed. *Postmodernism: a Reader* (New York: Columbia UP, 1993) also provide excellent discussions.

41 For an overview and in-depth analysis of the various manifestations of this refocusing on the self, see Richard McCormick's *Politics of the Self: Feminism and Postmodernism in West German Literature and Film* (Princeton, NJ: Princeton UP, 1991).

42 Habermas discusses much of his theory in a lecture he gave in both Frankfurt and New York in 1981, which was reprinted as "Modernity versus Postmodernity," *New German Critique* 22 (1981): 3–14.

43 Steinmetz cites here both Benjamin and Ricoeur as well as Sartre, the philosopher Wilhelm Schnapp and the critic Karlheinz Stierle as having contributed to this discussion (74). Michael Roemer also makes this claim, but from the standpoint of a narratologist. Roemer, *Telling Stories*, 11–19.

44 Ginia Bellafante, "Dostoyevsky and a Decaf," *Time* 5 June, 1995: 66–68.

45 See, for example, Robert Wright, "The Evolution of Despair," *Time*, 28 August, 1995: 50–57, as well as Wright's book *The Moral Animal: the New Science of Evolutionary Psychology.* (New York: Pantheon, 1994) and Jerome H. Barkow, Leda Cosmides, John Tooby, eds., *The Adapted Mind: Evolutionary Psychology and the Generation of Culture.* (New York: Oxford, 1992). These works all theorize that there exists an inequality between our genetic makeup and the social conditions of modernity. Central to our genetic constitution is the desire for social contact and communities, two aspects which have broken down due to the demands and constraints of modern society.

46 "Freedom and Community: The Politics of Restoration," *Economist*, 24 Dec. 1994–6 Jan. 1995: 33–36.
47 Jason DeParle, "Mountain Voice Shares Ageless, Magic Tales," *New York Times*, 22 June 1991: A1.
48 The reciprocal influence of the U.S. and Germany is not as tenuous as it may seem. Andreas Huyssen, for example, has argued that the European postmodern is in fact a manifestation of the American avant-garde movement of the 1960s. He establishes further a historical dialectic between North America and Europe beginning at the turn of the century, whereby cultural trends and theories reciprocally influenced each other, in many ways propelling the development of intellectual thought. See Huyssen, "Mapping the Postmodern," *After the Great Divide: Modernism, Mass Culture, Postmodernism* (Bloomington: Indiana UP, 1986) and in slightly reworked form, "Postmoderne—eine amerkanische Internationale?" *Postmoderne: Zeichen eines kulturellen Wandels*, Andreas Huyssen and Klaus R. Scherpe, eds. (Hamburg: Rowohlt, 1986). Moreover, in a *New York Times* article on Noah Gordon, an American writer enormously popular in Germany but relatively unknown in the States, Gordon's German publisher, Karl Blessing, explained the writer's popularity in the following manner: "the Anglo-Saxon tradition of strong storytelling often gives powerfully plotted American books like Mr. Gordon's more appeal than their sometimes plodding German competitors" (*New York Times* 21 May, 1996: B4), an analysis that further speaks to the mutual influence of American and German writing, but also indicates the importance of reception on literary trends, a point Steinmetz also makes.
49 Uwe Timm, "Das Erzählen muß wie Sand im Getriebe sein: Gespräch mit Uwe Timm." *Focus on Literatur* 2.1 (1995): 109.
50 Günter Grass makes a similar connection in his Nobel Prize acceptance speech. See Note 3.
51 For an excellent discussion of the sociopolitical issues surrounding the resurgence of narration, see Klaus Briegleb's "Weiterschreiben! Wege zu einer deutschen literarischen 'Postmoderne'?" in *Hansers Sozialgeschichte der deutschen Literatur*, Vol. 12, 340–381 as well as the chapter on this topic in Keith Bullivant's *The Future of German Literature* (Providence, RI: Berg, 1994.)
52 Uwe Timm designated his work *Die Entdeckung der Currywurst* (1993) a novella, as did Gerhard Kopf (*Borges gibt es nicht*, 1991), Bodo Kirchhoff (*Gegen die Laufrichtung*, 1993), Peter Hartling (*Bozena*, 1994), Norbert Gstrein (*O2*, 1993), Dieter Wellershoff (*Zikadengeschrei*, 1995) and many others in the 1990s.

Chapter 2 Notes

1 The original essays appeared separately under the titles *Versuch über die Müdigkeit* (1989), *Versuch über die Jukebox* (1990), and *Versuch über den geglückten Tag* (1991). As such they form a trilogy, a cycle for which Handke has a decided preference.
2 While the subtitle was added by the translators or the publisher, the dust jacket states that Handke has always worked very closely with his translators and was thus certainly in agreement with the subtitle.
3 This movement is sometimes referred to as "die neue Sensibilität."
4 The two most important and considered by critics to be among Handke's best works are *Der kurze Brief zum langen Abschied* (1972) and the memoir about his mother's death *Wunschloses Unglück* (1972). Also of importance for this period and for his development were the short novels *Die Angst des Tormanns beim Elfmeter* (1970), *Die Stunde der wahren Empfindung* (1975) and *Die linkshändige Frau* (1976).
5 As with most of Handke's works, there exists a very close correspondence between writer and narrator. This stems from Handke's belief that the writer must draw from life and experience for poetic inspiration. Most critics agree that the narrator usually is Handke, although a dis-

cretionary caution is always in order. I feel it is safe to assume, at least, that the narrator is generally male in all of Handke's works, as he has rarely displayed much of a feminist sensibility, with the notable exception of *Die linkshändige Frau*.
6   *Langsamer Heimkehr* (1979), *Die Lehre der Sainte-Victoire* (1980), *Kindergeschichte* (1981) and *Über die Dörfer* (1981). Two standard monographs, Richard Firda's *Peter Handke* (New York: Twayne, 1993) and Manfred Durzak's *Peter Handke und die deutsche Gegenwartsliteratur: Narziß auf Abwegen*. (Stuttgart: Kohlhammer, 1982) treat these works together as do Jerome Klinkowitz and James Knowlton's *Peter Handke and the Postmodern Transformation* (Columbia, MO: U of Missouri, 1983), abbreviated hereafter *PT*.
7   Klinkowitz and Knowlton, *PT*, 14.
8   Heinz Ludwig Arnold, "Gespräch mit Peter Handke," *Text und Kritik* 24/24a, 3rd Ed. (1975): 23.
9   See here Caroline Markolin's foreword to her study of the narrative act in *Langsamer Heimkehr*. Markolin offers a detailed study of narration in that novel, but little in the way of contextualizing the narrative structure within the larger body of Handke's works. She does state quite accurately that Handke has always been concerned with the problem of narration (Erzählen) even from with earliest works, whether it be through the rejection of it or the utilization of it. Caroline Markolin, *Eine Geschichte vom Erzählen: Peter Handkes poetische Verfahrungsweisen am Beispiel der Erzählung Langsamer Heimkehr* (Bern: Lang, 1991).
10 Peter Handke, *Ich bin ein Bewohner des Elfenbeinturms* (Frankfurt: Suhrkamp, 1972): 19–28. This volume will be abbreviated BE hereafter.
11 For a transcription of that encounter, see "Peter Handkes 'Auftritt' in Princeton und Hans Meyers Entgegnung,' in *Text und Kritik* 24, 5th Ed. (1989): 17–20.
12 "Zur Tagung der Gruppe 47 in USA," *Ich bin ein Bewohner des Elfenbeinturms* (Frankfurt: Suhrkamp, 1972): 29–34.
13 See, for example, Milo Dor's essay "Wie Peter Handke Peter Handke wurde" in: *Auf dem falschen Dampfer* or Nicholas Hern's monograph as typical of the cautious reception his early actions and writings received.
14 Handke maintains that he never intended any of his works to be novels: "[I]ch hab noch nie etwas, was ich geschrieben hab, mit reinem Gewissen als Roman bezeichnen können, das wurde dann vom Verlag ab und zu hinzugefügt, oder in Übersetzungen haben dann die ausländischen Verlage es 'Roman' genannt, aus diesen und jenen Gründen." *Aber ich lebe nur von den Zwischenräumen: Peter Handke im Gespräch mit Herbert Gamper* (Zürich: Ammann, 1987):127. Nevertheless, I will refer to Handke's prose works, which have no other genre categorization, as "novels" so as to distinguish the form of the work from the idea of "story." However one must be careful not to place too much importance on Handke's statement, I feel, for in another interview in 1993, he argues that the future of the novel, post-Joyce, Proust, and Musil, lies with short prose fiction: "Ich glaube, daß die Möglichkeit, Aufmerksamkeit für die Prosa zu erwecken, in kleinen Büchern liegt. Das bedeutet nicht, daß man nur so etwas zum Roman dieses Jahrzehnts erklären kann. Mir scheint auch, daß Prosa auf 20 oder 30 Seiten, die durchleuchtet und luftig genug ist, sehr schwer zu schreiben ist. Ich weiß aber wirklich nicht, wozu heute alle diese Romanschreiberei, die nur viel Platz einnimmt und vielleicht gerade deshalb nicht so viel Leser anzieht, wie sie Kurzprosa anziehen könnte" (Horvat 65). Two years later, however, he published *Mein Jahr in der Niemandsbucht*, an "epic" bestseller of more than 1,000 pages.
15 In a series of interviews conducted some years later, Handke acknowledges himself that he was very much a "child" or product of his time, and much of what he did and wrote was a reflection of the discourses of that time. This is a fact often overlooked by his critics, who view his changes more as opportunism than as a manifestation of current trends and ideas. See *Aber ich lebe nur von den Zwischenräumen*, 120–124.

16 "Die Literatur ist romantisch," *Ich bin ein Bewohner des Elfenbeinturms* (Frankfurt: Suhrkamp, 1972): 35–50.
17 See Klinkowitz and Knowlton's study for a discussion of Handke as a postmodern writer. They analyse his understanding and usage of language in his early works to establish the basis for what they term his "postmodern transformation."
18 See the lengthy interview with Herbert Gamper from April 10, 1986 where he discusses his development as a writer. *Aber ich lebe nur von den Zwischenräumen*, 105–168.
19 In an interview with June Schlueter in 1979 as well as in his interviews with Gamper, Handke defends his early essays as being important expressions of his beliefs at the time. He does not distance himself or retract his ideas, despite professing different views. June Schlueter, *The Plays and Novels of Peter Handke* (Pittsburgh: U of Pittsburgh P, 1981.)
20 These include his now famous *Publikumsbeschimpfung* (1966), *Weissagung* (1966), *Selbstbezichtigung* (1966), and *Hilferufe* (1967). For a discussion of these works see Hern, Firda, and Schlueter.
21 In Schlueter's interview with Handke from 1979, Handke admits that his reading of Barthes was crucial to his early poetics: "Es hat mir geholfen, auch Strukturen zu sehen, und das ist ein Vergnügen, es macht einen heiter; denn die Formlosigkeit, die sich einem bietet, ist in allen Phänomenen, jedes ist für sich und alle sind durcheinander" (166). See Schlueter, 163–170.
22 This strategy was used quite effectively in the cinema by Alexander Kluge, who around the same time, called for a new type of film which challenged the established conventions of cinematic narrative. Central to Kluge's narrative aesthetic was the idea as well that the logic and order of the film takes place in the mind of the viewer. See Chapter 3 for a lengthier discussion of this concept in the New German Cinema.
23 Half of the chapters deal in some way with *Ordnung* or *Unordnung*. In narratological terms this appears paradoxical, for narratives generally are a tool for establishing order or for imposing order on reality, yet, as an anti-narrative, the novel rejects notions of order, while attempting, thematically, to establish an order.
24 Compare this, for instance, to my discussion in the Conclusion of Uwe Timm's conception of an "Äsethetik des Alltags," the subtitle to his 1993 "Poetikvorlesungen" *Erzählen und kein Ende*, which forms the basis for the new narrative literature.
25 In fact, in one essay collected in Robbe-Grillet's groundbreaking *For a New Novel*, he sets out to address and counter the criticism and misunderstandings which had amassed with regard to this theory. See the chapter "New Novel, New Man" in Alain Robbe-Grillet, *For a New Novel: Essays on Fiction*, trans. Richard Howard. (New York: Grove Press, 1965.)
26 This interview was conducted in 1979 by which time Handke was beginning to change his views on narration. His interviews at this time reveal a redefined attitude which is important for the aesthetic and poetic program of his later works.
27 Many critics have written on this problematic in Handke's tetrology. Hugo Caviola outlines Handke's reassessment of the relationship of signifier to signified, by demonstrating Handke's appeal for a more concrete connection between script and object, whereby they become "consubstantial and saying approaches doing." Caviola terms this a "Ding—Bild—Schrift," in some ways reminiscent of many Asian languages in which the character physically represents an object, yet at this same time forms the basis for a language script. This is not unlike the phase Bloch reaches toward the end of *Angst des Tormanns* whereby language has failed him to the point that the narrator resorts to images to represent what Bloch is visualizing. Christoph Bartmann, on the other hand, examines this stage of Handke's writings in light of his quest for *Zusammenhang*, both thematically and structurally. Important here as well, Bartmann shows, is Handke's rejection of avant-garde aesthetics, which as I argue influenced his transition toward narrative; Bartmann, *Suche nach Zusammenhang: Handkes Werk als Prozeß* (Wien: Braunmüller, 1984). See also Ulrich

Wesche, "Peter Handke, Walker Percy, and the End of Modernity," *Essays in Literature* 19.2 (1992): 291–297, for a discussion on the breakdown of the relationship between language and object and Handke's attempts at bridging this gap through transubstantiation of a "Ding—Bild—Schrift."

28   They base their reading of this movement, in part, on Hans-Gerhard Winter's review essay "Von der Dokumentarliteratur zur 'neuen Subjektivität': Anmerkungen zur westdeutschen Literatur der siebziger Jahre," *Seminar* 17 (1981).

29   *Langsamer Heimkehr* is both the title of the first work as well as Handke's term for the tetrology.

30   For a discussion of the theme of redemption, see Caviola, "Ding—Bild—Schrift."

31   Loser would resurface in Handke's 1997 novel *In einer dunkeln Nacht ging ich aus meinem stillen Haus*, a novel which has many similarities to *Chinese des Schmerzes* both structurally and thematically.

32   This is especially true with regard to Holocaust narratives. Hannah Arendt, for example, has argued for the importance of storytelling as a means of representing and preserving the discourse of the Holocaust. For an in-depth discussion of this relationship, see Lisa Disch *Hannah Arendt and the Limits of Philosophy* (Ithaca : Cornell UP, 1994).

33   For the role of language in creating linguistic identity, see Herbert Gamper, "Stellvertreter des Allgemeinen? Über *Die Unvernünftigen sterben aus* und das Erzählprogram von *Die Wiederholung*," *Peter Handke: Die Langsamkeit der Welt*, ed. Gerhard Fuchs and Gerhard Melzer (Graz: Droschl, 1993): 165–200.

34   Gerhard Fuchs, "Sehnsucht nach einer heligen Welt. Zu einer 'Schreib-Bewegung' in den späteren Prosatexten Peter Handkes." In: *Peter Handke: Die Langsamkeit der Welt*, 115–136.

35   This idea is similar to Wenders's belief in the redemptive power of stories which will be discussed in Chapter 4. The connection, though, is here all the more interesting, as Wenders approached Handke to write the script for *Der Himmel über Berlin*, which deals quite extensively with the importance of storytelling, immediately after he had finished writing *Die Wiederholung*. Initially Handke declined, saying "Ich bin völlig erschöpft, ich habe keine Worte mehr in mir, alles, was ich hatte, habe ich zu Papier gebracht." But then, as Wenders recalls, added: "Vielleicht, wenn du herkommst und mir diese Geschichte [von dem Film] erzählst, kann ich dir helfen und einige Dialoge schreiben." Not surprisingly, the dialogues that Handke subsequently wrote dealt primarily with language and storytelling. See Wenders, "Le souffle de l'Ange," *Die Logik der Bilder* (Frankfurt: Verlag der Autoren, 1988) 133–138.

36   *Noch einmal vom Neunten Land: Peter Handke im Gespräch mit Joze Horvat.* (Klagenfurt: Wieser, 1993): 49. In June Schlueter's interview from 1979, he also terms *Langsamer Heimkehr* an "epische[s] Gedicht" (170).

37   Even stylistically, there are similarities. The opening lines of the Odyssey read: "Muse! Erzähl' mir vom wendigen Mann, der die heilige Feste Trojas zerstörten! . . . Greif in die Fülle, Göttin, Tochter des Zeus, auch uns davon zu erzählen!" *Odysee und Homerischen Hymen* trans. Anton Weiher (München: DTV/Artemis, 1990) 5. Not only is this plea to the storytelling Muse reminiscent of Handke's own praise to the Muse of narration, but it also closely resembles the passage he wrote for the figure of Homer in Wenders's *Himmel über Berlin*: "Erzähle, Muse, vom Erzähler, dem an den Weltrand verschlagenen kindlichen Uralten und mache an ihn kenntlich den Jedermann." Wenders and Handke, *Der Himmel über Berlin: Ein Filmbuch* (Frankfurt: Suhrkamp, 1987) 30.

38   Horkheimer and Adorno. *Dialectic of Enlightenment.* trans. John Cumming (New York: Continuum, 1972) 43–44. They argue as well, that one of the fundamental characteristics of Odysseus (and thus the Homeric protagonist) is that he "loses himself in order to find himself" (48), a tenet particular to Handke's protagonists as well. Implied here is the idea that the process of finding one's self results in self preservation and thus self-understanding, a theme central to all of Handke's works.

39 Interestingly, Habermas criticizes Handke directly for this very kind of thinking and for wanting to return to poetry a prophetic quality. See Iain Macdonald's discussion of this debate as well as Handke's mythic and utopian leanings in "Utopia and the Possibility of Place: Peter Handke and the Ambitions of a Storyteller," *Angelaki* 3.1 (1998): 137–144.

40 There have been many recent studies of the utopian in Handke's works, especially in dealing with his prose of the 1990s. See, among others, Thomas Kniesche, "Utopie und Schreiben zu Zeiten der Postmoderne: Peter Handke's 'Versuche,'" in: Rolf Jucker, ed. *Zeitgenössiche Utopieentwürfe in Literatur und Gesellschaft* (Amsterdam: Rodopi, 1997): 313–336 and Susanne Niemuth-Engelmann, "'Bleistift, Brücke nach Hause!' Alltag und Utopie in Peter Handkes Aufzeichnungssammlungen," in: *Alltag und Aufzeichnung. Untersuchungen zu Canetti, Bender, Handke und Schnurre* (Würzburg: Königshausen & Neumann, 1998): 89–104. To this end, many critics have cited his utopian thinking and tendency toward the mythic as having obscured his view of reality in his essays on Yugoslavia. The sharpest criticisms have been collected in *Die Angst des Dichters vor der Wirklichkeit: 16 Antworten auf Peter Handkes Winterreise nach Serbien*, ed. Tilman Zülch (Göttingen: Steidl, 1996).

41 Wenders, "Le souffle de l'Ange," *Die Logik der Bilder* (Frankfurt: Verlag der Autoren, 1988) 137. See Chapter 4 for a further discussion of the importance of Homer in the film.

42 "'Gelassen wär ich gern.' Ein Gespräch mit Peter Handke." *Spiegel* 49 (1994): 170.

43 This is also the underlying assumption of the polemic surrounding his publications on the crisis in the Balkans. Handke's argument is that the press had done an injustice to Serbia by unfairly portraying them as an aggressor nation, when in fact, they had been victimized by historical events. Further, he asserts an ability to posit an alternative "truth" by virtue of his first-hand experience, his *Winterreise* to Serbia, as he has titled the essays. What he is suggesting is a belief in the vailidity of observation and experience to impart truth to narration, a belief which his critics feel is myopic and distorted. See "Dichters Winterreise" *Spiegel* 5 (Feb. 1996): 190–193.

44 Handke, *Langsam im Schatten* (Frankfurt: Suhrkamp, 1992) 157. Handke's two essays dealing with John Berger and issues of narration are "Kleiner Versuch über den Dritten" (1988) and "Wir-Erzähler und Ich-Erzähler: Zu John Berger" (1991) both of which are collected in this volume.

45 Handke uses an interesting narrative technique of projecting himself into the writer yet distancing himself through the use of a third-person narrator. The narrator is clearly the protagonist and it is fairly evident that the protagonist is Handke, who is describing his action in the third person as a means of transforming his thoughts into story.

46 Gunther Pakendorf, "Writing about Writing: Peter Handke's Nachmittag eines Schriftstellers," *Modern Austrian Literature* 23.3/4 (1990): 77–86. Pakendorf cites in particular Jakobson's article "Der Doppelcharakter der Sprache. Die Polarität zwischen Metaphorik und Metonymik," in Jens Ihwe, ed. *Literaturwissenschaft und Linguistik. Ergebnisse und Perspektiven*, Band I (Frankfurt: Athenäum, 1972): 323–333.

47 See note 1.

48 Samuel Moser makes an important distinction here between the Platonic and Socratic forms of dialogue: "Nicht platonische Dialoge sind es, wo 'der fragende Sokrates insgeheim mehr von dem Problem wußte als der, zumindest zu Beginn, vom Vorurteils-Wissen geschwellte Antwortverkündler,' wie es im Versuch über die Jukebox (67) heißt. Aber es sind sokratische Dialoge, in denen vieles am Schluß ungesagt bleibt, und man aufsteht, um hinauszugehen" (142). The distinction is important for it reinforces Handke's understanding of narrative as a dynamic between teller and audience in which what is left unsaid is as important as what is said. See Samuel Moser, "Das Glück des Erzählens ist das Erzählen des Glücks: Peter Handke's Versuche." *Peter Handke: Die Langsamkeit der Welt*. ed. Gerhard Fuchs and Gerhard Melzer (Graz: Droschl, 1993): 137–154.

49 Moser argues further that these essays are not "Versuche über die Möglichkeit des Sprechens, sondern über die Möglichkeit des Schweigens. Sie sind Versuche über das Sein des Nichts" (137). The themes of emptiness and nothingness are ones that are important issues in Handke's writings, but are expressed as manifestations of, what Russel Berman terms, "a capacity that enables both sociability and history," for emptiness and nothingness exhibit themselves in his works as the abscence of boundaries and limits, a condition which fosters thought and expressibility. See Berman, "Refusal or Denial and the Sky of Europe: Literary Postmodernism in Peter Handke's Across." *Cultural Studies of Modern Germany: History, Representation and Nationhood*. (Madison: U of Wisconsin, 1993) 159.

50 Music has always played a major role in Handke's life and works, and the jukebox has served in his works as a symbol for both a politically and intellectually vital time period (the 1960s) as well as for American pop-culture. At one point in the essay, he even toys with the idea of using the song as a form for the essay: by creating a montage or conglomeration of scenes and feelings, the essay would become like a song, like a ballad of the jukebox, with the rhythms of thought flowing like a song.

51 Note here the similarities to the speech Handke wrote for the figure Homer in Wenders's *Himmel über Berlin*. See Chapter 4 and my discussion of the epics of peace.

Chapter 3 Notes

1 Wenders filmed two of Handke's short fictional works, *Die Angst des Tormanns beim Elfmeter* (1971) and *Falsche Bewegung* (1975). In addition, they collaborated on two other films, one of Wenders's early shorts *3 amerikanische LP's* (1969) and *Der Himmel über Berlin* (1986). Handke has directed three films on his own: *Chronik der laufenden Ereignisse* (1970), *Die linkshändige Frau* (1977) and *Die Abwesenheit* (1992).

2 From the beginning of film history many established writers have written screenplays and collaborated on film projects, including Gerhart Hauptmann, Hugo von Hofmannsthal, Else Lasker-Schuler, and Kurt Pinthus. For a representative sampling of early collaborative efforts, see *Das Kinobuch: Kinodramen von Bermann, Hasenclever, Langer, Lasker-Schuler, Keller, Asenijeff, Brod, Pinthus, Jolowicz, Ehrenstein, Pick, Rubiner, Zech, Hollriegel, Lautensack* (Leipzig: K. Wolff, 1914).

3 Joachim Paech, *Literatur und Film* (Stuttgart: Metzler, 1988).

4 Frank Kermode, *The Art of Telling: Essays on Fiction* (Cambridge, MA: Harvard UP, 1983): 10.

5 See Chapter 1 and the discussion of the novella's function in reifying the story.

6 See especially Siegfired Kracauer's discussion of this film in *From Caligari to Hitler*, 61–76.

7 Alexander Kluge, in an essay on the relationship between word and film, argues in fact that the cinema has modeled itself on the genre of the novella and thus become hampered from developing its epic possibilities. Kluge, "Word and Film," trans. Miriam Hansen *October* 46 (Fall, 1988): 85. One of the subtexts in Wenders's and Handke's *Himmer über Berlin* is the call for a new epic literature and conversely cinema, which, I argue later, Wenders attempts in the sequel to that film, *Far Away, So Close!* See Chapter 4.

8 See especially David Bordwell *Narration and the Fiction Film* (Madison: U of Wisconsin P, 1985) for an in-depth discussion of narration and the dominant cinema.

9 See Ruttmann, *Art and the Cinema*, in Walter Schobert, *Der deutsche avant-garde Film der 20er Jahre* (München: Goethe-Institut, 1989): 6–7.

10 Reprinted in Schobert, 7.

11 Ibid.

12 See my discussion in the Conclusion on neonarrative film at the end of the twentieth century as a model for reconciling commercial demands with the aesthetic contructs of the Art Film.

13 The term *Autorenfilm* comes from the French *auteur cinema* and means more exactly, "author's film," implying a direct correlation between the film as text and a singular author. Although there is no literal translation for either of these terms in English, the term "Art Film" in American film criticism has come to represent much of what is implied in the two terms. Ira Konigsberg defines the Art Film as a film "with serious artistic intentions as distinct from the commercial films made in Hollywood." Further, he notes, the term came into usage in the 1950s "largely to describe foreign films made with smaller budgets but with great originality in technique and greater emphasis on social and psychological reality than Hollywood's traditional and escapist products" Konigsberg, *The Complete Film Dictionary* (New York: Meridian, 1987): 18. The term is a useful one as it is often used in American (and British) film criticism and reflects the idea that European film is somehow more artistic and thus more meaningful and demanding, aspects often associated with the avant-garde as well as with non-narrative art forms in general.

14 See especially Jan Berg, ed., *Am Ende der Rolle: Diskussion über den Autorenfilm* (Marburg: Schüren, 1993) for a roundtable discussion on the subject.

15 Among the best monographs on Wenders and his career are those by Norbert Grob, Reinhold Rauh and Kolker and Beicken. All of these works examine the development of Wenders's career and offer insight and analysis of his individual films.

16 The earliest film exhibitions were often in conjunction with variety shows and the Kintopp, a sort of carnivalesque exhibition. These films were generally short, entertaining clips which demonstrated little or no narrative. For a good history of the early cinema shows, see Uta Berg-Ganschow and Wolfgang Jacobsen, eds. *Film, Stadt, Kino, Berlin* (Berlin: Argon, 1987).

17 Theodor Adorno, *Aesthetic Theory*. trans. C. Lenhardt (London: Routledge): 222; quoted in Kaes, *From Hitler to Heimat*, 116.

18 Thomas Kuchenbuch, *Bild und Erzählung: Geschichte in Bildern. Vom frühen Comic Strip zum Fernsehfeature* (Münster: MAkS, 1992).

19 Kuchenbuch traces the origins of the Bilderbücher from Comenius and to the nineteenth-century *orbis pictus*, which served a certain pedagogic function. Hoffmann's *Struwwelpeter* as well as Rodolphe Toepffer's *1847 Genfer Novellen* had a major impact on the development of picture narratives. Philosophically, Kuchenbuch demonstrates the influence of the development of semiology on the interconnection between image and narrative, beginning with Goethe's and Schiller's concerns with the aesthetic of "Visualismus" and continuing through the Romantic conception of "Anschaulichkeit." His thesis is that the idea of images telling stories was well ingrained in the minds of the German public by the turn of the century, thus the concept of narratives in silent film was not unfamiliar. See especially Section II of his study, "Von der Lust und Not, in Bildern zu erzählen," 65–114.

20 As David Bordwell and Kristen Thompson have shown, in the early years of the cinema, Hollywood films were more market driven than European films due primarily to the privatization of American studios which necessitated this sensitivity. Because many European film industries were consolidated by the government, there existed an ideology of furthering national culture, which allowed a greater degree of artistic freedom and less concern, in some cases, with commercial success. *Film as Art: An Introduction* (Reading, MA: Addison-Wesley, 1979): 293–298. This difference would play a major role in the postwar era as well, when Germany sought once again to develop a national cinema and thus provided federal financing for the film industry. This system of financing enabled the development and growth of the Autorenfilm. See Elsaesser's chapter "Film Industry-Film Subsidy," in *New German Cinema: a History*, (New Brunswick, NJ: Rutgers, 1989): 8–35.

21 Among the best known examples are the films of Oskar Fischinger, Hans Richter, and Viking Eggeling. See Walter Schobert, *Der deutsche avant-garde Film der 20er Jahre* (München:

Goethe-Institut, 1989) and Ingo Petzke, ed. *Das Experimentalfilm-Handbuch* (Frankfurt: Deutsches Filmmuseum, 1989).

22 For a more in depth discussion of the dominant cinema and narration, see David Bordwell, *Narration and the Fiction Film* (Madison: U of Wisconsin P, 1985), Bordwell, Kristin Thompson and Janet Staiger, *The Classical Hollywood Cinema: Film Style and Mode of Production to 1960* (New York: Columbia UP, 1985) and John Fell, *Film and the Narrative Tradition* (Norman: U of Oklahoma P, 1974).

23 Peter Wollen, "Godard and the Counter Cinema: *Vent d'Est*," *Readings and Writings: Semiotic Counter-Strategies* (London: Verso, 1982): 79–91.

24 See Christian Metz, *Language and cinema*. Trans. Donna Jean Umiker-Sebeok (The Hague: Mouton, 1974) for his discussion of semiotics in narrative film.

25 Kracauer, *From Caligari to Hitler*, 3–11.

26 The most famous example being the final scene in *L'Eclisse* (*The Eclipse*, 1962), in which the camera focuses on Monica Vitti's silent face for some 10 minutes. The image of her face is left to "tell" the rest of the story, albeit a fragmentary one. Wenders, too, made use of this same technique in many of his films, no doubt as influenced by Antonioni.

27 For an in-depth study of the state of the German film industry in the 1950s and 60s, see Heide Fehrenbach, *Cinema in Democratizing Germany : Reconstructing National Identity after Hitler* (Chapel Hill: U of North Carolina P, 1995) as well as the first chapter to Thomas Elsaesser's *New German Cinema: a History* (New Brunswick, NJ: Rutgers, 1989); for a discussion of the immediate postwar period, see Ralph Willet, *The Americanization of Germany, 1945–1949* (London: Routledge, 1989): 28–44.

28 See Truffaut, *Hitchcock*, trans. Helen Scott (New York: Simon and Schuster, 1984); Fassbinder, *The Anarchy of the Imagination* Michael Töteberg and Leo Lensing, eds. (Baltimore: Johns Hopkins, 1992); Wenders, *Emotion Pictures* (Frankfurt: Verlag der Autoren, 1986).

29 In Kluge's essay "Was wollen die 'Oberhausener'?," he states that there is a close connection between the Oberhausener and the *Gruppe 47*: "Wir haben zahlreiche Gespräche mit Mitgliedern der *Gruppe 47* geführt und dabei festgestellt, daß das Interesse am Film bei den in anderen Bereichen Tätigen ganz außerordentlich ist" in: Hans Helmut Prinzler and Eric Rentschler, eds. *Augenzeugen: 100 Texte deutscher Filmemacher* (Frankfurt: Verlag der Autoren, 1988): 47. Moreover, the group also sought contact with the Kölnerschule, the avant-garde music movement led by Karlheinz Stockhausen.

30 Wenders belonged to the first class of the newly created Hochschule für Film und Fernsehen, a film school created by the government to promote a national cinema. Ironically, Fassbinder was rejected based on insufficient knowledge of film history.

31 See especially Thomas Elsaesser's overview of postmodernism and the New German cinema: "American Graffiti und Neuer Deutscher Film: Filmemacher zwischen Avantgarde und Postmoderne" in *Postmoderne: Zeichen eines kulturellen Wandels*, Andreas Huyssen and Klaus R. Scherpe, eds. (Hamburg: Rowohlt, 1986): 302–328.

32 There have been many studies of the French cinema and the *nouvelle vague* too numerous to name. However, Alan Williams' *Republic of Images: A History of French Filmmaking* (Boston: Harvard UP, 1992) and Roy Armes, *French Cinema* (London: Oxford, 1985) both provide very good overviews. I am also indebted to Anne Marie Freybourg's comparison of the *Autorenkino* of Godard and Fassbinder for its discussion of the similarities between the French and German conceptions of the *Autorenkino*: Freybourg, "Film und Autor: Eine Analyse des Autorenkinos von Jean-Luc Godard und Rainer Werner Fassbinder," diss. U Hamburg, 1993.

33 See Freybourg, 52–55.

34 Truffaut once stated: "I don't see how you can define the New Wave except by age," implying that the generational conflict was central to the development of the new cinema. Quoted

in Sorlin, 142. Similarly, Norbert Grob, subtitles his chapter on the German film history of the 1960s "Abschied von den Eltern." *Geschichte des deutschen Films*, Wolfgang Jakobsen, Anton Kaes, and Hans Helmut Prinzler, eds. (Stuttgart: Metzler, 1993): 211–248.

35 Reprinted in Prinzler and Rentschler, *Augenzeugen*, 29.
36 Most German film histories treat the period after 1962 in great length. For a more specific discussion of the ramifications of the Oberhausener Manifest, though, see Krischan Koch, *Die Bedeutung des "Oberhausener Manifestes" für die Filmentwicklung in der Bundesrepublik Deutschland* (Frankfurt: Peter Lang, 1985).
37 Especially problematic and controversial was his representation of women and the use of (an often male) voice-over narration as an authorial voice. On this debate, see the special issue of *New German Critique*, No. 59 (Winter, 1999) and especially Helke Sander's essay.
38 Most historians and critics distinguish between the Young German cinema of the 1960s, that is the generation of the signers of the Oberhausener Manifest, and the New German Cinema, the next generation which included directors like Herzog, Fassbinder, Schlöndorff and Wenders. While both groups shared similar views, international success and recognition came to the second wave of filmmakers. See Elsaesser's *New German Cinema* as well as *Geschichte des deutschen Films*, eds. Jakobsen, Kaes, and Prinzler, for detailed discussions of these movements.
39 Quoted in Rainer Lewandowski, *Alexander Kluge* (Munich: C.H. Beck, 1980): 51–52.
40 Kaes has, in fact, compared him to Robert Musil and has speculated that Kluge's rejection of narrative follows the philosophical leanings of Jean-François Lyotard. See *From Hitler to Heimat*, 108.
41 For a discussion of the struggles of the Young German Cinema, see especially Norbert Grob's "Abschied von den Eltern," in: *Geschichte des deutschen Films*, 211–248.
42 Silbermann, "Beyond Spectacle: Alexander Kluge's Artists under the Big Top: perplexed," *German Cinema: Texts in Context* (Detroit: Wayne State UP, 1995): 192.
43 On this topic, see especially Kaes *From Hitler to Heimat*, in which he takes up these issues and explores the degree to which public history and private stories intermingle. With regard to Kluge, Kaes shows that Kluge is not concerned with history as a backdrop to private stories, rather aims to shed light both on the past and the present (108).
44 Grob, "Film der sechziger Jahre: Abschied von den Eltern," *Geschichte des deutschen Films*, ed. Jakobson, et. al., 229.
45 Also of importance in the development of the New German Cinema were many female directors who also played an active role, but had to struggle with other factors and with a different set of circumstances. See Julia Knight, *Women and the New German Cinema* (New York: Verso, 1992).
46 Elsaesser, "American Graffiti und Neuer Deutscher Film" in Huyssen and Scherpe, 302–328.
47 This section is based largely on my article "From Aesthetics to Commercialism: Narration and the New German Comedy," *Seminar* 33.4 (1997): 356–373.
48 Susan Sontag, "The Decay of Cinema," *New York Times Magazine* 25 Feb. 1996: 60–61.
49 Quoted from Rentschler, "Film der achtziger Jahre: Endzeitspiele und Zeitgeistszenerien," *Geschichte des deutschen Films*, 288.
50 "Wenders wants curbs on U.S. pix in Europe," *Variety* (18 May, 1992): 5.
51 Elsaesser has made this same point in his analysis of postmodernism and the New German Cinema, arguing that the fact that the films of the NGC specifically rejected the traditional form of a begininng, middle and an end reflected the fact that the American Hollywood film was an important point of reference for these filmmakers and that by consciously rejecting this structure, they were purposefully rejecting the dominant cinema and consequently, the hegemony of American culture. See "American Graffitti und Neuer Deutscher Film," in Huyssen and Scherpe, 318.

52 "New Pix tickle Teutons," *Variety* 17 July, 1995: 34–35. Dörrie's *Keiner liebt mich* and von Garnier's *Abgeschminkt* have similarly achieved both commercial and critical success and have found U.S. distributors, something unusual for German films.
53 For a analysis of the New German Comedy from a production and publicist view point, see the essays collected in *Der bewegte Film: Aufbruch zu den neuen deutschen Erfolgen*, Heike Amend and Michael Bütow, eds. (Berlin: Vistas, 1997).
54 "Up close with Wim Wenders," *Everybody's News* (Cincinnati, OH) 11 Feb. 1994:10–11. Following a set of rules is also a distinguishing characteristic of the narrative cinema. Part of Wenders's transformation to traditional narrative cinema had to do with his acceptance of rules and structuring principles. See Chapter 4 for a lengthy discussion of this shift.
55 Elsaesser makes this distinction based on the tendency of many critics to divide the thematics of the Autorenfilm into two types (*New German Cinema* 52–56). He states, however, that as a whole, the films of the 1970s and 1980s defy categorization. In either case, they nonetheless developed a reputation as being difficult or intellectually challenging, something which did not increase their commercial viability.
56 This is especially true of Katja Riemann, Veronica Ferres, and Til Schweiger, who have individually or collectively participated in most of the new comedies. Moreover, Sönke Wortmann, Detlev Buck, and Doris Dörrie have achieved a certain degree of name recognition as directors. Stars and known directors are crucial for establishing a popular cinema. While the New German Cinema also had a set of regular actors and directors, the themes and structuring principles of the films detracted from it ever achieving the same degree of popularity.
57 "'Gepäck abgeworfen': Interview mit Regisseur Hark Bohm über die neue deutsche Lachlust," *Spiegel*, 19 Feb. 1996: 182.
58 "Ich habe nichts gegen Männer" *Frankfurter Rundschau*, 14 Sept. 1998, on-line.
59 These are elements that are central over all to the new literary and cinematic narratives which I discuss in the Conclusion.
60 Christiane Peitz, "Das Kino, eine Baustelle," *Die Zeit*, 5 April, 1996: 15.

Chapter 4 Notes

1 This rather widely accepted view can be seen in the number of monographs on Wenders, which begin with this premise. Among the more recent books on Wenders are Reinhold Rauh's *Wim Wenders und seine Filme* (München: Heyne, 1990), Norbert Grob's *Wenders* (Berlin: Edition Filme, 1991), Robert Kolker and Peter Beicken's *The Films of Wim Wenders* (New York: Cambridge, 1993) and the essay collection *The Cinema of Wim Wenders: Image, Narrative, and the Postmodern Condition*, edited by Roger F. Cook and Gerd Gemünden (Detroit: Wayne State UP, 1997). Works dealing with postwar German cinema also treat Wenders and there are numerous articles on Wenders and his films. Each of the aforementioned works has an excellent bibliography.
2 In his interview with Wenders, Gerd Gemünden confronts Wenders specifically on this issue pointing out that the moral aspect of his films in the mid-1990s (*Wings of Desire* and *Far Away, So Close!*, specifically, but the point pertains to *The End of Violence* as well) has shifted from the level of form to that of content. Moreover, he cites critics who have faulted Wenders for the lack of subtlety in those films. Wenders responds: "The images can no longer carry the message. That's why I wanted to be more specific with *Far Away, So Close!* than with *Wings of Desire*. If I take the liberty to use angels a second time and to continue their story, then I have to say something that too often remains unsaid." He goes on to say that films have refrained from "saying" anything in the previous decade and that he thus feels an obligation to make moral statements in his films. Cook and Gemünden, 80.

3   See Chapter 1 for a discussion of Benjamin's conception of storytelling as a means of sharing communal experience and wisdom.
4   The connection between wisdom and childhood innocence will be explored later in this chapter with regard to the film as a whole and especially to Handke's *Lied vom Kindsein*, the poem which serves as a leitmotif for the film.
5   Grob, "'Life Sneaks out of Stories': *Until the End of the World*," in Cook and Gemünden, 191–192.
6   References to Wenders's essay collections will be abbreviated as follows: *Emotion Pictures*: *EP*; *Die Logik der Bilder*: *LB*; and *The Act of Seeing*: *AS*.
7   Cinema, like the theater, is one of the few remaining art forms which has maintained its ability to address a group audience. Benjamin argued that the novel led, in part, to the demise of the oral tradition by isolating both the reader and the writer. Video has done the same to cinema; with the advent of the VCR, the viewer has become isolated and can watch films without the dynamic of an audience. Although Wenders has not addressed this aspect of video technology directly, he has expressed his dismay with video as a technology in numerous interviews as well as in his essay film, *Notebook on Cities and Clothes*, and in his film *Lisbon Story*, which, even more so than the former, praises the aesthetic nature of film and condemns the isolation of the filmmaker as well as the viewer.
8   Today, he quite readily recognizes this change. In an interview in *Die Zeit* about his love of music, he recounts his decision early on to give up music in favor of filmmaking. When asked what he would have missed most had he chosen music instead, Wenders responds "das Geschichtenerzählen." Before the mid-1980s, he would certainly have given a quite different answer. In the same interview, he confesses his early preference for music as a structuring principle, as opposed to story: "Ich habe oft gedacht, es muss eigentlich reichen, wenn man eine Situation an die andere hängt und daraus ein Weg entsteht, der am Schluss auch so etwas wie eine Geschichte ist. Ich habe verhältnismäßig spät damit angefangen, an Geschichten zu glauben. Erst mit *Paris, Texas* ist mir stringentes Erzählen gelungen." "Ständiger Wohnsitz: Rock 'n' Roll," *Die Zeit*, 7 Dec. 2000.
9   See Balázs' *Theory of the Film: Character and Growth of a New Art*, Edith Bone, trans. (New York: Dover, 1970) as well as Kracauer's *Theory of Film: The Redemption of Physical Reality* (New York: Oxford, 1960).
10 In Grob's monograph of Wenders, a large section is devoted to the theoretical basis behind Wenders's "filmischen Blick." Grob sights Kracauer's conception of cinematic realism as central to understanding Wenders, but also André Bazin, who as part of a later realist movement, saw in film the creation of an illusion of reality. As for the ability of the viewer to absorb this illusion and create his/her own reality, Grob cites the semiotic theories of Edgar Morin and Christian Metz, who suggest that this illusion of reality then actually becomes the reality of the viewer by creating the experience of reality. Thus the chain comes full circle.
11 This characterization interestingly recalls Walter Ruttmann's conception of avant-garde and absolute filmmaking in the 1920s: "Malerei mit der Zeit." See his essay of the same name in Walter Schobert, *The German Avant-Garde Film of the 1920s*, 102–105.
12 See Chapter 1 for a discussion of both Benjamin's and Price's understanding of the importance of stories for society and humans.
13 This idea is an extenuation of Nietzsche's argument in *Geburt der Tragödie* that the world as we know it is a false, cruel, contradictory world without meaning, and thus lies are necessary in order to conquer reality and to enable us to live. Handke deals with many of the same issues in *Über die Dörfer*, a dramatic poem which, coincidentally, Wenders directed at the Salzburg Festival in 1982. For a lengthy discussion on the Nietzschean elements in Handke's works see *Aber ich lebe nur von den Zwischenräumen: Ein Gespräch, geführt von Herbert Gamper* (Zürich: Ammann, 1987): 198–209.

14 For a lengthier discussion, see Anton Kaes' reading of *Die Patriotin* and his discussion of Kluge's constructivist method in *From Hitler to Heimat*, 113–121.
15 Roger Cook, "Angels, Fiction, and History in Berlin," in Cook and Gemünden, 163–190.
16 In addition to his collaborations with Handke (*Die Angst des Tormanns beim Elfmeter*, *Falsche Bewegung*, and *Himmel über Berlin*), he has worked with Tankred Dorst on *The Scarlet Letter* and Sam Shepard on *Paris, Texas*.
17 Kluge was a practicing lawyer and student of Adorno and thus combined an unusual array of philosophy and sharp, political commentary and critique in his films. Fassbinder was an established playwright and came to cinema via the theater. Only Herzog shares the same visual, aesthetic approach as Wenders, but on a different, fantastical level, as opposed to Wenders roots in a realist tradition.
18 In 1972 he did adapt another literary work, *The Scarlet Letter* from a screenplay by Tankred Dorst. Wenders has since distanced himself from this film and considers it a failure, primarily due to the conditions under which he was forced to work. Nevertheless, it represents an important caesura within his body of work, the second coming after Hammett, a film which represented similarly suffocating production conditions. See "I wish my life was a nonstop movie show . . . " and "Le souffle de l'Ange" in *Die Logik der Bilder* for Wenders own commentary on these two films.
19 In fact the title of one interview in *The Act of Seeing* expresses his sentiments: "Ein Drehbuch zu schreiben, das ist die Hölle" (235–245).
20 Schlöndorff has maintained in numerous essays as well as in his diaries that he sees himself as a "German" filmmaker and thus has an affinity to filming works of German literature in the hopes of (re)creating a national cinema. See Schlöndorff, "*Die Blechtrommel*": *Tagebuch einer Verfilmung*, (Darmstadt: Luchterhand, 1979): 37, as well as a 1995 interview, "Ich dachte, das mache ich im Schlaf," *Die Zeit*, 8 Sept. 1995: 13–14.
21 Once again Werner Herzog appears to be a notable exception. However, recent reevaluations of his films, especially under the rubric of neocolonialist studies, suggest that Herzog's films are perhaps more contemporary and political then seen at the time. See, for example, articles by John Davidson and Lutz Koepnick in the special issue, "German Film History" of *New German Critique*, 60 (Fall 1993).
22 See Richard McCormick's *Politics of the Self*, for a discussion of the most notable example of this style of filmmaking, Wenders's *Falsche Bewegung*.
23 Almost every interview collected in *The Act of Seeing* deals, at least overtly, with stories and storytelling. In more recent interviews his discussion of storytelling and the need for stories has become even more impassioned. See especially "Reden über Deutschland" in *Act of Seeing*, 187–200.
24 Berys Gaut's review article "Making Sense of Films: Neoformalism and its Limits," *Forum for Modern Language Studies* 30.1 (1995): 8–23, summarizes the basic ideas that David Bordwell and Kristin Thompson, two of the leading exponents of this theory, have developed in a series of books and articles. Although Gaut is critical of their constructivist ideas, the article presents a good introduction and overview of the basic tenets.
25 See for example the interviews "Das Wahrnehmen einer Bewegung" and "Der Zeit einen Sprung voraus sein" in *The Act of Seeing*, in which Wenders talks about the affinity he feels toward painting.
26 For a lengthier discussion of Wenders's biography, see Kathe Geist's and Reinhold Rauh's monographs.
27 In his speech from 1991 entitled "Reden über Deutschland," Wenders mentions that his favorite scene in film history is from *Fahrenheit 451* (*AS* 197). In another speech from 1988, "Nicht allein in einem großen Haus," he lists "einige der großen europäischen Künstler," in which he includes both Truffaut and Godard (*AS* 181).
28 Kathe Geist, *The Cinema of Wim Wenders; from Paris, France to "Paris, Texas*," 5.

29 Kolker and Beicken, for instance, argue that while Wenders would often quote Godard in his films, "his sympathies are finally not with him" (22). The difference, they maintain, is that Wenders was, until his America experience in the late-1970s with Hammett, infatuated with America, whereas Godard was critical of America and especially American capitalism. While this is true, Wenders nonetheless was stylistically influenced by not only Godard, but the other members of the *nouvelle vague*, especially Truffaut, Chabrol, and Rohmer.
30 Quoted in Geist, 5. Wenders made this statement in 1982.
31 Some thirty years later, Wenders turned again to filming music, first in video clips for U2, then in his documentaries on Cuban music, *Buena Vista Social Club* and on the German rock band BAP.
32 Another important similarity is the love of classic American cinema. Wenders shared the same passion for Hollywood that the young French directors did, something that separated Wenders from his German colleagues, however. Wenders's many references and homages to Hollywood cinema—another hallmark of the *nouvelle vague*—can be seen in almost every film, from the quick shots of cinemas showing John Ford films in *Tormann* and *State of Things*, to his tribute to Nicholas Ray in *Nick's Film*.
33 Many of these essays are collected in *Emotion Pictures*, including his review of Thome's *Rote Sonne*, 54–55.
34 Wenders even gives this as the subtitle of the essay: "Nashville: Ein Film, bei dem man Hören und Sehen lernen kann." *Emotion Pictures*, 102–112.
35 Geist, Rauh, Grob, and Kolker and Beicken all view this film as part of a trilogy of films beginning with *Alice in den Städten*, 1974, and *Falsche Bewegung*, 1975, which uses the Bildungsroman as its basic structuring principle. These films have been discussed in great detail, perhaps more than any other of Wenders's films, save *Himmel über Berlin*, in the many monographs on Wenders. Thus I will not undertake a lengthy analysis here, but am especially indebted to Rauh and Grob and their reading of these films. For further discussion, see Dawson, Grob and Rauh (in German) and Geist and Kolker and Beicken (in English). Beginning with *The State of Things* and *Paris, Texas*, Wenders's career takes a new turn in which he begins reevaluating his methodology and approach to filmmaking. This is not to say, however, that the image becomes devalued; his visual acuity and the purity of the image continue to be hallmarks of all of his films.
36 For an analysis of Wenders's Hollywood experience, see both Rauh and Geist. Wenders himself has written about his experiences and has expressed his frustration in various interviews collected in both *Logik der Bilder* and *Act of Seeing*.
37 Both Godard and Truffaut had made films previously about the process of filmmaking, (*Le mépris*, 1964 and *La nuit américaine*, 1973, respectively). Moreover, the film within a film motif was popular with young directors in Europe in the 1960s because of its self-reflective nature, an aspect important for the *nouvelle vague* as well as for the students of the HFF. See Geist's discussion of the early HFF theories, 9–17.
38 The similarities between Wenders and Munro are quite obvious. Both had been living and working in the U.S. and both had made ten feature films. Moreover, in one scene, we see a list of Munro's films: the first was entitled *Schauplätze* (the title of Wenders's first short) and the second *Der lange Brief* (a play on Handke's novel *Der kurze Brief zum langen Abschied*). Wenders's second film was, of course, an adaptation of another Handke novel, *Die Angst des Tormanns beim Elfmeter*. Rauh makes this connection as well (85). Murnau had, like Munro, gone to Hollywood, but died tragically in a car accident. At one point in the film, Munro also recites a line attributed to Murnau: "I'm at home nowhere, in no house, in no country."
39 Wim Wenders, *The State of Things*. Videorecording. Pacific Arts, 1987. All following quotes are from the videocassette release.
40 In an interview from this time, Wenders recognizes this distinction. Furthermore, he admits that making a film with the title "Directed by Wim Wenders" instead of "Ein Film von Wim

Wenders" was also a lifelong dream, a reference to the distinction between the role of the European and the American director. When asked what the fundamental difference between the American and European cinema is, he answers, not surprisingly, "Die Einstellung zum Drehbuch!" Wim Wenders, Interview: New York, May 1982. (unpublished; in archives of the Stiftung Deutsche Kinemathek, Berlin used by permission).

41 In the original English version of this scene, Munro makes this speech in a monotone voice while Gordon is loudly singing a song entitled "Hollywood, Hollywood," which extols the virtues and hypocrisies of the town. In the German version, Munro's speech is slightly different. Rauh transcribes it as follows: "Ich habe zehn Filme gemacht. Und immer die gleiche Geschichte erzählt. Am Anfang war es ganz leicht. Da ging's von Einstellung zu Einstellung. Aber jetzt habe ich Angst am Abend vorher. Jetzt weiß ich, wie das Erzählen geht—und unweigerlich läuft den Geschichten das Leben aus und sie sind tot. Geschichten haben einfach zu viel Regeln, Mechanismen. Tod, das ist die große Geschichte. Davon handeln sie alle. Todesboten" (83). Wenders often spoke in interviews around this period of the rules associated with screenplays and his preference for the freedom of improvisation, echoing his sentiments that stories kill life and thus reality. See especially "Unmögliche Geschichten" in *Logik der Bilder* (68–77) for a discussion of the problems of screenplays.

42 In 1995, Wenders would resurrect Munro for his second Portuguese film, *Lisbon Story*, a film which would continue the ideas developed and problematized in *State of Things*. *Lisbon Story* also incorporates a figure, Philip Winter, from *Until the End of the World*, thus acknowledging the metafictional nature of his own films.

43 Shawn Levy, "*Until the End of the World*. Wim Wenders's Dance Around the Planet," *American Film* Jan.–Feb. 1992: 51–52.

44 "Das war eine historisch bedingte Position damals, eine absichtlich eingenommene, recht krasse Position." (*AS* 256).

45 Alexander Kluge would continue to work in Germany under many of the principles of the New German Cinema, as would other directors. However, only Wenders, Fassbinder, Schlöndorff, Herzog and Margarethe von Trotta had reached the level of international acclaim that brought attention to the New German Cinema. Von Trotta lived for a short time in Italy, making highly personalized Italian films. In the mid-1990s, she returned to Germany and once again began making films in and about Germany. Wenders's many international awards, though, thrust him, for better or for worse, into the forefront of German directors. For an excellent overview of the NGC, see Elsaesser's *New German Cinema: a History* (New Brunswick, NJ: Rutgers, 1989) and Eric Rentschler's *West German Cinema in the Course of Time: Reflections on Twenty Years since Oberhausen* (Bedford Hills, NY: Redgrave, 1984).

46 In a 1982 interview, shortly after making *State of Things*, Wenders remarks that he was at that time reading Homer's *Odysee*. This was during his production of Handke's *Über die Dörfer* at the Salzburg Festival. Wenders's reading of Homer would profoundly influence the plot of *Paris, Texas*, in that Wenders saw in Homer an imperative for affirmative stories (*LB* 61). Moreover, his renewed collaboration with Handke on *Über die Dörfer* as well as on his next project *Himmel über Berlin*, would result in a further reworking of various aspects of the Homerian archtype, which will be discussed in more detail later.

47 Wenders's portrayal of women has been often criticised and questioned. Indeed, most of his films portray male characters whereby women function primarily as a reflection of male desire. Geist's critique is very well made, for she notes that while this scene is indeed a breakthrough for Wenders in that he is able for the first time to sustain a strong dramatic conversation between the sexes, it is in conversation only. Wenders still "shows himself as ignorant of women's reality as he was formerly uninterested" (121). Kolker and Beicken develop a similar critique based on the family politics that the film promotes (114–137). German critiques have more often overlooked the male-oriented nature of his films, but *Paris, Texas* was criticized for its view of the family (see Rauh, 103). Like Handke, Wenders has

rarely shown a feminist sensibility, being a "male-centric director" as Geist has referred to him (123). Although his films are not overtly degrading to women, they are, with few exceptions, not films about women. This changes somewhat with *Until the End of the World*, where personal narrative serves to cure Claire, the female protagonist, but in general, narratives and story-telling are associated with males in Wenders's films. When asked about the lack of a female voice in his works, he generally asserts that he makes films about what he knows, namely men and male stories.

48 Wim Wenders, *Until the End of the World*. Videocassette. Warner Bros., 1991.
49 Siegfried Kracauer, *Theory of Film: The Redemption of Physical Reality*. (New York: Oxford, 1960).
50 Wenders has on numerous occasions expressed his dismay with regard to the overabundance of images in society, be it television, advertising or even video images. See, for example, Walter Donohue's interview with Wenders, as well as various essays and interviews in *The Act of Seeing*, especially "I'm nowhere at home" (210–212), and "Die Wahrheit der Bilder" (57–87).
51 Wenders refers to this genre of filmmaking as "Tagebuchfilme" and most critics refer to them as essay films, a genre which has yet to be treated in greater depth with regard to Wenders. These films also include his 1980 film on Nicholas Ray *Nick's Film/Lightning over Water* and his 1985 film *Tokyo-Ga*.
52 "Thought was born blind, but Thought knows what is seeing./Its careful touch, deciphering forms from shapes,/Still suggests form as aught whose proper being/Mere finding touch with erring darkness drapes./ Yet whence, except from guessed sight, does touch teach/That touch is but a close and empty sense?/ How does mere touch, self-uncontented, reach/For some truer sense's whole intelligence? The thing once touched, if touch be now omitted,/Stands yet in memory real and outward known,/So the untouching memory of touch is fitted/With the sense of a sense whereby far things are shown./ So, by touch of untouching, wrongly aright,/Touch' thought of seeing sees not things but Sight." Fernando Pessoa, *Esoterische Gedichte, Mensagem, Englische Gedichte* (Frankfurt: Fisher, 1994): 156.
53 See Benjamin's essay "Der Erzähler" *Gesammelte Werke* Vol. II.2 (Frankfurt: Suhrkamp, 1977):
54 At the U.S. premiere of *Far Away, so Close!* Wenders read passages from the Bible and talked about his sense of religion. Although he has mentioned this in some interviews around the time of that film, it is not something he has dwelled upon since. Nevertheless, the "Christian" act that Cassiel commits can be clearly seen in the context of the film. Here I am indebted to Simon Richter for discussions about this aspect.

Conclusion Notes

1 Mann, "Die Kunst des Romans," *Gesammelte Werke*, Vol. 11, Berlin: Aufbau, (1960) 457–471.
2 The necessity of stories for recounting the past and the importance of the preterit in literary storytelling is perhaps best summarized in Thomas Mann's "Vorsatz" to *Der Zauberberg*: "Geschichten müssen vergangen sein, und je vergangener, könnte man sagen, desto besser für sie in ihrer Eigenschaft als Geschichten und für den Erzähler, den raunenden Beschwörer des Imperfekts" *Gesammelte Schriften* Vol. 2 (Berlin: Fischer, 1965): 5.
3 Here O'Neill relies on Seymour Chatman's conception of narratology as his theoretical basis (5). See Chatman, *Story and Discourse: Narrative Structure in Fiction and Film*, Ithaca: Cornell UP, 1978. The argument of the unreliability of the narrator as a postmodernist trope is also made by Theodore Ziolkowski in *Dimensions of the Modern Novel: German Texts and European Contexts*, (Princeton, NJ: Princeton UP, 1969.)

4   This is also the case in Tom Tykwer's 1998 film *Lola rennt*, a film which I will argue later, is typical of the new narrative cinema. Traditional oral storytelling uses this device quite often, but it is rarely found in novels or film.
5   This argument is best summarized in Judith Ryan's study, "The Problem of Pastiche: Patrick Süskind's *Das Parfum*," *German Quarterly* 63 (1990): 396–403.
6   Moritz writes: "Es bedarf keiner intellektuellen Hilfestellung, um diesen Roman zumindest an seiner Oberfläche zu begreifen" (16). Klaus Zeyringer and Mirjam Schaub make similar arguments in their contributions to the same volume of essays. See Rainer Moritz, ed. *Über Schlafes Bruder: Materialien zu Robert Schneiders Roman*. (Leipzig: Reclam, 1996.)
7   See Brooks's "The Tale vs. the Novel," *Novel: A Forum on Fiction* 21.2–3 (1988): 285–292 and in expanded form, his *Psychoanalysis and Storytelling*. (Oxford: Blackwell, 1994.)
8   They have subsequently been published under the title *Erzählen und kein Ende: Versuche zu einer Ästhetik des Alltags*.
9   See "Das Erzählen muß wie Sand im Getriebe sein: Ein Gespräch mit Uwe Tim." Interview with David Coury and Herman DeVries. *Focus on Literatur* 2.1 (1995): 101–112.
10 See Nadolny's "'Us and Them': Stories about Strangers," *World Literature Today*. Summer (1995): 482–486.
11 See especially Sabine von Dirke's "West meets East: Narrative Construction of the Foreigner and Postmodern Orientalism in Sten Nadolny's *Selim oder die Gabe der Rede*," *Germanic Review*. 69 (1994): 61–69, as well as a recent debate in the *German Quarterly*'s forum section.
12 See my discussion in the Introduction. Wittstock is not alone in his concern and with this assessment. Keith Bullivant documents much of the debate on German literature, especially in the 1980s, in his excellent study *The Future of German Literature*, Oxford: Berg, 1994.
13 Here Alexander and thus Nadolny seem to follow in the tradition of Hannah Arendt, who maintained that Holocaust testimony and the reality of the horrors required the construction of narrative. See Lisa J. Disch, "More Truth than Fact: Storytelling as Critical Understanding in the Writings of Hannah Arendt," *Political Theory* 21.3 (1 Nov. 1993): 665–694.
14 This is the very point with which von Dirke takes issue with Nadolny in regard to his representation of Turks in the greater narrative frame. In her criticism of the novel she argues that Nadolny reinforces stereotypes of an Oriental culture and idealizes many cultural attributes. Specifically she sees Selim's portrayal as a gifted storyteller as a manifestation of a Western cliché of Orientalist culture. See note 11.
15 Wittstock, 160. See also Bullivant's arguments in *Realism Today* and *The Future of German Literature* as well as an article on the subject in the *Neue Zürcher Zeitung*: "Reisender Schnee oder Realismus ohne Resignation; die deutschsprachige Literatur und 'das Authentische.'" *NZZ* 30 Nov. 1996: 65.
16 "Von Momo, Mythen und Moneten: Robert Schneider's *Die Luftgängerin* verliert einen alten Kampf. *Die Welt* 3 Jan. 1998 on-line.
17 "Ich bin der König: Der österreichische Schriftsteller Robert Schneider über Kitsch, Vampire und sein neues Buch *Die Luftgängerin*." *Süddeutsche Zeitung*, 4 Feb. 1998, on-line.
18 "Filmemacherin Sanders-Brahms - das deutsche Kino ist öde," *DPA* 18 June, 2000.
19 Ibid.
20 This has been the case with a number of films in the past decade as diverse as Lars von Trier's *Breaking the Waves* to several of Luc Bresson's films. Furthermore several more recent German films, such as Caroline Link's *Jenseits der Stille*, have been released by Buena Vista, a division of Disney. In addition, a number of French filmmakers have begun making films in English so as to appeal to a wider audience as well as to achieve greater access into American markets. See Kristen Hohenadel, "European Films are Learning to Speak English," *New York Times* 30 Jan. 2000.

21 With regard to the cinema, Duncan Petrie's *Screening Europe: Image and Identity in Contemporary European* Cinema (London: BFI, 1992) has taken up many of these issues from different perspectives. See also Pierre Sorlin *European Cinemas, European Societies* (London: Routledge, 1991), Wendy Everett, *European Identity in Cinema* (Exeter: Intellect Books, 1996), and Richard Dyer and Ginette Vincendeau, eds. *Popular European Cinema* (London: Routledge, 1992).
22 See Petrie, 1, as well as Dyer and Vincendeau, 6.
23 Susan Sontag, "L'idée d'Europe (un élégie de plus)," *Les Temps Modernes*, 510 (Jan. 1989): 80, quoted in David Morley and Kevin Robins, "No Place like Heimat: Images of Home(land) in European Culture," *New Formations* 12 (Winter 1990): 3.
24 See my article, "From Aesthetics to Commercialism: Narration and the New German Comedy," *Seminar* 33.4 (Nov. 1997): 356–373.
25 "Die Zeit und Flimmer," *FAZ* (20 Aug. 1998): 31.
26 "Ein Narr, wer den Zufall Schicksal nennt," *Süddeutsche Zeitung* (19 Aug. 1998): n.p.
27 "Zeit des Aufbruchs: Tendenzen im deutschen Kino 1998/1999," *epd-film* (March 1999): 26–31.
28 Clearly Tykwer's placement of the version with the happy end as the third story preferences it over the first two. This may be a conceit to viewer desire or simply an ironic acknowledgement of the tendency in the dominant cinema to require a happy end. This ending does not seem to make the film more believable, rather more like a fairy tale.
29 In January 2001 The Gene Siskel Film Center in Chicago (formerly the Film Center at the Art Institute of Chicago) programmed a series on this "New Narrative Order" which showcased such examples of neonarrative and permutational cinema. While the series concentrated on American films (Tarantino's *Reservoir Dogs*, Jim Jarmusch's *Mystery Train* and Steven Soderbergh's *The Limey*, among others), it made reference to this phenomenon in international cinema, including mention of Tykwer's film. Taken from the Film School's web site: www.artic.edu/saic/art/filmcntr/narrative.html (stand: 1 February 2001).
30 "Botschafter ohne festen Wohnsitz: Wim Wenders, Oscar-Kandidat," *Süddeutsche Zeitung*, 24 March 2000: 3.

~ BIBLIOGRAPHY ~

Primary Works

Handke, Peter. *Abschied des Träumers vom neuten Land*. Frankfurt: Suhrkamp, 1991.
———. *Die Abwesenheit: Ein Märchen*. Frankfurt: Suhrkamp, 1987.
———. *Die Angst des Tormanns beim Elfmeter*. Frankfurt: Suhrkamp, 1970.
———. *Der Chinese des Schmerzes*. Frankfurt: Suhrkamp, 1983.
———. *Ich bin ein Bewohner des Elfenbeinturms*. Frankfurt: Suhrkamp, 1972.
———. *The Jukebox: And Other Essays on Storytelling*. Trans. Ralph Manheim and Krishna Winston. New York: Farrar, Straus and Giroux, 1994.
———. *Kindergeschichte*. Frankfurt: Suhrkamp, 1981.
———. *Der kurze Brief zum langen Abscheid*. Frankfurt: Suhrkamp, 1972.
———. *Langsam im Schatten*. Frankfurt: Suhrkamp, 1992.
———. *Langsamer Heimkehr*. Frankfurt: Suhrkamp, 1979.
———. *Die Lehre der Sainte-Victoire*. Frankfurt: Suhrkamp, 1980.
———. *Die linkshändige Frau*. Frankfurt: Suhrkamp, 1976.
———. *Lucie im Walde mit Dingsda*. Frankfurt: Suhrkamp, 1999.
———. *Mein Jahr in der Niemandsbucht*. Frankfurt: Suhrkamp, 1994.
———. *Nachmittag eines Schriftstellers*. Salzburg: Residenz, 1987.
———. *Peter Handke: Prosa, Gedichte, Theaterstücke, Hörspiel, Aufsätze*. Frankfurt: Suhrkamp, 1969.
———. *Die Stunde der wahren Empfindung*. Frankfurt: Suhrkamp, 1975.
———. *Über die Dörfer*. Frankfurt: Suhrkamp, 1981.
———. *Versuch über den geglückten Tag*. Frankfurt: Suhrkamp, 1991.
———. *Versuch über die Jukebox*. Frankfurt: Suhrkamp, 1990.
———. *Versuch über die Müdigkeit*. Frankfurt: Suhrkamp, 1989.
———. *Die Wiederholung*. Frankfurt: Suhrkamp, 1986.
———. *Wunschloses Unglück*. Frankfurt: Suhrkamp, 1972.
Wenders, Wim. *The Act of Seeing*. Frankfurt: Verlag der Autoren, 1992.
———. *Einmal: Bilder und Geschichten*. Frankfurt: Verlag der Autoren, 1994.
———. *Emotion Pictures*. Frankfurt: Verlag der Autoren, 1986.
———. *Die Logik der Bilder*. Frankfurt: Verlag der Autoren, 1988.

Secondary Works

Abrahams, Roger D. *The Man-of-Words in the West Indies: Performance and the Emergence of Creole Culture*. Baltimore: Johns Hopkins UP, 1983.
Adorno, Theodor W. *Noten zur Literatur*. Frankfurt: Suhrkamp, 1958.
Amend, Heike and Michael Bütow, eds. *Der bewegte Film: Aufbruch zu den neuen deutschen Erfolgen*. Berlin: Vistas, 1997.
Armes, Roy. *French Cinema*. London: Oxford, 1985.
Arnold, Heinz Ludwig. *Text und Kritik: Peter Handke* 24/24a, 3d ed. 1975.

———. *Text und Kritik: Peter Handke* 24, 5th ed. 1989.
Balázs, Bela. *Theory of the Film: Character and Growth of a New Art*. Trans. Edith Bone. New York: Dover, 1970.
Bance, Alan, ed. *Weimar Germany: Writers and Politics*. Edinburgh: Scottish Academic P, 1982.
Barkow, Jerome H., Leda Cosmides, and John Tooby, eds. *The Adapted Mind: Evolutionary Psychology and the Generation of Culture*. New York: Oxford, 1992.
Baron, Stephaine, ed. *"Degenerate Art": The Fate of the Avant-Garde in Nazi German*. Los Angeles: Los Angeles County Museum of Art, 1991.
Barthes, Roland. *Image—Music—Text*. Trans. Stephen Heath. New York: Hill and Wang, 1977.
Bartmann, Christoph. *Suche nach Zusammenhang. Handkes Werk als Prozeß*. Wien: Braumuller, 1984.
Bellafante, Ginia. "Dostoyevsky and a Decaf," *Time*, 5 June 1995, 66–68.
Benjamin, Walter. *Gesammelte Schriften*. Eds. Rolf Tiedemann and Hermann Schweppenhäuser. 8 Vols. Frankfurt: Suhrkamp, 1977.
Berg, Jan, ed. *Am Ende der Rolle: Diskussion über den Autorenfilm*. Marburg: Schüren, 1993.
Berg-Ganschow, Uta, and Wolfgang Jacobsen, eds. *Film, Stadt, Kino, Berlin*. Berlin: Argon, 1987.
Berger, John, and Jean Mohr. *Another Way of Telling*. New York: Pantheon, 1982.
Berman, Russell A. "Refusal or Denial and the Sky of Europe: Literary Postmodernism in Peter Handke's *Across*." *Cultural Studies of Modern Germany: History, Representation and Nationhood*. Madison: U of Wisconsin, 1993. 159–174.
———. *The Rise of the Modern German Novel: Crisis and Charisma*. Cambridge, MA: Harvard U.P., 1986.
Bernofsky, Susan. "'The Threshold is the Source': Handke's *Der Chinese des Schmerzes*." *Critique* 32.1 (1990): 58–65.
Best, Alan, and Hans Wolfschütz, eds. *Modern Austrian Writing: Literature and Society after 1945*. London: Wolff, 1980.
Borchert, Wolfgang. *Das Gesamtwerk*. Reinbek, Rowohlt, 1959.
Bordwell, David. *Narration in the Fiction Film*. Madison: U of Wisconsin, 1985.
Bordwell, David, and Kristin Thompson. *Film Art: An Introduction*. Reading, MA: Addison-Wesley, 1979.
Bordwell, David, Kristin Thompson, and Janet Staiger. *The Classical Hollywood Cinema: Film Style and Mode of Production to 1960*. New York: Columbia UP, 1985.
"Botschafter ohne festen Wohnsitz: Wim Wenders, Oscar-Kandidat," *Süddeutsche Zeitung* 24 March 2000, 3.
Branigan, Edward. *Narrative Comprehension and Film*. New York: Routledge, 1992.
Briegleb, Klaus, and Sigrid Weigel, eds. *Hansers Sozialgeschichte der deutschen Literatur*, Vol. 12. Munich: Hanser, 1980.
Brooks, Peter. *Psychoanalysis and Storytelling*. Oxford: Blackwell, 1994.
———. "The Tale vs. the Novel." *Novel: A Forum on Fiction* 21.2–3 (1988): 285–292.
Bullivant, Keith. *The Future of German Literature*. Providence, RI: Berg, 1994.
———. *Realism Today: Aspects of the Contemporary West German Novel*. Leamington Spa, U.K.: Berg, 1987
Cassirer, Ernst. *The Myth of the State*. New Haven: Yale UP, 1946.
Caviola, Hugo. "*Ding—Bild—Schrift*: Peter Handke's Slow Homecoming to a 'Chinese' Austria." *Modern Fiction Studies* 39 (1990): 381–394.
Cook, Roger F., and Gerd Gemünden, eds. *The Cinema of Wim Wenders: Image, Narrative, and the Postmodern Condition*. Detroit: Wayne State UP, 1997.
Corrigan, Timothy. *New German Cinema: The Displaced Image*. Austin: U of Texas P, 1983.
Coury, David. "From Aesthetics to Commercialism: Narration and the New German Comedy," *Seminar* 33.4 (1997): 356–373.

DeMeritt, Linda. "Peter Handke: From Alienation to Orientation." *Modern Austrian Literature* 20 (1987): 53–71.
DeParle, Jason. "Mountain Voice Shares Ageless, Magic Tales." *New York Times*, 22 June 1991, A1.
"Dichters Winterreise," *Spiegel*, 5 Feb. 1996, 190–193.
"Die Zeit und Flimmer," *FAZ*, 20 Aug. 1998, 31.
Dirke, Sabine von. "West meets East: Narrative Construction of the Foreigner and Postmodern Orientalism in Sten Nadolny's *Selim, oder die gabe der rede.*" *Germanic Review* 69 (1994): 61–69.
Disch, Lisa. *Hannah Arendt and the Limits of Philosophy*. Ithaca: Cornell UP, 1994.
———. "More Truth than Fact: Storytelling as Critical Understanding in the Writings of Hannah Arendt," *Political Theory* 21.3 (1 Nov. 1993): 665–694.
Döblin, Alfred. *Aufsätze zur Literatur*. Ed. Walter Muschg. Olten und Freiburg im Breisgau: Walter-Verlag, 1963.
Docherty, Thomas, ed. *Postmodernism: a Reader*. New York: Columbia UP, 1993.
Donohue, Walter. "Revelations. An Interview with Wim Wenders." *Sight and Sound*, April 1992, 8–13.
Dor, Milo. *Auf dem falschen Dampfer*. Wien: Zsolnay, 1988.
Durzak, Manfred. *Peter Handke und die deutsche Gegenwartsliteratur: Narziß auf Abwegen*. Stuttgart: Kohlhammer, 1982.
Dyer, Richard, and Ginette Vincendeau, eds. *Popular European Cinema*. London: Routledge, 1992.
"Ein Narr, wer den Zufall Schicksal nennt," *Süddeutsche Zeitung* on-line 19 Aug. 1998.
Elsaesaer, Thomas. "The European Art Movie," *Sight and Sound*, April 1994, 22–29.
———. *New German Cinema: a History*. New Brunswick, NJ: Rutgers, 1989.
Emrich, Wilhelm. "Die Erzählkunst des 20. Jahrhunderts und ihr geschichtlicher Sinn." *Deutsche Literatur in unserer Zeit*. Göttingen: Vandenhoeck & Ruprecht, 1966.
Fassbinder, Rainer Werner. *The Anarchy of the Imagination*. Eds. Michael Töteberg and Leo Lensing. Baltimore: Johns Hopkins, 1992.
Fehrenbach, Heide. *Cinema in Democratizing Germany: Reconstructing National Identity after Hitler*. Chapel Hill: U of North Carolina P, 1995.
Fell, John. *Film and the Narrative Tradition*. Norman: U of Oklahoma P, 1974.
Fellinger, Raimund, ed. *Peter Handke*. Frankfurt: Suhrkamp, 1985.
"Filmemacherin Sanders-Brahms—das deutsche Kino ist öde." *DPA*, 18 June 2000.
Finnegan, Ruth H. *Limba Stories and Storytelling*. Oxford: Clarendon, 1967.
Firda, Richard Arthur. *Peter Handke*. New York: Twayne, 1993.
"Freedom and Community: The Politics of Restoration," *Economist*, 24 Dec. 1994–6 Jan. 1995, 33–36.
Freybourg, Anne Marie. *Film und Autor: Eine Analyse des Autorenkinos von Jean-Luc Godard und Rainer Werner Fassbinder*. diss. U Hamburg, 1993.
Fuch, Gerhard, and Gerhard Melzer, eds. *Peter Handke: Die Langsamkeit der Welt*. Graz: Droschl, 1993.
Gamper, Herbert. *Aber ich lebe nur von den Zwischenräumen: Peter Handke im Gespräch mit Herbert Gamper*. Zürich: Ammann, 1987.
Gaut, Berys. "Making Sense of Films: Neoformalism and its Limits." *Forum for Modern Language Studies* 30.1 (1995): 8–23.
Geist, Kathe. *The Cinema of Wim Wenders: from Paris, France to "Paris, Texas."* Ann Arbor, MI: UMI Research Press, 1987,
"'Gelassen wär ich gern.' Ein Gespräch mit Peter Handke." *Der Spiegel*, 49 (1994), 170–176.
"'Gepäck abgeworfen': Interview mit Regisseur Hark Bohm über die neue deutsche Lachlust," *Spiegel*, 19 Feb. 1996, 182.
Grass, Günter. *Die Blechtrommel*. Frankfurt: Fischer, 1963.

Grimm, Jacob and Wilhelm. *Deutsches Wörterbuch*. Munich: DTV, 1984.
Grob, Norbert. *Wenders*. Berlin: Edition Filme, 1991.
Habermas, Jürgen. "Modernity versus Postmodernity," *New German Critique* 22 (1981): 3–14.
Harrell, John. *Origins and Early Traditions of Storytelling*. Kensington, CA: York House, 1983.
Harvey, David. *The Condition of Postmodernity: an Enquiry into the Origins of Cultural Change*. Cambridge, MA: Blackwell, 1989.
Hatfield, Henry. *Crisis and Continuity in Modern German Fiction*. Ithaca, NY: Cornell, 1969.
Hern, Nicholas. *Peter Handke: Theater and Anti-theater*. London: Oswald Wolff, 1971.
Hesse, Hermann. *Gesammelte Schriften*. Frankfurt, Suhrkamp, 1957.
Hohenadel, Kristen. "European Films are Learning to Speak English," *New York Times* on-line, 30 Jan. 2000.
Horkheimer, Max, and Theodore W. Adorno. *Dialectic of the Enlightenment*. Trans. John Cummings. New York: Continuum, 1972.
Horvat, Joze. *Noch einmal vom Neunten Land: Peter Handke im Gespräch mit Joze Horvat*. Klagenfurt: Wieser, 1993.
Hutcheon, Linda. *The Poetics of Postmodernism*. New York: Routledge, 1988.
Huyssen, Andreas. *After the Great Divide: Modernism, Mass Culture, Postmodernism*. Bloomington, IN: Indiana UP, 1986.
Huyssen, Andreas and Klaus R. Scherpe, eds. *Postmoderne: Zeichen eines kulturellen Wandels*. Hamburg: Rowohlt, 1986.
"Ich bin der König: Der österreichische Schriftsteller Robert Schneider über Kitsch, Vampire und sein neues Buch *Die Luftgängerin*." *Süddeutsche Zeitung* on-line, 4 Feb. 1998.
"'Ich dachte, das mache ich im Schlaf,' Interview with Volker Schlöndorff." *Die Zeit*, 8 Sept. 1995, 13–14.
"Ich habe nichts gegen Männer" *Frankfurter Rundschau* on-line, 14 Sept. 1998.
Jakobsen, Wolfgang, Anton Kaes, and Hans Helmut Prinzler, eds. *Geschichte des deutschen Films*. Stuttgart: Metzler, 1993.
Jencks, Charles, ed. *The Post-Modern Reader*. New York: St. Martin's, 1992.
Jucker, Rolf, ed. *Zeitgenössiche Utopieentwürfe in Literatur und Gesellschaft*. Amsterdam: Rodopi, 1997.
Kaes, Anton. *Deutschlandbilder: Die Wiederkehr der Geschichte als Film*. Munich: Text und Kritik, 1987.
———. *From Hitler to Heimat: the Return of History as Film*. Cambridge, MA: Harvard UP, 1989.
Kahler, Erich. *The Inward Turn of Narrative*. Trans. Richard and Clara Winston. Princeton, NJ: Princeton UP, 1973.
Kayser, Wolfgang. *Entstehung und Krise des modernen Romans*. Stuttgart: Metzler, 1955.
Kermode, Frank. *The Art of Telling: Essays on Fiction*. Cambridge, MA: Harvard UP, 1983.
———. *The Sense of an Ending: Studies in the Theory of Fiction*. New York: Oxford UP, 1967.
Klinkowitz, Jerome, and James Knowlton. *Peter Handke and the Postmodern Transformation*. Columbia, MO: U of Missouri, 1983.
Kluge, Alexander, Edgar Reitz, and Wilfred Reinke. "Word and Film." Trans. Miriam Hansen. *October* 46 Fall, 1988. 83–95.
———. *Bestandsaufnahme: Utopie Film. 20 Jahre neuer deutscher Film*. Frankfurt: Zweitausendeins, 1983.
Knight, Julia. *Women and the New German Cinema*. London: Verso, 1992.
Koch, Krischan. *Die Bedeutung des "Oberhausener Manifestes" für die Filmentwicklung in der Bundesrepublik Deutschland*. Frankfurt: Peter Lang, 1985.
Kolker, Robert and Peter Beicken. *The Films of Wim Wenders*. New York: Cambridge, 1993.
Konigsberg, Ira. *The Complete Film Dictionary*. New York: Meridian, 1987.
Koskella, Gretel A. *Die Krise des deutschen Romans: 1960– 1970*. Frankfurt: R.G. Fischer, 1986.

Kracauer, Siegfried. *From Caligari to Hitler: A Psychological History of the German Film*. Princeton, NJ: Princeton UP, 1974.

———. *Theory of Film: The Redemption of Physical Reality*. New York: Oxford, 1960.

Kuchenbuch, Thomas. *Bild und Erzählung: Geschichte in Bildern. Vom frühen Comic Strip zum Fernsehfeature*. Münster: MAkS, 1992.

Kundera, Milan. *The Art of the Novel*. Trans. Linda Asher. New York: Grove Press, 1986.

Langenbucher, Wolfgang R., Ralf Rytlewski, and Bernd Weyergraf, eds. *Kulturpolitisches Wörterbuch: Bundesrepublik Deutschland/Deutsche Demokratische Republik im Vergleich*. Stuttgart: Metzler, 1983.

Levy, Shawn. "*Until the End of the World*: Wim Wenders' Dance Around the Planet." *American Film*, Jan.–Feb.1992, 51–52.

Lewandowski, Rainer. *Alexander Kluge*. Munich: C.H. Beck, 1980.

Lukàcs, Georg. *Die Theorie des Romans*. Berlin: Luchterhand, 1965.

Lyotard, Jean-François. *The Postmodern Condition: A Report on Knowledge*. Geoff Bennington and Brian Massumi, trans. Minneapolis: U of Minnesota, 1984.

Macdonald, Iain. "Utopia and the Possibility of Place: Peter Handke and the Ambitions of a Storyteller," *Angelaki* 3.1 (1998): 137–144.

Magenau, Jörg. "Die neue Lust am Erzählen," *Deutschland: Zeitschrift für Politik, Kultur, Wirtschaft und Wissenschaft* (Oct/Nov 2000): 29.

Mann, Thomas. *Gesammelte Werke*. 13 Vols. Berlin: Aufbau, 1965.

Markolin, Caroline. *Eine Geschichte vom Erzählen: Peter Handkes poetische Verfahrungsweisen am Beispiel der Erzählung Langsamer Heimkehr*. Bern: Lang, 1991.

Mayer, Hans. *Zur deutschen Literatur der Zeit: Zusammenhange, Schriftsteller, Bucher*. Reinbek: Rowohlt, 1967.

McCormick, Richard W. *Politics of the Self: Feminism and the Postmodern in West German Literature and Film*. Princeton, N.J.: Princeton UP, 1991.

Medicus, Thomas. "Populäres Sprachrohr der Katharsis: Warum der Schirftsteller Bernhard Schlink bei uns auch und anderswo so erfolgreich ist," *Frankfurter Rundschau* on-line, 16 Feb. 2000.

Metz, Christian. *Language and cinema*. Trans. Donna Jean Umiker-Sebeok. The Hague: Mouton, 1974.

Monoco, James. *How to Read a Film*. New York: Oxford, 1981.

Moritz, Rainer, ed. Über *Schlafes Bruder: Materialien zu Robert Schneiders Roman*. Leipzig: Reclam, 1996.

Morley, David, and Kevin Robins, "No Place like Heimat: Images of Home(land) in European Culture," *New Formations* 12 (Winter 1990) 1–23.

Moser, Samuel. "Das Glück des Erzählens ist das Erzählen des Glücks: Peter Handkes Versuche." *Peter Handke: Die Langsamkeit der Welt*. Eds. Gerhard Fuchs and Gerhard Melzer. Graz: Droschl, 1993. 137–154.

Musil, Robert. *Gesammelte Werke in neun Bänden*. Reinbek: Rowohlt, 1978.

Nadolny, Sten. "'Us and Them': Stories about Strangers." *World Literature Today*. Summer (1995): 482–486.

Nash, Cristopher, ed., *Narrative in Culture: the Uses of Storytelling in the Sciences, Philosophy, and Literature*. New York: Routledge, 1990.

"New Ideas Flourish in an Old Venue: The Return of the Literary Salon" *This Week in Germany*, 17 Dec 1999.

"New Pix tickle Teutons," *Variety*, 17 July 1995, 34–35.

Niemuth-Engelmann, Susanne. *Alltag und Aufzeichnung. Untersuchungen zu Canetti, Bender, Handke und Schnurre*. Würzburg: Königshausen & Neumann, 1998.

O'Neill, Patrick. *Acts of Narrative: Textual Strategies in Modern German Fiction*. Toronto: U of Toronto, 1996

Oxford Dictionary of English Etymology. Oxford: Clarendon, 1966.
Paech, Joachim. *Literatur und Film.* Stuttgart: Metzler, 1988.
Pakendorf, Gunther. "Writing about Writing: Peter Handke's *Nachmittag eines Schriftstellers,*" *Modern Austrian Literature* 23.3/4 (1990): 77–86.
Pascal, Roy. *The German Novel.* Toronto: U of Toronto P, 1965.
Peitz, Christiane. "Das Kino, eine Baustelle," *Die Zeit,* 5 April 1996, 15.
Pessoa, Fernando. *Esoterische Gedichte, Mensagem, Englische Gedichte.* Frankfurt: Fisher, 1994.
Petrie, Duncan. *Screening Europe: Image and Identity in Contemporary European Cinema.* London: BFI, 1992.
Petzke, Ingo, ed. *Das Experimentalfilm-Handbuch.* Frankfurt: Deutsches Filmmuseum, 1989.
Price, Reynolds. *A Palpable God.* New York: Atheneum, 1978.
Prinzler, Hans Helmut, and Eric Rentschler, eds. *Augenzeugen: 100 Texte deutscher Filmemacher.* Frankfurt: Verlag der Autoren, 1988.
Pütz, Peter. *Peter Handke.* Frankfurt: Suhrkamp, 1982.
Rauh, Reinhold. *Wim Wenders: und seine Filme.* Munich: Heyne, 1990.
"Reisender Schnee oder Realismus ohne Resignation; die deutschsprachige Literatur und 'das Authentische.'" *Neue Zürcher Zeitung.* 30 (Nov. 1996): 65.
Rentschler, Eric. *West German Film in the Course of Time.* Bedford Hills: Redgrave, 1984.
Ricoeur, Paul. *Time and Narrative,* vol. 2. Chicago: U of Chicago P, 1985.
Robbe-Grillet, Alain. *For a New Novel: Essays on Fiction.* Trans. Richard Howard. New York: Grove Press, 1965.
Roemer, Michael. *Telling Stories: Postmodernism and the Invalidation of Traditional Narrative.* Lanham, MD: Rowman and Littlefield, 1995.
Rooth, Anna Birgitta. *The Importance of Storytelling: A Study based on Field work in Northern Alaska.* Uppsala: Almqvist and Wiksell, 1976.
Ryan, Judith. "The Problem of Pastiche: Patrick Süskind's *Das Parfum,*" *German Quarterly* 63 (1990): 396–403.
Schlöndorff, Volker. "*Die Blechtrommel*": *Tagebuch einer Verfilmung.* Darmstadt: Luchterhand, 1979.
Schlueter, June. *The Plays and Novels of Peter Handke.* Pittsburgh: U of Pittsburgh P, 1981.
Schobert, Walter. *Der deutsche avant-garde Film der 20er Jahre.* Munich: Goethe-Institut, 1989.
Schulte-Sasse, Jochen. "Modernity and Modernism, Postmodernity and Postmodernism: Framing the Issue." *Cultural Critique* 5 (1986–1987): 5–21.
Silbermann, Marc. *German Cinema: Texts in Context.* Detroit: Wayne State UP, 1995.
Sontag, Susan. *Against Interpretation.* New York, Anchor, 1990.
———. "The Decay of Cinema," *New York Times Magazine,* 25 Feb. 1996, 60–61.
Sorlin, Pierre. *European Cinemas, European Societies: 1939– 1990.* London: Routledge, 1991.
"Ständiger Wohnsitz: Rock 'n' Roll," Interview with Wim Wenders. *Die Zeit* on-line, 7 Dec. 2000.
Steiner, Wendy. "Look Who's Modern Now," *New York Times Book Review,* 10 Oct. 1999, 18–19.
Steinmetz, Horst. "Die Rückkehr des Erzählers. Seine alte neue Funktion in der modernen Medienwelt." *Funktion und Funktionswandel der Literatur im Geistes- und Gesellschaftsleben.* Bern: Lang, 1989. 67–82.
Stiegler, Bernd. "Peter Handke: Der Traum von der Überwindung der Zeit durch die Erzählung als neuen Mythos," *Dasselbe noch einmal : die Ästhetik der Wiederholung,* eds. Carola Hilmes and Dietrich Mathy, 244–258. Opladen: Westdeutscher Verlag, 1998.
Stiller, Klaus. "Die Verwandschaft des Erzählers. Peter Handkes Prosa." *Text und Kritik* 24 (1969): 43–59.
"Tempo, Tempo, Tempo. Die Regisseurin Katja von Garnier über ihren Überraschungserfolg *Abgeschminkt.*" *Der Spiegel,* 6 Sept. 1993, 214.
Timm, Uwe. "'Das Erzählen muß wie Sand im Getriebe sein': Ein Gespräch mit Uwe Tim," interview by David Coury and Herman DeVries, *Focus on Literatur* 2.1 (1995): 101–112.

———. *Erzählen und kein Ende: Versuch zu einer Ästhetik des Alltags.* Cologne: Kiepenheuer & Witsch, 1993.
Truffaut, Francois. *Hitchcock.* Trans. Helen Scott. New York: Simon and Schuster, 1984.
"Up close with Wim Wenders," *Everybody's News* (Cincinnati, OH), 11 Feb. 1994, 10–11.
"Von Momo, Mythen und Moneten: Robert Schneider's *Die Luftgängerin* verliert einen alten Kampf." *Die Welt* on-line, 3 Jan. 1998.
Welsch, Wolfgang. *Unsere postmoderne Moderne.* Weinheim: Acta humaniora, 1988.
———. *Wege aus der Moderne.* Weinheim: Acta humaniora, 1988.
Welzig, Werner. *Der deutsche Roman im 20. Jahrhundert.* Stuttgart: Kröner, 1970.
"Wenders wants curbs on U.S. pix in Europe," *Variety*, 18 May 1992, 5.
Wenders, Wim, and Peter Handke. *Der Himmel über Berlin: Ein Filmbuch.* Frankfurt: Suhrkamp, 1989.
Wesche, Ulrich. "Peter Handke, Walker Percy, and the End of Modernity." *Essays in Literature* 19.2 (1992): 291–297.
Willet, Ralph. *The Americanization of Germany, 1945–1949.* London: Routledge, 1989.
Williams, Alan. *Republic of Images: A History of French Filmmaking.* Cambridge, MA: Harvard UP, 1992.
Winter, Hans-Gerhard. "Von der Dokumentarliteratur zur 'neuen Subjektivität': Anmerkungen zur westdetuschen Literatur der siebzigen Jahre." *Seminar* 17 (1981).
Wittstock, Uwe. *Leselust: Wie unterhaltsam ist die neue deutsche Literartur?* Munich: Luchterhand, 1995.
Wollen, Peter. *Readings and Writings: Semiotic Counter-Strategies.* London: Verso, 1982.
"'Zauber des Bildes': Wim Wenders über hämische Kritiker, Humor und seinen neuen Film." *Der Spiegel*, 15 May 1995, 241–243.
Wright, Robert. "The Evolution of Despair," *Time*, 28 August 1995, 50–57.
———. *The Moral Animal: the New Science of Evolutionary Psychology.* New York: Pantheon, 1994.
"Zeit des Aufbruchs: Tendenzen im deutschen Kino 1998/1999," *epd-film* (March 1999): 26–31.
Ziolkowski, Theodore. *Dimensions of the Modern Novel.* Princeton, NJ: Princeton UP, 1969.
Zülch, Tilman, ed. *Die Angst des Dichters vor der Wirklichkeit: 16 Antworten auf Peter Handkes Winterreise nach Serbien.* Göttingen: Steidl, 1996.

~ INDEX ~

A

À Bout de Souffle, 96–97
Abgeschminkt!, 107, 110
Absolute Film, 87–88, 91, 95
Absolute Giganten, 167–168
Adorno, Theodor, 4–5, 32–33, 34, 35–36, 39, 44, 71, 90, 157
"Afternoon of a Writer," 74, 76
Akin, Fatih, 167
Alabama: 2000 Light Years, 128
Alekan, Henri, 123
All Along the Watchtower, 128
Almodóvar, Pedro, 106
Alphaville, 127
Altman, Robert, 130
American Zoetrope studio, 131
Andric, Iva, 66
Angelus Novus, 116
Annaud, Jean–Jacques, 106
Another Way of Telling, 73
Anti–narrative, 5, 7, 13, 43, 153, 167
    and Döblin, Alfred, 32
    films, 8, 10–11, 13, 85, 89, 115, 167
    and Handke, Peter, 51, 55–62
    and Wenders, Wim, 89, 115
Anton Reiser, 60
Antonioni, Michelangelo, 93, 143, 144, 151
Aristotle, 92, 107
Artisten in der Zirkuskuppel, 100
Auteur cinema, 88, 95, 105
Autorenfilm, 88–89, 92–109, 109–110, 112–114, 123, 124–125, 133, 149, 167, 168, 169
    See also New German Cinema (NGC)
Autorenkino, 89, 101–102, 104, 113, 131, 135, 136, 149

B

Balázs, Béla, 120
Bance, Alan, 36
Barthes, Roland, 6, 42–43, 57
Bartmann, Christoph, 63
Baudrillard, Jean, 6, 43
Bauhaus School, 87
Bazin, André, 96
Begrüßung des Aufsichtsrats, 49
Beicken, Peter, 134, 136
Benjamin, Walter, 3, 4, 7, 9–10, 36
    narrative, demise of, 19–22, 24, 25–30, 46, 72, 85 116–117, 118, 147–148
    narrative, importance of, 44, 45–47, 81, 90, 121, 149
    and Wenders, Wim, 116–117, 118, 121, 140, 143, 147–148, 151
Berger, John, 73, 74, 78
Berlin Alexanderplatz, 25, 26, 29–32
Berlin–Brandenburg Academy of Arts, 12
Berman, Russell, 33–34, 65–66
Bernhard, Thomas, 6
Bernofsky, 65
Beslandsaufnahme: Utopie Film, 104
Bildungs, 27
Bildungsroman, 23, 30, 60, 63, 66–67
Blue Angel, 167
Boccaccio, 157
Bohm, Hark, 111
Bois, Curt, 118
Bordwell, David, 105
Brecht, Bertolt, 37
Broch, Hermann, 28, 39
Brooks, Peter, 2, 7, 9, 20–21, 48, 156
Bullivant, Keith, 5
Buñuel, Luis, 166

C

Cahiers du Cinéma, 96
Campbell, Mary Schmidt, 1, 2
Campos de Castilla, 79
Camus, Albert, 60
Caviola, Hugo, 62–63
Chambre 666, 127, 143
Cinéma de papa, 98
Cinématheque Française, 96
Citizen Kane, 166
Cook, Roger, 122
Coppola, Francis Ford, 131

D

Dadaists, 36
Das Gewicht der Welt, 63
Das Kabinet des Dr. Caligari, 87
Das Kalkwerk, 6
Das Parfum, 3, 153–156, 162
De Sica, Vittori, 94
Decamerone, 157
Der bewegte Mann, 110
Der Chinese des Schmerzes, 63–66
"Der Erzähler," 4, 19, 25, 26
Der Hausierer, 49, 56, 57–58
Der Himmel über Berlin, 8, 72, 81, 85, 109, 116–118, 123, 147–149, 150–151
Der kurze Brief zum langen Abscheid, 60–61
Der Scharlachroten Buchstabe, 124
Der Spiegel, 107
Der Stand der Dinge, 104, 131
Der Vorleser, 3, 161
Deutschlandromane, 37
Dichtung und Wahrheit, 26–27
Die Abwesenheit, 63, 72
Die Angst des Tormanns beim Elfmeter, 6, 59–60, 123, 137
Die Blechtrommel, 5, 6, 136, 154–155, 156, 166
Die Entdeckung der Currywurst, 153, 156–158, 161
Die Hornissen, 49, 56–57
Die Lufigangerin, 161
"Die Patriotin," 101, 122
Die Rättin, 48
Die Wiederholung, 63, 66–70, 74, 158–159
Dietrich, Marlena, 167
Döblin, Alfred, 4, 23, 25–26, 29–32, 34, 36, 39, 128
    anti-narrative, 32
Dörrie, Doris, 110, 111–112

3 amerikanische LP's, 127–128
Durzak, Manfred, 50

E

Easy Rider, 128
Economist, 2
Einmal, 119, 147
Einstellung, 129
Elsaesser, Thomas, 102–103, 104–107
Empfindung, 77, 125
Emrich, Wilhelm, 28–31
Enlightenment, 2, 6, 30, 53–54, 163
Entwicklungsroman, 38
Erzähler, 25, 32–34, 35, 156
Erzählkunst, 28
Erziehungsroman, 27
European Art Film, 88, 91, 94–96, 103–107, 113–114, 135, 164, 166, 167, 168
European Film Academy, 105, 114, 115
Evans, Walker, 123, 137–138
Exilromane, 37

F

Fahrenheit 451, 126, 141
Falk, Peter, 149–150
Falsche Bewegung, 67, 123–124, 137
Fassbinder, Rainer Werner, 95, 96, 101, 102, 103, 104, 110, 136, 167
Fellini, Federico, 94–95
Firda, Richard Arthur, 57, 67
Fitzgerald, F. Scott, 74, 76
Fonda, Peter, 128
Fontane, Theodor, 23
Förderrungssystem, 108
Forum Stadtpark, 52
Foucault, Michel, 6
Frankfurter Allgemeine Zeitung, 3, 164
Fuller, Samuel, 95, 108

G

Gamper, Herbert, 70
Gegenkultur, 142
Geist, 23–24, 26
Geist, Kathe, 127–128, 139–140
Geschichte, 17, 101
Geschichten–Erzählen, 139
Gide, André, 29, 36
Godard, Jean–Luc, 8, 126, 143
    films, 101, 112, 127, 146, 147
    nouveau roman, 4–5, 39–41, 58, 97
    nouvelle vague, 10–11, 96–98

Goethe, Johann, 23–24, 26, 156
Gorbachev, Mikhal, 151
Grass, Gunter, 5, 6, 16, 39, 48, 136, 154–156
Graz, Austria, 11–12
Grazer Gruppe, 52, 65–66
Grimm, Brothers, 17, 21, 47
Grob, Norbert, 101–102, 117, 123, 125, 128
Gruppe 47, 40–41, 52, 53, 63, 65

H

Habermas, Jürgen, 6, 30, 43–44
Haltung, 129
Hamburger Erklärung, 102
Hammett, 124, 131–132, 138
Handke, Peter, 6, 7, 8–9, 10, 48
    anti-narrative, 51, 55–62
    films, 60–61, 85–86, 89, 111
    interior monologues, 49–50
    narrative, 51–55, 63–72, 83
    nouveau roman, 49, 50, 53, 56, 85
    self-expression, 73–75
    and Wenders, Wim, 59, 60, 72, 85–86, 115–116, 123–124, 125, 127, 138
Heimat, 94, 128
Heimatfilme, 93
Herzog, Werner, 102, 103, 136, 138
Hesse, Hermann, 38
Hicks, Ray, 47
High Noon, 168
Higson, Andrew, 164
Hiroshima mon amour, 166
Hitchcock, Alfred, 95
Homer, 71, 72, 122, 137
Hopper, Edward, 123, 137–138
Huyssen, Andreas, 43, 44

I

Im Lauf der Zeit, 124, 130–131, 137
In weiter Ferne, so nah!, 8, 147, 149–151

J

Jakobson, Roman, 76
James, Henry, 2
Jeder für sich und Gott gegen alle, 138
Jenseits der Wolken, 151
Johnson, Uwe, 6
Joyce, James, 31, 36, 39

K

Kaes, Anton, 93–94
Kafka, Frank, 28
Kahglschlag, 38, 39
Kahlschlagliteratur, 38
Kayser, Wolfgang, 34–35
Kermode, Frank, 36–37, 86
Kinder- und Hausmärchen, 21
Klee, Paul, 116
Klinkowitz, Jerome, 50, 56, 62
Kluge, Alexander, 96, 99–101, 104, 112, 113, 119, 122
Knowlton, James, 50, 56, 62
Koeppen, Wolfgang, 39
Kolker, Robert, 134, 136
Konrad, Györgi, 12
Koskella, Gretel, 52–53
Kracauer, Siegfried, 92, 109, 120, 142, 143
Kuchenbuch, Thomas, 91
Kulturpolitik, 164
Kundera, Milan, 34
Kurz un Schmerzlos, 167–168

L

Lacan, Jacques, 98
Langsam im Schatten, 73
Langsamer Heimkehr, 60, 62– 63, 78
L'Année dernière a Marienbad, 97
L'art pour l'art, 18
Leselust, oder Wie unterhaltsam ist die neue deutsche Literatur?, 3
Lewandowski, Rainer, 100
Lichtefeld, Peter, 167, 168
Lisbon Story, 135, 145–147, 151
Literary salon, 12
Littérature engagée, 54
Lola rennt, 164–167, 168
Lukàcs, George, 33–34, 35–36, 46, 116–117
Lyotard, Jean-Francois, 5, 44

M

Machado, Antonio, 79
Made in the USA, 127
Mann, Thomas, 4, 23–29, 30, 31, 32, 37, 38, 39, 154
Männer, 110
Mauern, 136
Mein Jahir der Niemandsbucht, 72, 82–83
Meister, Wilhelm, 137
Metz, Christian, 92

Mohr, Jean, 73
Moritz, Karl Philipp, 60
Müller, Robby, 123
Musil, Robert, 4, 23, 28–29

N

Na Drini cuprija, 66
Nachdenkenüber über Christa T., 158
Nachmittag eines Schriftstellers, 63, 74–76, 78–80
Nadolny, Sten, 153–154, 158–161
Nashville, 130
National Socialism, 37–38, 38–39, 87, 89, 92
Neoformalist, 126
Neue Subjektivitat, 49, 52, 62, 127
"Neuer Realismus," 52
New German Cinema (NGC), 8, 10, 11, 60, 88–89, 94, 111, 136, 162
  decline of, 102–103, 108–109, 110, 164
  and Wenders, Wim, 115, 123, 151–152
  See also Autorenfilm
New German Comedy, 89, 109–114
New German Filmmakers, 89, 101, 109, 162, 164, 168
New York Times, 46–47
New York Times Book Review, 1–2
New York Times Magazine, 1, 103
Nick's Film: Lightning over Water, 131
Notebook on Cities and Clothes, 143–144
Nouveau roman, 6, 39
  films, 10–11, 97, 98
  and Godard, Jean–Luc, 4–5, 39–41, 58, 97
  and Handke, Peter, 49, 50, 53, 56, 85
  and Robbe–Grillet, Alain, 4–5, 39–41, 53, 58
  and Wenders, Wim, 130
Nouvelle vague
  films, 8, 10–11, 88, 89, 93, 96–99
  and Goddard, Jean–Luc, 10–11, 96–98
  and Robbe–Grillet, Alain, 97
  and Wenders, Wim, 89, 108, 115, 126–131, 132–134

O

Oberhausener Manifest, 98–99, 101, 104, 136–137, 151
O'Neill, Patrick, 5–6, 154, 155

Oxford Dictionary of English Etymology, 16–17
Ozu, Yazujiro, 118

P

Paech, Joachim, 86, 90
Pakendorf, Gunther, 76
Paris, Texas, 120, 124, 134–135, 136–140
Pictures of Europe, 106
Pinselführung, 123
Plater, Edward, 148, 149, 150
Price, Reynolds, 16–17, 18, 45, 121, 153
Puttnam, David, 106

R

Rahmenezählung, 86–87
Rashomon, 166
Rauh, Reinhold, 135
Ray, Nicholas, 95, 108
Reading for the Plot, 2
Reitz, Edger, 113
Resnais, Alain, 166
Reverse Ange—New York City, 129
Richter, Hans, 87
Ricouer, Paul, 5, 9, 22, 43
Rilke, 28
Robbe–Grillet, Alain, 4–5, 39–41, 53, 58
  nouveau roman, 4–5, 39–41, 53, 58
  nouvelle vague, 97
Roemer, Michael, 17, 20
Roman pur, 29, 36
Rote Sonne, 129
Rubin, Martin, 166
Rühmann, Heinz, 151
Ruttmann, Walter, 87

S

Sanders–Brahms, Helma, 162–163, 164, 167, 168
Sarraute, Nathalie, 40
Sarte, Jean–Pau;, 54
Schamoni, Peter, 101
Schelmenroman, 154
Schimpfwort, 167
Schipper, Sebastian, 167
Schlafes Bruder, 3, 153–156
Schlink, Bernhard, 3, 6, 161
Schlöndorff, Volker, 96, 102, 103, 109, 112, 124, 136
Schneider, Robert, 3, 153–154, 155, 156, 161–162

Schopenhauer, Arthur, 27
Schrader, Paul, 106
Schreiben für den Film: Das Drehbuch als eine andere Art des Erzählens, 135–136
Schulze, Ingo, 3, 6, 161
Schwelle, 65
Seghers, Anna, 37
Seidelmann, Susan, 143
Selim, oder die Gabe der Rede, 153, 158–160, 161
Shepard, Sam, 124, 137
Silbermann, Marc, 100
Silent film, 11, 86–87, 90–91, 97
Simple Stories, 3, 161
Sirk, Douglas, 95
Society for Friends of the Academy of Arts, 12
Socrates, 50, 76, 81
Sontag, Susan, 42, 103, 163
Sorlin, Pierre, 94–95, 96
Speilberg, Steven, 143
SprachlosigKeit, 51
Sprechstück, 55–56, 77
Steiner, Wendy, 1–2
Steinmetz, Horst, 4, 7–8, 44–45, 48, 81
Sterne, Laurence, 34
Stiegler, Bernd, 68
Stiller, Klaus, 58
Störfall, 48
Straub, Jean-Marie, 119
Stunde Null, 38, 109
Sukowa, Barbara, 167
Summer in the City, 123, 127, 128, 137
Süskind, Patrick, 3, 153–156, 161, 162

T

Tales of Mother Goose, 20–21
Tarkovsky, Andrei, 118, 151
Tavernier, Bertrand, 106
Tegetthoff, Folke, 12
"The Jukebox: And Other Essays on Storytelling," 7, 49
   See also *Versuch über die Jukebox*
The State of Things, 131–134, 135, 136, 138, 145
The Survivors, 132
Theorie des Romans, 33–34
Thome, Rudolf, 129
Time, 46
Time and Narrative, 22
Timm, Uwe, 7, 47–48, 153–154, 156–158, 160–161
Tristram Shandy, 34

Truffaut, François, 95, 96, 118, 126, 141, 151
Two or Three Things I Know about Her, 127
Tykwer, Tom, 164–167

U

Über den Begriff der Geschichte, 116–117
Ullmann, Liv, 106
Ulysses, 31
Unterhaltung, 3
Unterhaltungskino, 104
Until the End of the World, 107, 135, 140–142, 144, 150–151

V

Verfallsform, 24–25
Vergangenheitsbewältigung, 94
Verhoeven, Paul, 106
Verinnerlichung, 27
Verlag, S. Fisher, 3
Versuch über den geglückten Tag, 80–81
Versuch über die Jukebox, 77, 78–80
Versuch über die Müdigkeit, 76, 77, 78
Versuche, 7, 76
von Garnier, Katja, 107–108, 110–111
von Trotta, Margarethe, 103
Vorwort, 33–34

W

Weimar, 39, 87, 99, 167
Welles, Orson, 166
Welzig, Werner, 32
Wenders, Wim, 8–9, 11
  American films, 105, 115, 126, 127, 131–134, 135–136, 147, 149
  anti–narrative, 89, 115
  and Benjamin, Walter, 116–117, 118, 121, 140, 143, 147–148, 151
  comedy, 109–110
  and Handke, Peter, 59, 60, 72, 85–86, 115–116, 123–124, 125, 127, 138
  literary works in film, 122–124
  narrative, images and, 119–126
  narrative, importance of, 112, 115, 116–118, 131, 135–142, 147–152
  New German Cinema (NGC), 115, 123, 151–152
  nouveau roman, 130
  nouvelle vague, 89, 108, 115, 126–131, 132–134
  video, 143–147
Weyrauch, Wolfgage, 38

Williams, Alan, 97–98
Wings of Desire, 122
 See also Der Himmel über Berlin
Wittstock, Uwe, 3, 159, 161, 162
Wolf, Christa, 48, 158–159
Wörterbuch, 17
Wortmann, Sönke, 110

X

X–Filme Creative Pool GmbH, 112–113, 167

Y

Yamamoto, Yohji, 143, 144
Young German Cinema, 88, 94, 99, 101, 119
Young German Filmmakers, 100–101, 103, 168

Z

Zeitgeist, 24
Zinnemann, Fred, 168
Ziolkowski, Theodore, 32
Zugvögel, 167, 168
Zusammenhang, 122
Zwei Ansichten, 6

STUDIES IN GERMAN LANGUAGE AND LITERATURE

1. Ulrich Goebel and Oskar Reichmann (eds.) in collaboration with Peter I. Barta, **Historical Lexicography of the German Language, Volume 1**
2. Christoph Meckel, *Zünd* **and Other Stories**, Carol Bedwell (trans.)
3. Christoph Meckel, *Snow Creatures* **and Other Stories**, Carol Bedwell (trans.)
4. Hasan Dewran, *A Thousand Winds May Make A Storm/Tausend Winde-Ein Sturm, Poems and Aphorisms/Gedichte und Aphorismen*, Hans W. Panthel (trans.)
5. William C. McDonald, **The Tristan Story in German Literature of the Late Middle Ages and Early Renaissance: Tradition and Innovation**
6. Ulrich Goebel and Oskar Reichmann (eds.) in collaboration with Peter I. Barta, **Historical Lexicography of the German Language, Volume 2**
7. Ian F. Roe, **An Introduction to the Major Works of Franz Grillparzer, 1791-1872, Austrian Dramatist and Poet**
8. Margaret Littler, **Alfred Andersch (1914-1980) and the Literary, Philosophical, and Cultural Life of the Federal Republic of Germany**
9. *The Nibelungenlied*, Robert Lichtenstein (trans.)
10. Eva Wagner, **An Analysis of Franz Grillparzer's Drama: Fate, Guilt, and Tragedy**
11. Erich W. Schaufler, **Elias Canettis Autobiographie in Der Deutschen Presse**
12. Patrick T. Murray, **The Development of German Aesthetic Theory from Kant to Schiller: A Philosophical Commentary on Schiller's** *Aesthetic Education of Man* **(1795)**
13. Edelgard E. DuBruck, **Aspects of Fifteenth-Century Society in the German Carnival Comedies: Speculum Hominis**
14. Ulrich Goebel and David Lee (eds.), **The Ring of Words in Medieval Literature** (paperback)
15. Albrecht Classen, **The German Volksbuch: A Critical History of a Late-Medieval Genre**
16. Martin Swales, **Studies of German Prose Fiction in the Age of European Realism**
17. **The Alsfeld Passion Play,** Larry E. West (trans.)
18. **Ludwig Achim von Arnim's Novellas of 1812 - Isabella of Egypt, Melück Maria Blainville, The Three Loving Sisters and the Lucky Dyer, Angelika the Genoese and Cosmus the Tightrope-Walker**, Bruce Duncan (trans.)
19. Karl A. Bernhardt and Graeme Davis, **The Word Order of Old High German**
20. Barbara Burns, **The Short Stories of Detlev von Liliencron: Passion, Penury, Patriotism**
21. J.W. Thomas (trans.), **Fables, Sermonettes, and Parables by The Stricker, 13th Century German Poet, in English Translation**
22. **Theodor Storm–Narrative Strategies and Patriarchy; Theodor Storm–Erzählstrategien und Patriarchat**, herausgegeben von David A. Jackson und Mark G. Ward

23. Gordon J.A. Burgess, **A Computer-Assisted Analysis of Goethe's** *Die Wahlverwandtschaften*: **The Enigma of Elective Affinities**
24. Rainer Maria Rilke, *The Duino Elegies*, translated by John Waterfield
25. Paul Bishop, **The World of Stoical Discourse in Goethe's Novel** *Die Wahlverwandtschaften*
26. Heike Bartel and Brian Keith-Smith (eds.), **'Nachdenklicher Leichtsinn'– Essays on Goethe and Goethe Reception**
27. Roger Kingerlee, **Psychological Models of Masculinity in Döblin, Musil, and Jahnn: Männliches, Allzumännliches**
28. Otto Weininger (1880-1903), **A Translation of Weininger's** *Über die letzten Dinge* **(1904/1907)** / *On Last Things*, translated from the original German, and with an introduction by Steven Burns
29. G. Peter McMullin, **Childhood and Children in Thomas Mann's Fiction**
30. Gillian Pye, **Approaches to Comedy in German Drama**
31. Hajo Drees, **A Comprehensive Interpretation of the Life and Work of Christa Wolf, 20th-Century German Writer**
32. Regina Angela Wenzel, **Changing Notions of Money and Language in German Literature from 1509-1956**
33. Joan Wright, **The Novel Poetics of Goethe's** *Wilhelm Meisters Wanderjahre*: **Eine zarte Empirie**
34. Kathleen M. Condray, **Women Writers of the Journal** *Jugend* **from 1919-1940: "Das Gehirn unsrer lieben Schwestern"**
35. Jeffrey L. High, **Schillers Rebellionskonzept und die Französische Revolution**
36. David N. Coury, **The Return of Storytelling in Contemporary German Literature and Film–Peter Handke and Wim Wenders**